System Standards

Volume One

PUBLISHED BY KACHINA PRESS, P.O. BOX 50011, DALLAS, TEXAS 75250

System Standards, Volume One

Copyright © 1978 by Kachina, Incorporated. All rights reserved. No part of this book may be transmitted or reproduced in any form or by any means, electronic or mechanical, including photocopy, recording, or any information storage and retrieval system, without express permission in writing from the publisher, except in the case of brief quotations embodied in critical articles and papers.

Printed and bound in the United States of America.
ISBN No. 0-930724-03-8

Library of Congress Catalogue Card Number 78-52235

Acknowledgements

The publishers are deeply indebted to the many officers and employees of the Atchison, Topeka and Santa Fe Railway Company who encouraged and provided assistance in this undertaking. Special thanks are due those individuals in the public relations department, the engineering department, the signal department, the valuation department, the operating department, and the executive department. Without their help and support, this project could not have been completed.

Foreword

To the casual "railfan," this publication will be of only nominal interest, but to the dedicated railway transportation buff and historian, as well as the serious model railroader, this first of three volumes on the engineering and architectural standards of the Santa Fe Railway will be a welcome addition to the library as well as a source of academic pleasure provided by perusal of the data contained herein. The Santa Fe is highly regarded in the railroad world as a model of operating and financial efficiency. Lesser known is the fact that it, too, was a very professional "standard" railway whose designs were based on the best operating and engineering knowledge. The standard designs presented here relate primarily to buildings, trackside facilities, roadbed and roadway, track, bridges, and similar appurtenances commonly seen but not so commonly recognized and understood. Standards in any line of endeavor have a way of improving and upgrading as time passes, and railway standards are no different. That's why notations of revision are made along with the revisions themselves. In preparing this three-volume series, the publishers have not attempted to present every standard — only select ones that reflect the character of the railroad itself and ones that, hopefully, will provide inspiration and background to those who model this old friend — *the Santa Fe Railway.*

The Santa Fe herald appearing in this publication is a registered trademark and is used by permission of the Atchison, Topeka and Santa Fe Railway Company.

Index To Volume One, System Standards

Standard Signs:
- Lettering 5
- Standard trademark, square 6
- Standard trademark, circle 7
- State line monuments 8
- Highway crossing signs 9
- Railroad crossing signs 14
- Whistle/derail/switch signs 15
- Speed/slow/stop signs 16
- Yard limit signs 17
- Miscellaneous 18
- Clearance markers 22
- Underpass clearance 24
- Tresspass/danger signs 25
- Bridge numbering 27
- Station names, heralds 28
- Siding names 29
- Train bulletins 32
- Baggage/waiting room signs 33
- Bridge advertisements 34
- Emblem on water tanks 35
- Signal signs 36
- Fire prevention signs 39
- Stock scale signs 41

Mail Crane 42
Cut Track Spikes 43
Bunk House 44
Frame Hose Cart House 45
Frame Hose House 46
Steel Hose Reel House 47
Rail Rack 48
Switch Stands:
- High Star, Single Crank 49
- High Star, Double Crank 50
- Low Star, Single Crank 51
- Low Star, Double Crank 52
- Ramapo 53
- Switch Lamp Fork & Target Rod Tip 54

Way Bill Box 55
Breyley Friction Car Stop 56
Tell Tales 57
Step Stile 58
Location of Dating Nails 59
Loading of Cross Ties, Piling & Rails 60
Stockyard No. 1 61
Stockyard No. 2 62
Stockyard No. 3 63
Stockyard Details 64
Double Deck Stock Chute 68
Scale House, Metal 71
Scale House, Transite 72
Track Layouts for Scales 73
56-Foot, 150-Ton Track Scale 75
66-Foot, 150-Ton Track Scale 79
46-Foot, 100-Ton Track Scale 84
50-Foot, 150-Ton Track Scale 88
Selection of Bridges & Culverts 93
Assignment of Rail (1939) 95
Assignment of Cross Ties (1963) 96
Cross Tie Standards 97
Road Crossings, Planked 98
Road Crossings, Sectional Panel 99
Inside Steel Guard Rail for Bridges 100
Walk & Handrail – Existing T-Rail Bridges With Ballasted Deck ... 101
Open Deck Timber Trestle Bridges 105
Ballasted Deck Timber Trestle Bridges 117

Contents of Volume Two

- Dwarf Signals, all types
- Signals on Lattice Girder 3-Track Bridge
- Signals on 2-Track C&NW Type Bridge
- Signals on Cantilever Mast
- Signals on Standard 2-Track Bridge
- Train Order Signal Using HC-33 Units
- Colorlight Spring Switch Lamp
- Signals With Siding Signs
- Bi-Directional Signals
- Signal Ladders
- Inoperative Approach Signal
- Semaphore Signals, A.C. and D.C.
- Switch Indicators
- "Automatic Flagman" of 1918
- Torpedo and Fusee Box
- Thermometer Shelter
- Right-of-Way Fence Standards
- 4-Room Section House
- 5-Room Section House
- Standard Section House
- 10-Room Concrete Block Bunkhouse
- 10-Room Brick Bunkhouse
- 10-Room Tile Bunkhouse
- 10-Room Concrete Bunkhouse
- Instructions For Use of Switch Targets and Switch Lights
- Railroad Crossing Gate
- 2-Track Signal Bridge Foundations
- 4-Track Signal Bridge Foundations
- Single Ground Signal on Battery Cellar
- Cantilever Semaphore Signal
- Highway Crossing Signals
- Standard Signal Blades
- Searchlight Signals, all common locations
- No. 1 Branch Line Depot
- No. 2 Branch Line Depot
- No. 3 Branch Line Depot
- No. 4 Branch Line Depot
- No. 5. Branch Line Depot
- No. 1 Main Line Depot
- No. 2 Main Line Depot
- No. 3 Main Line Depot
- No. 4 Main Line Depot
- No. 5 Main Line Depot
- Combination Frame 2-A Depot
- Six Room Operators Cottage No. 2
- Six Room Operators Cottage, Coast Lines
- Standard Wood Block Tower
- Standard Interlocking Tower, Frame
- Standard Interlocking Tower, Concrete
- Interlock Tower Material House

Contents of Volume Three

- Low Type Frame Roundhouse
- Low Type Roundhouse, Later Version
- 92-Foot Low Type Concrete Roundhouse
- 132-Foot Engine House
- 5-Stall Roundhouse for Mallet Engines
- 85-Foot Turntable
- Engine Supply House
- Standard Sand House
- Standard Sand House, Mechanical
- Frame Lumber Shed, 26-Foot
- Frame Lumber Shed, 40-Foot
- Brick Lumber Shed, 80-Foot
- Brick Store House, No. 1
- Brick Store House, No. 2
- Brick Store House, No. 3
- Single Boiler House
- Double Boiler House
- 46-Foot Derrick & Pump House
- Poage 10-Inch Water Column
- Standard 12-Inch Water Column
- Standard 12-Inch Oil Column
- "Otto" 10-Inch Stand Pipe
- Derrick & Pump House
- Standard Water Tanks
- Concrete Oil Storage Reservoir
- Concrete Cistern
- Water Treating Plant
- Water Treating Plant & Boiler House
- Buildings Used At Terminals:
- Bar Iron and Pipe House
- Flue and Sheet Metal House
- Lumber Shed
- Coal and Coke House
- Arch Brick and Fire Clay House
- Combination Pipe-Flue-Iron-Sheet Metal House
- Coal House for Depot
- Standard Depot Closet
- Yard Closets, Single and Double
- Material Houses for Signal Maintainers
- Mail Crane — Pierce Style
- Hog Chute
- Stock Chute, Single and Double Deck
- Lumber Specifications
- Crossing Gates — Painting
- Bumping Posts
- Track Tools
- Section House Fence
- Track Car Set-Off
- Concrete Abutments and Piers
- Section Tool House
- Cast Iron Chimneys
- Cotton Platforms
- Auto Unloading Platforms
- Heavy Machinery Platforms & Docks
- Passenger Motor Car Fuel Station
- Dating of Concrete Bridges and Tunnels
- Portable Snow Fences
- Standard Ladders
- Concrete Arch Culverts
- Cross-Tie Spacing
- Planked Road Crossings
- Switch Machine Layouts
- Freight House & Baggage Room Scales
- Stock Scales, 5-Ton & 10-Ton
- Supports for Outside Overhead Pipe Lines

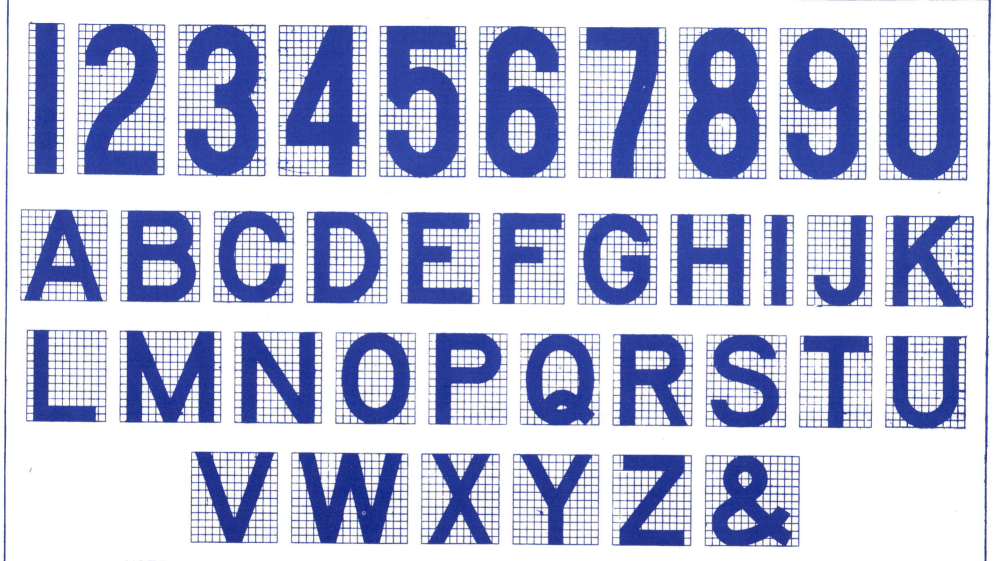

NOTE:
This sheet indicates the style of letter to be used generally.
In special cases full size patterns of the alphabet will be furnished for use in station names, interlocking towers, etc. Full size patterns will also be supplied for arms of crossing, whistle posts and other roadway signs.

THE A T & S F RY SYSTEM

STANDARD SIGNS

TOPEKA, MARCH-1911

Revised Jan. 1923.

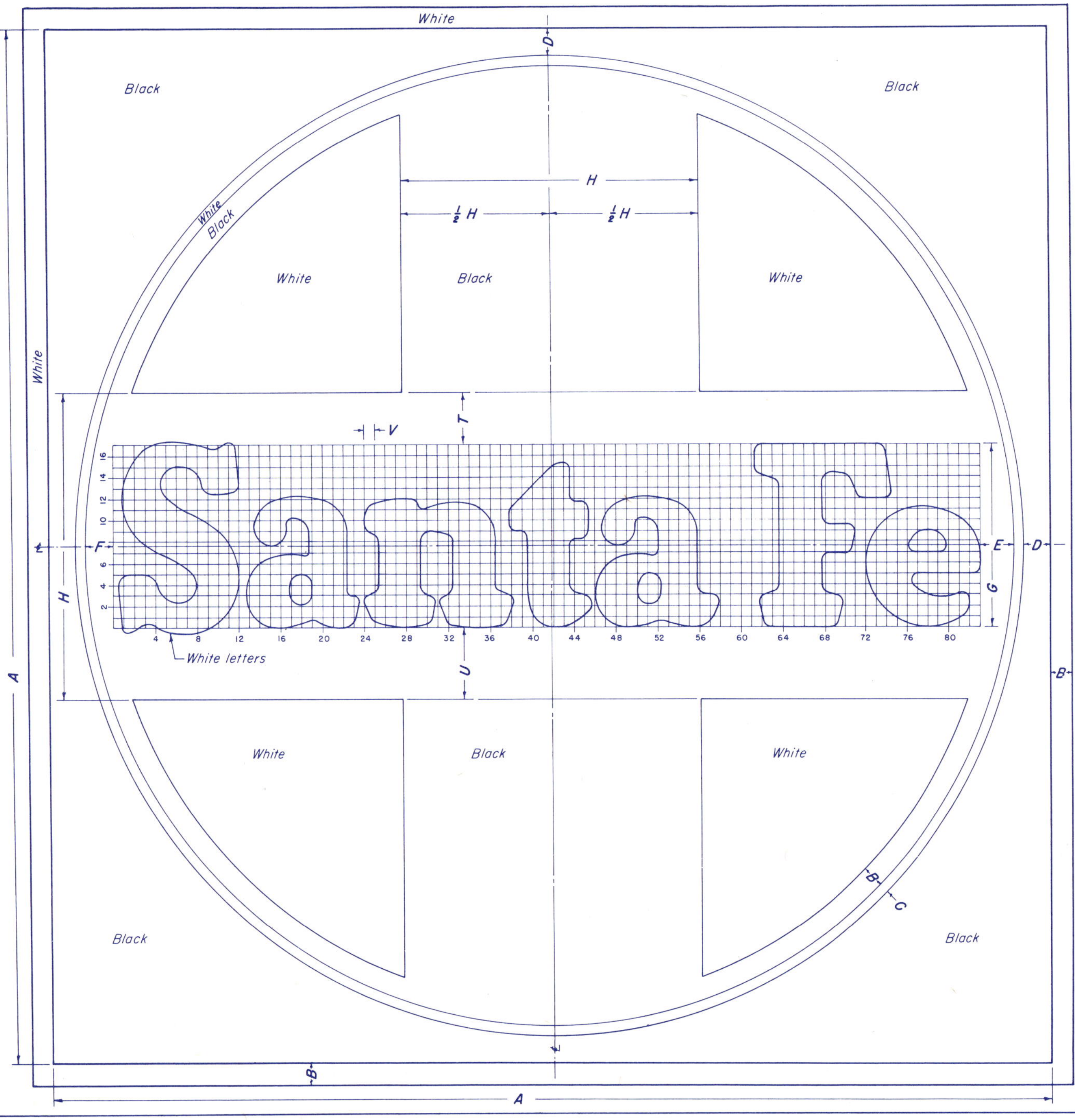

NOTES

1- This emblem is the registered trademark of the Santa Fe Railway System including all of its subsidiaries and shall be used on all structures and roadway machines requiring trademark emblems.

2- The emblem shall be black and white, preferably as shown on this plan; however in cases where the white border does not properly contrast with the background, the colors may be reversed, for example, the white border changed to black etc.

3- For sizes of trademark emblems not shown in the table on this plan, the dimensions, lettering etc. shall be proportional to those shown in the table.

4- The trademark emblem as shown on this plan (white border) shall be used on the following standard plans:
  C.E.S. 5059, Sheet No. 21, Station Sign, No. 83.
  C.E.S. 5059, Sheet No. 16-A and 27, Black Steel Girder Bridges.
  C.E.S. 5059, Sheet No. 28, Black Steel Tanks.

5- The trademark emblem with colors reversed (black border) shall be used on C.E.S. 5059, Sheet No. 25, Timetable and Bulletin Board.

TABLE OF DIMENSIONS FOR VARIOUS SIZES OF EMBLEMS

A	B	C	D	E	F	G	H	T	U	V
3.750"	.078"	.040"	.098"	.087"	.067"	.680"	1.110"	.187"	.243"	.040"
9.600"	.200"	.100"	.250"	.325"	.275"	1.700"	2.850"	.475"	.675"	.100"
1'-2 1/2"	5/16"	5/32"	3/8"	17/32"	29/64"	2 9/16"	4 5/16"	3/4"	1"	.150"
2'-0"	1/2"	1/4"	5/8"	13/16"	11/16"	4 1/4"	7 1/8"	1 3/16"	1 11/16"	1/4"
2'-6"	5/8"	5/16"	25/32"	1"	7/8"	5 5/16"	8 29/32"	1 1/2"	2 3/32"	5/16"
3'-0"	3/4"	3/8"	15/16"	1 7/32"	1 1/32"	6 3/8"	10 11/16"	1 25/32"	2 17/32"	3/8"
4'-0"	1"	1/2"	1 1/4"	1 5/8"	1 3/8"	8 1/2"	14 1/4"	2 3/8"	3 3/8"	1/2"
5'-0"	1 1/4"	5/8"	1 9/16"	2 1/32"	1 23/32"	10 5/8"	17 13/16"	2 31/32"	4 7/32"	5/8"
6'-0"	1 1/2"	3/4"	1 7/8"	2 7/16"	2 1/16"	12 3/4"	21 3/8"	3 9/16"	5 1/16"	3/4"
7'-0"	1 3/4"	7/8"	2 3/16"	2 27/32"	2 13/32"	14 7/8"	2'-0 15/16"	4 5/32"	5 29/32"	7/8"
8'-0"	2"	1"	2 1/2"	3 1/4"	2 3/4"	17"	2'-4 1/2"	4 3/4"	6 3/4"	1"

REVISIONS OR ADDITIONS

Date	Changed Items	Approved
12-1970	Note 6 deleted. A = 9.600" added.	W.S.Q.

NOTICE

The Santa Fe herald is a registered trademark and can not be reproduced in any manner without express permission of the Atchison, Topeka and Santa Fe Railway Company.

THE A. T. & S. F. RY. SYSTEM

STANDARD SIGNS

SANTA FE SQUARE TRADEMARK

CHICAGO, MAY 1963

APPROVED: R.D. Shelton
VICE PRESIDENT

APPROVED: R.H. Beeder
CHIEF ENG'R SYSTEM

NOTES

1- This emblem is the registered trademark of the Santa Fe Railway System including all of its subsidiaries and shall be used on special occasions when authorized by the Advertising or Engineering Departments.

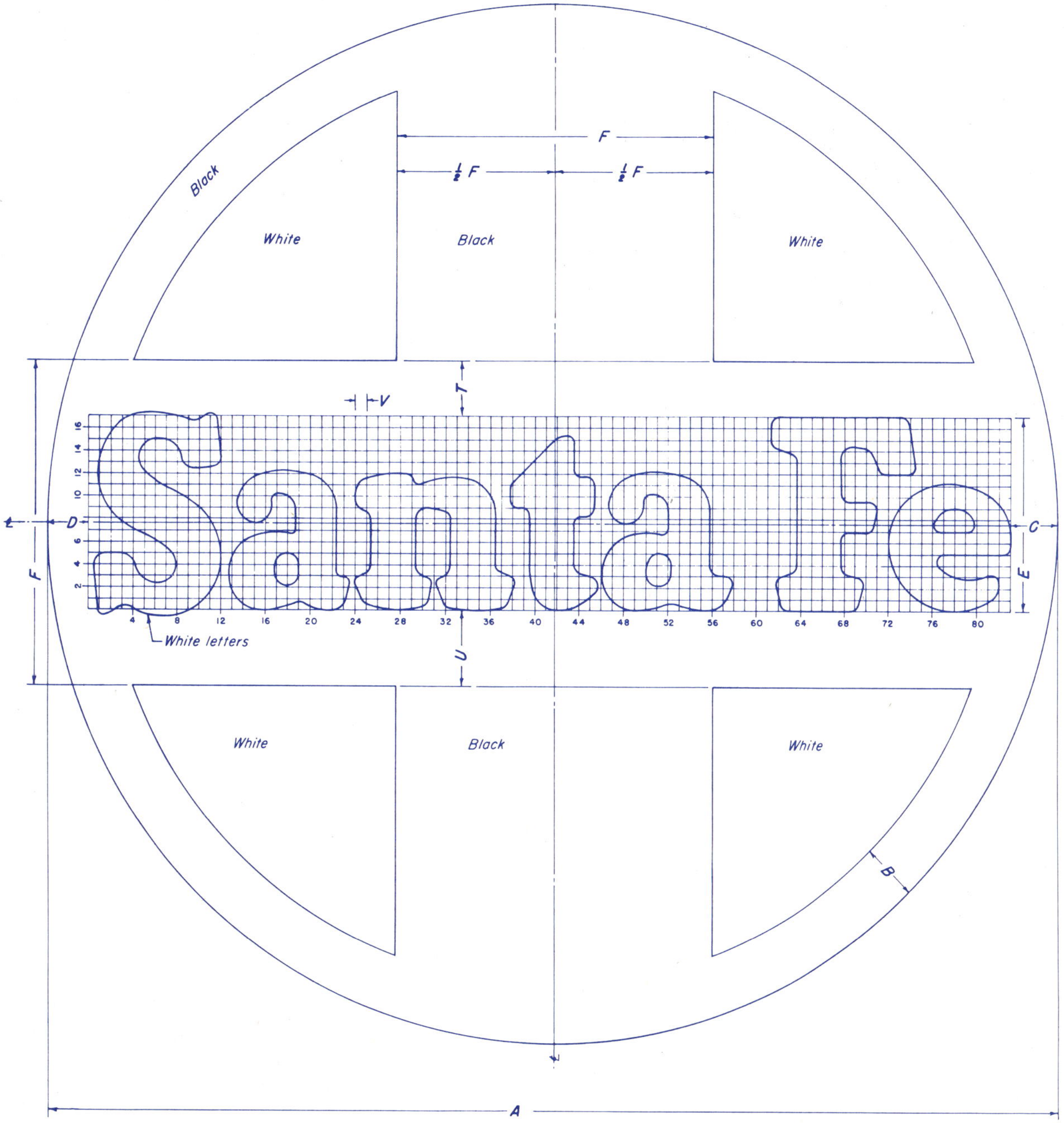

F
½ F
½ F
Black
White
Black
White
Santa Fe
T
V
D
C
E
F
U
White letters
White
Black
White
B
A

TABLE OF DIMENSIONS FOR VARIOUS SIZES OF EMBLEMS								
A	B	C	D	E	F	T	U	V
3.554"	.205"	.127"	.107"	.680"	1.110"	.187"	.243"	.040"
1'-1 3/4"	51/64"	11/16"	39/64"	2 9/16"	4 5/16"	3/4"	1"	.150"
1'-10 3/4"	1 5/16"	1 1/16"	15/16"	4 1/4"	7 1/8"	1 3/16"	1 11/16"	1/4"
2'-4 7/16"	1 41/64"	1 5/16"	1 3/16"	5 5/16"	8 29/32"	1 1/2"	2 3/32"	5/16"
2'-10 1/8"	1 31/32"	1 19/32"	1 13/32"	6 3/8"	10 11/16"	1 25/32"	2 17/32"	3/8"
3'-9 1/2"	2 5/8"	2 1/8"	1 7/8"	8 1/2"	14 1/4"	2 3/8"	3 3/8"	1/2"
4'-8 7/8"	3 9/32"	2 21/32"	2 11/32"	10 5/8"	17 13/16"	2 31/32"	4 7/32"	5/8"
5'-8 1/4"	3 15/16"	3 3/16"	2 13/16"	12 3/4"	21 3/8"	3 9/16"	5 1/16"	3/4"
6'-7 5/8"	4 19/32"	3 23/32"	3 9/32"	14 7/8"	2'-0 15/16"	4 5/32"	5 29/32"	7/8"
7'-7"	5 1/4"	4 1/4"	3 3/4"	17"	2'-4 1/2"	4 3/4"	6 3/4"	1"

REVISIONS OR ADDITIONS		
Date	Changed Items	Approved
12-1970	D for A = 4'-8 7/8"	W.S.A.

THE A. T. & S. F. RY. SYSTEM

STANDARD SIGNS

SANTA FE CIRCLE TRADEMARK

CHICAGO, MAY 1963

APPROVED: R. D. Shelton — VICE PRESIDENT

APPROVED: R. H. Beeder — CHIEF ENG'R SYSTEM

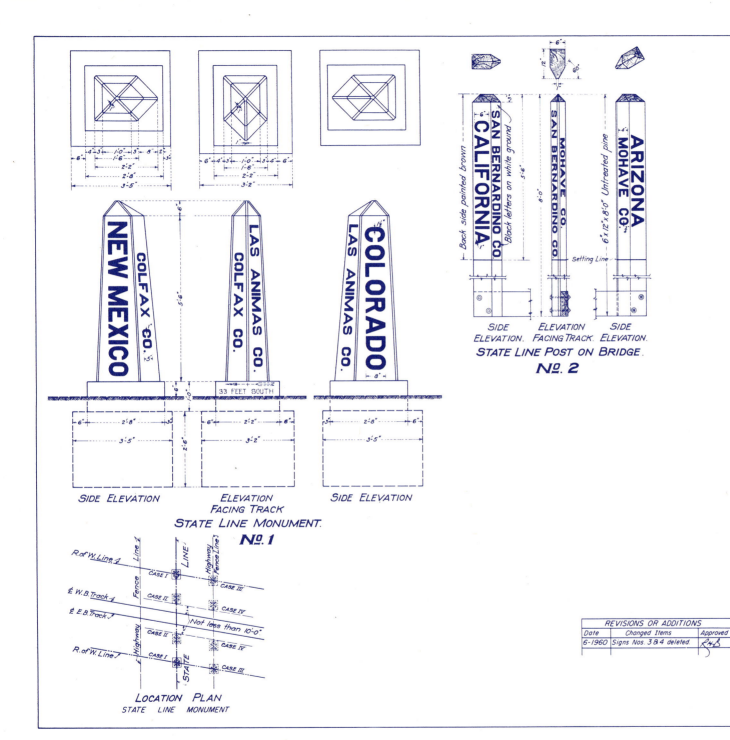

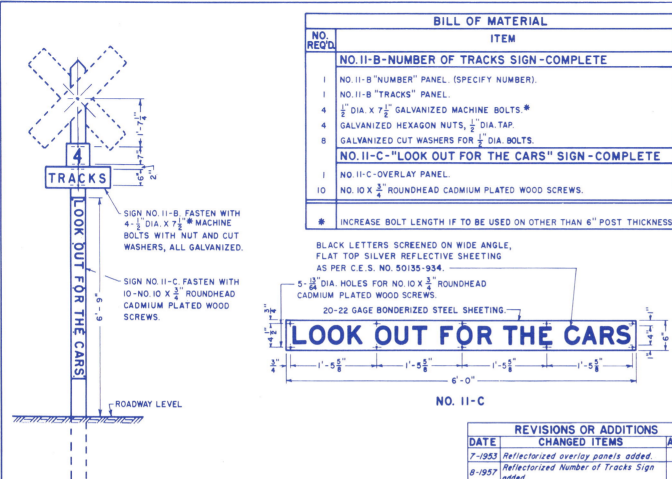

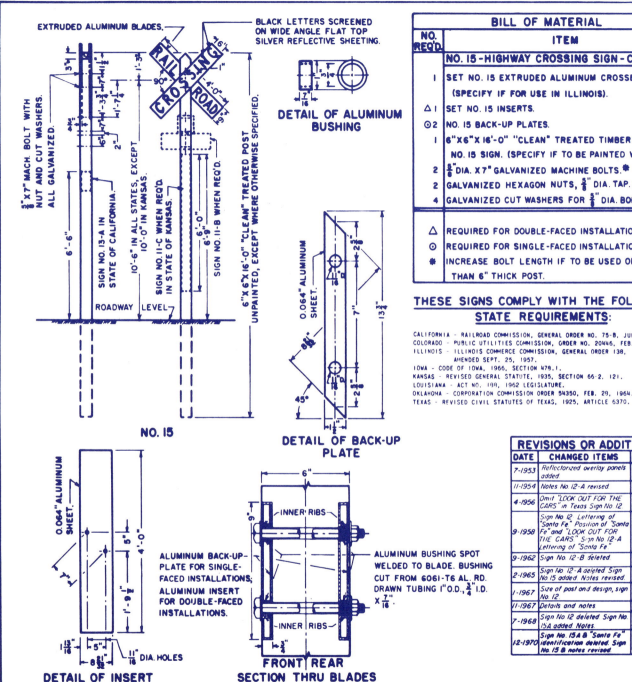

NOTES

NO. 15 - HIGHWAY CROSSING SIGN:

FOR USE IN ALL STATES WITH THE EXCEPTION THAT IN THE STATE OF CALIFORNIA, SIGN NO. 15 MAY BE USED ONLY AT CLOSE CLEARANCE LOCATIONS IN LIEU OF SIGN NO. 13.

SIGN NO. 15 WILL BE USED ON NEW INSTALLATIONS AND FOR THE REPLACEMENT OF EXISTING HIGHWAY CROSSING SIGNS, ON AN ATTRITION BASIS, AS RENEWALS ARE REQUIRED. EXISTING WOODEN CROSSBUCK BLADES WILL BE REPLACED WITH EXTRUDED ALUMINUM BLADES, PER THIS DRAWING, WHEN RENEWAL OF SIGN MESSAGE IS REQUIRED.

SIGNS NO. 11-B, 11-C AND 13-A SHALL BE USED IN CONJUNCTION WITH SIGN NO. 15, WHEN REQUIRED.

IN THE STATES OF ARIZONA, CALIFORNIA, ILLINOIS AND OKLAHOMA, POST WILL BE PAINTED WHITE FROM TOP TO POINT ONE FOOT ABOVE ROADWAY LEVEL.

AT GRADE CROSSING OF PARALLEL MULTIPLE TRACKS, TWO HIGHWAY CROSSING SIGNS SHALL BE PROVIDED, ONE ON EACH SIDE OF TRACKS WITH MESSAGE ON APPROACHING FACE ONLY. ON SINGLE TRACK, EXCEPT IN THE STATE OF ILLINOIS, ONE SIGN WITH MESSAGE ON BOTH FACES WILL BE USED UNLESS TWO SIGNS ARE REQUIRED TO PROTECT THE HIGHWAY FROM BOTH DIRECTIONS.

IN THE STATE OF ILLINOIS, TWO SIGNS ARE REQUIRED FOR EACH GRADE CROSSING, ONE ON EACH SIDE OF THE TRACK. BACKS OF CROSSBUCK BLADES FOR USE IN ILLINOIS WILL HAVE A STRIP OF REFLECTIVE SHEETING APPLIED BETWEEN INNER RIBS OF EACH BLADE.

SIGN IS TO BE SET IN SUCH POSITION AS TO GIVE THE BEST VIEW TO ONE APPROACHING THE CROSSING FROM EITHER DIRECTION ON THE HIGHWAY WITH FACE OF POST LOCATED NOT LESS THAN 14 FEET NOR MORE THAN 20 FEET FROM NEAREST RAIL, EXCEPT IN ILLINOIS, WHERE MAXIMUM DISTANCE FROM FACE OF POST TO NEAREST RAIL SHALL BE 15 FEET, AND IN KANSAS, WHERE MAXIMUM DISTANCE FROM FACE OF POST TO CENTERLINE OF TRACK SHALL BE 15 FEET.

FOR GRADES AND SPECIES OF LUMBER, SEE C.E.S. 5783. LUMBER DIMENSIONS ON THIS PLAN ARE STANDARD SIZES, BOARD MEASURE; NOT DRESSED DIMENSIONS.

THE A.T.& S.F. RY. SYSTEM
STANDARD SIGNS
HIGHWAY CROSSING SIGNS

CHICAGO, JULY 1951

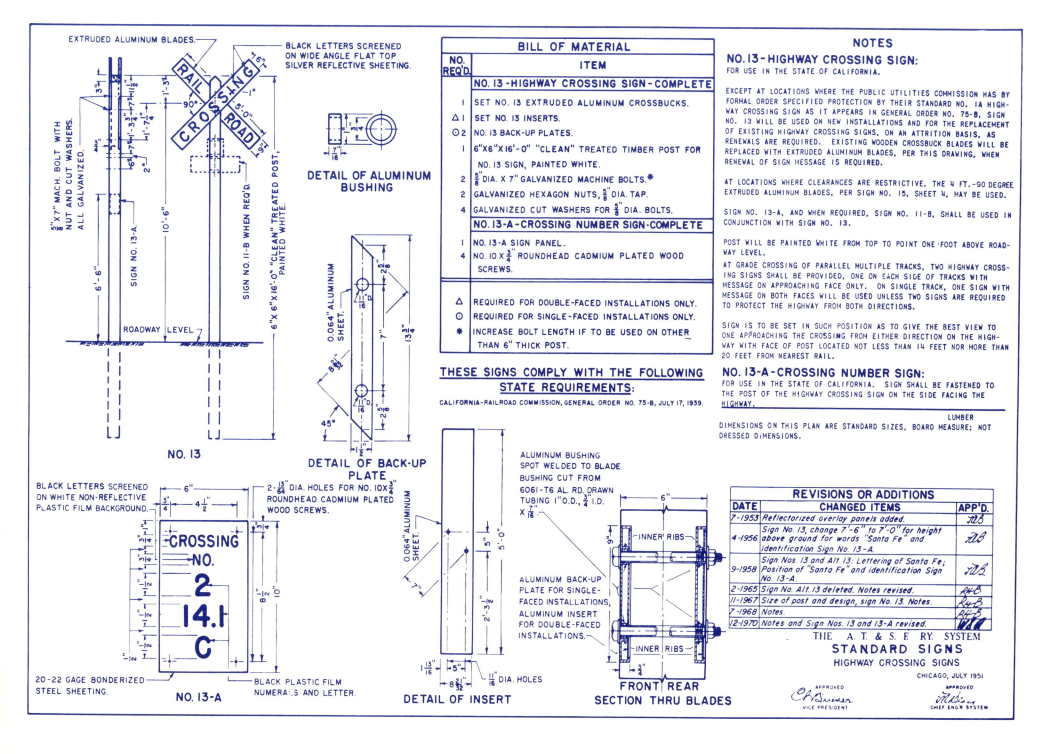

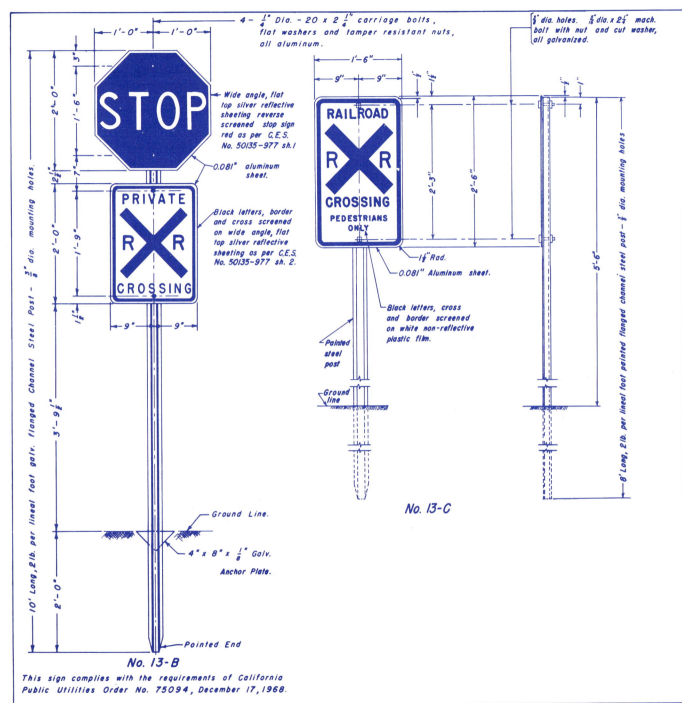

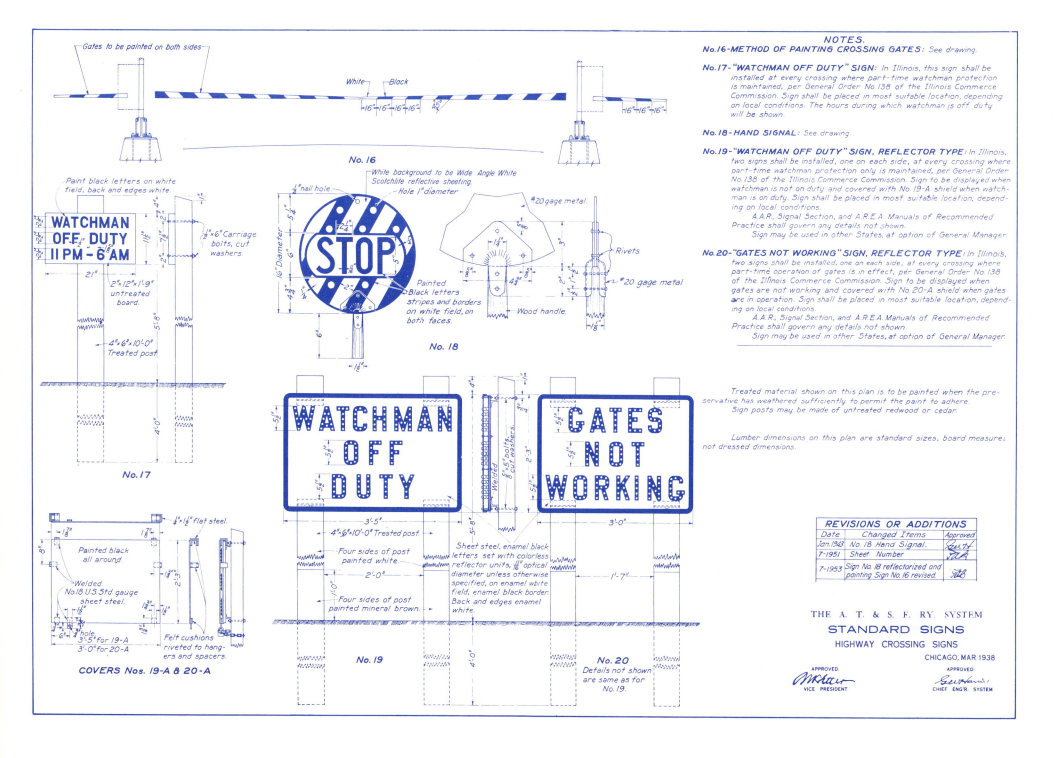

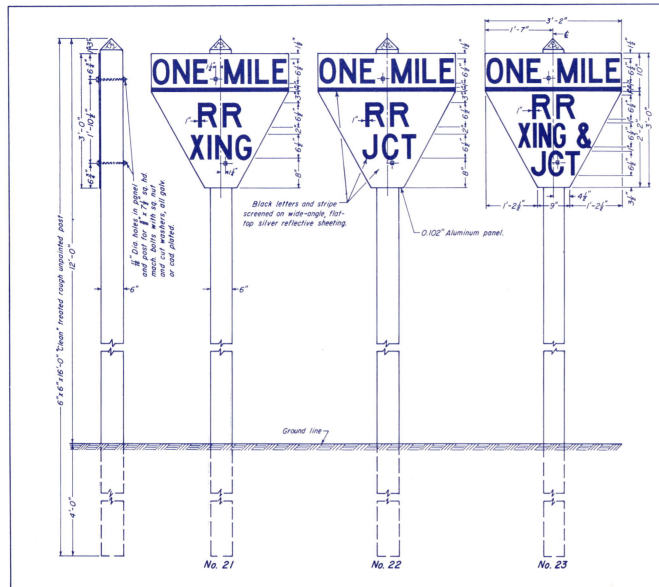

NOTES

No. 21 – RAILROAD CROSSING SIGN: Sign to be set at right angles to the track at a distance of 12'-0" from near rail to side of post, on the right hand side of the track as one faces the railroad crossing at grade and at distance of one mile in each direction from the crossing. Sign may be placed at a shorter distance from the crossing where required by local conditions and in such case, distance to nearest hundred feet to be painted on sign in lieu of one mile. Lettered side of the sign to be set facing trains approaching the crossing. (For exception, see additional note.)

No. 22 – RAILROAD JUNCTION SIGN: Sign to be set at right angles to the track at a distance of 12'-0" from near rail to side of post, on the right hand side of the track as one faces the junction and at distance of one mile in each direction from the junction, considering the junction to be the switch where normal main track train movements join. Sign may be placed at a shorter distance from the junction where required by local conditions and in such case, distance to nearest hundred feet to be painted on sign in lieu of one mile. Lettered side of sign to be set facing trains approaching the junction. (For exception, see additional note.)

No. 23 – RAILROAD CROSSING AND JUNCTION SIGN: This combination sign may be used where the distance between a railroad crossing and junction is not more than 500 feet.
Sign to be set at right angles to the track at a distance of 12'-0" from near rail to side of post, on the right hand side of the track as one faces the crossing and junction and at a distance of one mile in each direction from the crossing or junction, considering the junction to be the switch where normal main track train movements join. Sign may be placed at a shorter distance from the crossing and junction where required by local conditions, and in such case, distance to nearest hundred feet to be painted on sign in lieu of one mile. Lettered side of sign to be set facing trains approaching the crossing and junction. (For exception, see additional note.)

Nos. 21, 22 & 23 – EXCEPTION: Where railroad crossings at grade or junctions are protected by interlocking signals for at least one mile from same, or where they are within yard limits, or junctions are similarly protected by block signals, the placing of Signs 21, 22 & 23 is optional with the General Manager.

Existing signs Nos. 21, 22 and 23 of the triangular type will be replaced with the above design on an attrition basis. Where it becomes necessary to renew wornout reflectorized overlay panels of existing signs in this group, new aluminum panels with message to conform with this plan will be furnished provided existing posts are in serviceable condition. Requisitions should clearly indicate whether complete signs or only the reflectorized panels to include fastening bolts are required.

As complete signs of the above design are installed distance of side of post to near rail will be 12'-0". Existing posts in serviceable condition located at a distance of 14'-0" from near rail to side of post to agree with previous standard plan will not be moved to the 12'-0" distance from near rail when wornout reflectorized overlay panels are replaced with the aluminum panels.

REVISIONS OR ADDITIONS		
Date	Changed Items	Approved
9-1937	Location of signs Nos. 21, 22 & 23	
7-1951	Sheet number.	
8-1952	Scotchlite overlay panels added.	
8-1966	Change of design.	

THE A. T. & S. F. RY. SYSTEM

STANDARD SIGNS

CHICAGO, APRIL, 1932.

APPROVED: VICE PRESIDENT
APPROV'D: CHIEF ENG'R. SYSTEM

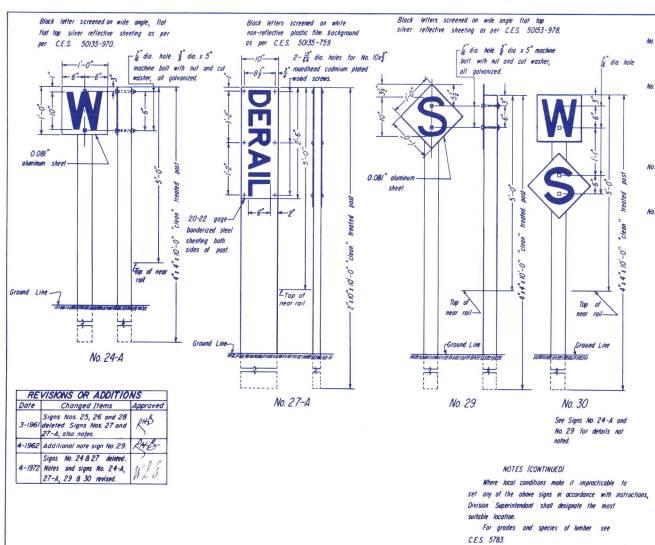

NOTES

No. 24-A-WHISTLE SIGN FOR HIGHWAY CROSSINGS: Sign is to be set, with message side of sign mounted facing trains approaching the grade crossing, at right angles to the track, 7 feet 6 inches from the near rail to the side of post, on the right hand side of the track as one faces the crossing, at points 1320 feet in each direction from the crossing. On high speed main track General Mananager may increase this distance to a maximum of 2000 feet.

No. 27-A-DERAIL SIGN: Sign is to be set, with message on both sides of post, at right angles to the track, 7 feet 6 inches from the near rail to the side of post, at all derails (not interlocking) at which there is no high stand to indicate position of derail. Derails which are pipe connected with switch stand, while considered as interlocked, will nevertheless require placing of sign.

In the State of California sign shall be used at all derails on sidings, derailing switch or other operating device whether the derailer is operated where located or from a distance.

Where "Derail" overlay panels of this design are used on existing posts having semi-circular tops, top of overlay panel shall be placed 5 inches from top of post.

No. 29-WHISTLE SIGN FOR STATIONS: Sign shall be used at the discretion of the General Manager and when used shall be located approximately one mile from the station in each direction with message side of sign set facing trains approaching the station. Sign to be set at right angles to the track, 7 feet 6 inches from the near rail to the side of the post and on the right hand side of the track as one faces the station.

No. 30-COMBINATION HIGHWAY CROSSING AND STATION WHISTLE SIGN: When Signs No. 24-A and No. 29 are required within 500 feet of each other, this dual sign may be used instead of these separate signs at the discretion of the General Manager. The location of the sign will conform to the location requirements for Sign No. 24-A.

NOTES (CONTINUED)

Where local conditions make it impracticable to set any of the above signs in accordance with instructions, Division Superintendent shall designate the most suitable location.

For grades and species of lumber see C.E.S. 5783.

Lumber dimensions on this plan are standard sizes, board measure, not dressed dimensions unless otherwise indicated.

BILL OF MATERIAL		
No. REQ'D	ITEM	
	No. 24-A-WHISTLE SIGN FOR HIGHWAY CROSSINGS-COMPLETE	
1	No. 24-A sign panel.	
1	4"x 4"x 10'-0" "clean" treated timber post for No. 24-A sign.	
2	⅜" dia. x 5"* galvanized machine bolts.	
2	Galvanized hexagon nuts, ⅜" dia. tap.	
2	Galvanized cut washers for ⅜" dia. bolts.	
	No. 27-A-DERAIL SIGN-COMPLETE	
2	No. 27-A overlay, sign panel.	
1	2"x10"x10'-0" "clean" treated timber post for No. 27-A sign.	
12	No. 10 x ¾" roundhead cadmium plated wood screws.	
	No. 29- WHISTLE SIGN FOR STATIONS-COMPLETE	
1	No. 29 sign panel.	
1	4"x 4"x 10'-0" "clean" treated timber post for No. 29 sign.	
2	⅜" dia. x 5"* galvanized machine bolts.	
2	Galvanized hexagon nuts, ⅜" dia. tap.	
2	Galvanized cut washers for ⅜" dia. bolts.	
	No. 30-COMBINATION HIGHWAY CROSSING AND STATION WHISTLE SIGN-COMPLETE	
1	No. 24-A sign panel.	
1	No. 29 sign panel.	
1	4"x 4"x 10'-0" "clean" treated timber post for No. 30 sign.	
4	⅜" dia. x 5"* galvanized machine bolts.	
4	Galvanized hexagon nuts, ⅜" dia. tap.	
4	Galvanized cut washers for ⅜" dia. bolts.

* Change bolt length if to be used on other than 4" thick posts.

THE A. T. & S. F. Ry. SYSTEM
STANDARD SIGNS
CHICAGO, JAN. 1923

APPROVED
VICE PRESIDENT

APPROVED
CHIEF ENGINEER SYSTEM

REVISIONS OR ADDITIONS

Date	Changed Items	Approved
3-1961	Signs Nos. 25, 26 and 28 deleted. Signs Nos. 27 and 27-A, also notes.	RHB
4-1962	Additional note sign No. 29.	RHB
4-1972	Signs No. 24 & 27 deleted. Notes and signs No. 24-A, 27-A, 29 & 30 revised.	WLS

REVISIONS OR ADDITIONS

Date	Changed Items	Approved
6-1935	No. 30 added.	GWH
9-1937	Notes on Nos. 26,27,29	GWH
9-1943	Notes on No. 24	GWH
7-1951	Notes on No. 29. Sign No. 30. Sheet number	JLB
11-1954	Signs No 24, 29 and 30 reflectorized on main lines	JLB
4-1956	Note sign No. 30	JLB
8-1957	Sign No 24-A and notes Sign Nos. 24,29,30 added.	JLB

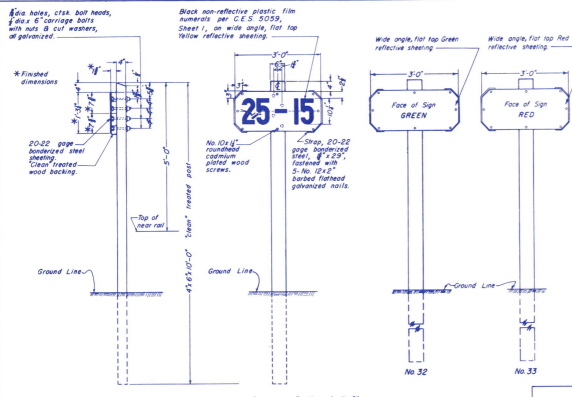

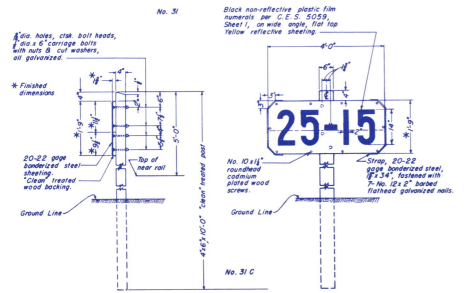

NOTES

No. 31 - PERMANENT SLOW SIGN: Points where speed is to be reduced, and the speeds to be indicated on sign, in multiples of five miles per hour, to be determined by Superintendent. The numerals nearest the track show the speed limit for passenger trains and the other numerals for freight trains, except where speed restriction is the same for both, only one set of numerals will be shown.

Sign to be set at right angles to the track, 7'-6" from the near rail to the side of post, setting line at same elevation as top of near rail, on the right hand side of the track as one faces the point where speed is to be reduced and at a sufficient distance, to be designated by the Superintendent, (not less than 2500 feet, when practicable) in each direction from the slow track, the variable distance for such location to depend upon the grade and other physical conditions, the normal speed and the speed allowed over the slow track. Face of sign to be set facing trains approaching the slow track.

Where a succession of stretches of slow track occurs and there is not sufficient distance between the same for resumption of normal speed, only one "Slow" sign will be set, as specified, preceding the first stretch of slow track.
(see "Rules Maintenance of Way and Structures")

No. 32 - PERMANENT RESUME SPEED SIGN: Sign to be set at right angles to the track, 7'-6" from the near rail to side of post, setting line at same elevation as top of near rail on the right hand side of the track as one faces away from the slow track, at point where rear of train having passed, normal speed may be resumed. Face of sign to be set facing train proceeding away from the slow track.

Where a succession of stretches of slow track occurs and there is not sufficient distance between the same for the resumption of normal speed, only one "Resume Speed" sign will be set, as specified, following the final stretch of slow track.
(see "Rules Maintenance of Way and Structures")

No. 33 - PERMANENT STOP SIGN: Sign to be set at right angles to the track, 7'-6" from the near rail to side of post, setting line at same elevation as top of near rail, on the right hand side of the track as one faces the point requiring a stop (as designated by Superintendent) and about 200' from such point. Face of sign to be set facing trains approaching point requiring a stop.

No. 31C - SPECIAL SLOW SIGN: Sign will have message approximately one third larger than Sign No. 31. To be used at locations where construction projects, for other than brief durations, have introduced safety hazards in the existing operating condition requiring reduction of train speeds from the normal.

Instructions shown above for No. 31 Permanent Slow Sign will apply also for Sign No. 31C except that setting distance from near rail to side of post will be 8'-0" instead of 7'-6" as required for Sign. No. 31.

The superintendent will designate locations where these special signs are required.

BILL OF MATERIAL		
No. REQD		ITEM
		No. 31 - PERMANENT SLOW SIGN - COMPLETE
1		No. 31 Overlay sign panel (Specify speed limits).
1		No. 31 Wood backing.
1		4"x6"x10'-0" "clean" treated timber post for No. 31 sign.
8	△	No. 10x1¼" roundhead cadmium plated wood screws.
4		¼" dia. x 6" galvanized carriage bolts.
4		Galvanized hexagon nuts, ¼" dia. tap.
4		Galvanized cut washers for ¼" dia. bolts.
		No. 31C SPECIAL SLOW SIGN - COMPLETE
1		No. 31C Overlay sign panel (Specify speed limits).
1		No. 31C Wood backing.
1		4"x6"x10'-0" "clean" treated timber post for No. 31C sign.
10		No. 10x1¼" roundhead cadmium plated wood screws.
4		¼" dia. x 6" galvanized carriage bolts.
4		Galvanized hexagon nuts, ¼" dia. tap.
4		Galvanized cut washers for ¼" dia. bolts.
		No. 32 - PERMANENT RESUME SPEED SIGN - COMPLETE
1		No. 32 Overlay sign panel.
△		Same material as required for No. 31 sign.
		No. 33 - PERMANENT STOP SIGN - COMPLETE
1		No. 33 Overlay sign panel.
△		Same material as required for No. 31 sign.

REVISIONS OR ADDITIONS		
Date	Changed Items	Approved
6-1958	Sign No. 31C added, changed width sign Nos. 31, 32 and 33.	HB
1-1960	Added Nos. 37 and 37A.	RHB
8-1966	Alternate sign material, Nos. 31, 32, 33 and 36. Post design Nos. 34, 34A, 35, 35A, 37 and 37A.	RHB
7-1968	Note Sign No. 31.	RHB
8-1971	Revised No. 31, 32, 33 & 31C. Moved Nos. 34, 34A, 35, 35A, 36, 37 & 37A to sh. 12.	WSQ
11-1972	Bolt length, Signs No. 31 & 31C.	WSQ

THE A.T. & S.F. RY. SYSTEM
STANDARD SIGNS
CHICAGO, AUG. 1957

APPROVED:
VICE PRESIDENT

APPROVED:
CHIEF ENG'R SYSTEM

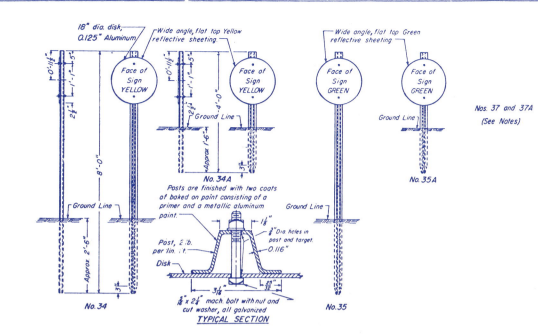

NOTES

No. 34 - TEMPORARY SLOW SIGNAL: To be set at right angles to the track, 7'-6" from the near rail to side of metal post, on engineman's side of track on single or multiple track territory (See also notes for Sign 34A) and not less than one mile in each direction from slow track. Face of sign to be set facing trains approaching the slow track.

Where a succession of stretches of slow track occurs and there is not sufficient distance between the same for the resumption of normal speed, only one "Slow" sign will be set, as specified, preceding the first stretch of slow track.
(see "Rules Maintenance of Way and Structures")

No. 34A - "LOW" TEMPORARY SLOW SIGNAL: To be used at points where there is not sufficient clearance for Sign 34. Top of metal post must not be higher than 2'-0" above top of rail, and side of metal post must not be nearer than 4'-0" from the near rail.
(see "Rules Maintenance of Way and Structures")

No. 35 - TEMPORARY RESUME SPEED SIGNAL: To be set at right angles to the track, 7'-6" from the near rail to side of metal post, on engineman's side of track on single or multiple track territory (see also notes for Sign 35A), at point where rear of train having passed, normal speed may be resumed. Face of sign to be set facing trains proceeding away from the slow track.

Where a succession of stretches of slow track occurs and there is not sufficient distance between the same for the resumption of normal speed, only one "Resume Speed" sign will be set, as specified, following the final stretch of slow track.
(see "Rules Maintenance of Way and Structures")

No. 35A - "LOW" TEMPORARY RESUME SPEED SIGNAL: To be used at points where there is not sufficient clearance for Sign 35. Top of metal post must not be higher than 2'-0" above top of rail, and side of metal post must not be nearer than 4'-0" from the near rail.
(see "Rules Maintenance of Way and Structures")

No. 36 - YARD LIMIT SIGN: Sign to be set at right angles to the track, 7'-6" from near rail to side of post, on the right hand side of the track as one faces the yard. Face of sign to be set facing trains approaching the yard. Superintendent will designate stations at which signs will be used and the distances they will be set outside the head blocks.

Nos. 37 and 37A - TEMPORARY STOP SIGNALS: Similar to Nos. 34, 34A, 35 and 35A except face to be red reflective sheeting. To be set at right angles to the track, 7'-6" from the near rail to side of metal post, on engineman's side of track on single or multiple track territory and not less than 300 feet in advance of the impassable track. For use of low signal No. 37A, follow instructions for Nos. 34A and 35A as to setting with respect to rail.
(see "Rules Maintenance of Way and Structures")

For grades and species of lumber see C.E.S. 5783. Lumber dimensions on this plan are standard sizes, board measure, not dressed dimensions.

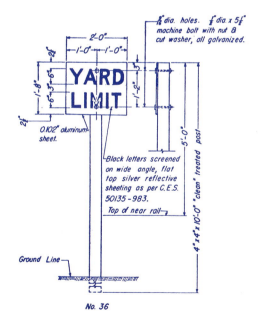

	BILL OF MATERIAL
No. REQ'D	ITEM
	No. 34 - TEMPORARY SLOW SIGNAL - COMPLETE
1	No. 34 Disk.
1	2 Lb. per lin. foot flanged channel steel post, painted, 8 feet long, pointed end, with 3/8" dia. mounting holes.
*2	3/8" dia. x 2 1/4" galvanized machine bolts.
2	Galvanized hexagon nuts, 3/8" dia. tap.
2	Galvanized cut washers for 3/8" dia. bolts.
	No. 34A - "LOW" TEMPORARY SLOW SIGNAL - COMPLETE
1	No. 34A Disk.
1	2 Lb. per lin. foot flanged channel steel post, painted, 4 feet long, pointed end, with 3/8" dia. mounting holes.
△2	3/8" dia. x 2 1/4" galvanized machine bolts.
2	Galvanized hexagon nuts, 3/8" dia. tap.
2	Galvanized cut washers for 3/8" dia. bolts.
	No. 35 - TEMPORARY RESUME SPEED SIGNAL - COMPLETE
1	No. 35 Disk.
*	Same material as required for No. 34 signal.

	BILL OF MATERIAL (CONT.)
No. REQ'D	ITEM
	No. 35A - "LOW" TEMPORARY RESUME SPEED SIGNAL - COMPLETE
1	No. 35A Disk.
△	Same material as required for No. 34A signal.
	No. 36 - YARD LIMIT SIGN - COMPLETE
1	No. 36 Sign panel.
1	4"x 4"x 10'-0" "clean" treated timber post for No. 36 sign.
2	3/8" dia. x 5 1/2" galvanized machine bolts.
2	Galvanized hexagon nuts, 3/8" dia. tap.
2	Galvanized cut washers for 3/8" dia. bolts.
	No. 37 - TEMPORARY STOP SIGNAL - COMPLETE
1	No. 37 Disk.
*	Same material as required for No. 34 signal.
	No. 37A - "LOW" TEMPORARY STOP SIGNAL - COMPLETE
1	No. 37A Disk.
△	Same material as required for No. 34A signal.

REVISIONS OR ADDITIONS		
Date	Changed Items	Approved
1-1960	Added Nos 37 and 37A.	RHB
8-1966	Post design Nos. 34, 34A, 35, 35A, 37 and 37A.	RHB
8-1971	Sheet No. changed. No. 36 revised.	WSQ

THE A.T. & S.F. RY. SYSTEM
STANDARD SIGNS

CHICAGO, AUG. 1957

APPROVED: _____ VICE PRESIDENT

APPROVED: _____ CHIEF ENG'R SYSTEM

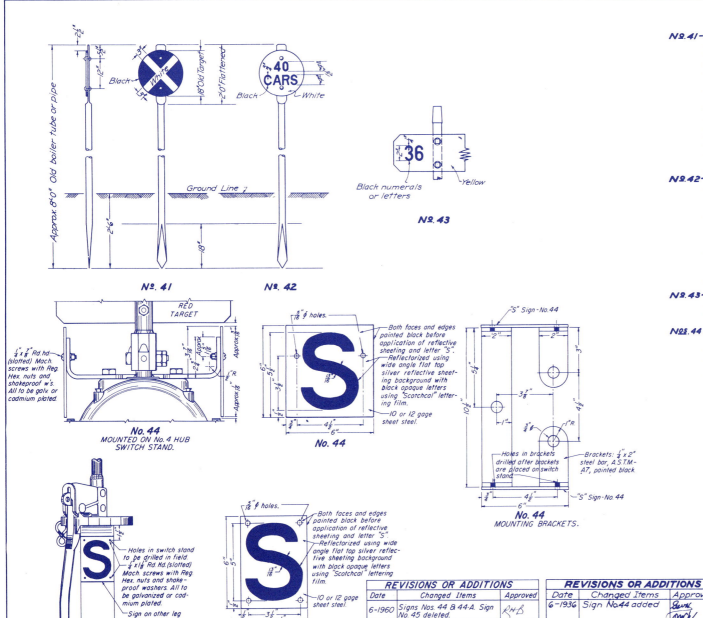

NOTES

No. 41 - SIGN FOR RAISING SNOW FLANGERS: To be made from an 18" old switch target or other suitable material, riveted to an 8 foot section of old boiler tube, or pipe, flattened at each end as shown. Face of target to be painted black with white stripes, 3 inches wide, diagonally across the face. Back of target and tube, or pipe, to be painted mineral brown.

Sign to be set at right angles to the track, 7 feet 6 inches from the near rail to side of post, on the right hand side of the track as one faces the object to be protected and at a distance of 150 feet in each direction from all public and private road crossings, outside switches of station grounds and bridges with inside steel guard rails or plank deck.

Sign to be set in territory designated by General Managers.

No. 42 - CAR CLEARANCE SIGN: Material and construction same as Sign for Raising Snow Flangers, No. 41. Face of sign to be painted white with black letters and figures 4 inches high, width of stroke ⅞ inches. Back of target and tube or pipe to be painted mineral brown.

Number of cars to be indicated in multiples of ten.

Sign to be set at right angles to the main track, 7 feet 6 inches from the near rail to side of tube or pipe, and at such a distance from the headblock of passing track as to allow the number of cars indicated on sign to approximately clear the headblock as train is leaving passing track.

Sign may be used where view of switch is obstructed.

No. 43 - TRACK NUMBERS ON SWITCH TARGETS: In yards designated by the General Manager, the number (so given for operating reasons) of track will be indicated on the face of switch stand target.

Nos. 44 & 44-A - SPRING SWITCH MARKERS: To be used only for automatic spring switches, reflectorized metal panels with letter "S" for mounting, respectively, on No. 4 Hub switch stands and No. 6 High or Low Star switch stands. The panels will be provided in pairs and requisitions should specify by number identification for which stand intended. Requisitions should also call for the required hardware for fastening.

REVISIONS OR ADDITIONS

Date	Changed Items	Approved
6-1960	Signs Nos. 44 & 44-A. Sign No. 45 deleted.	R+B

Date	Changed Items	Approved
6-1936	Sign No. 44 added	
12-1944	Sign No. 45 added	
7-1951	Sheet No. changed	
Apr. 1956	No. 6 High Star switch stand removed, type of spring switch marker No. 44 changed.	

THE A. T. & S. F. RY. SYSTEM

STANDARD SIGNS

CHICAGO, APRIL, 1931.

APPROVED:
VICE PRESIDENT

APPROVED:
CHIEF ENG'R. SYSTEM

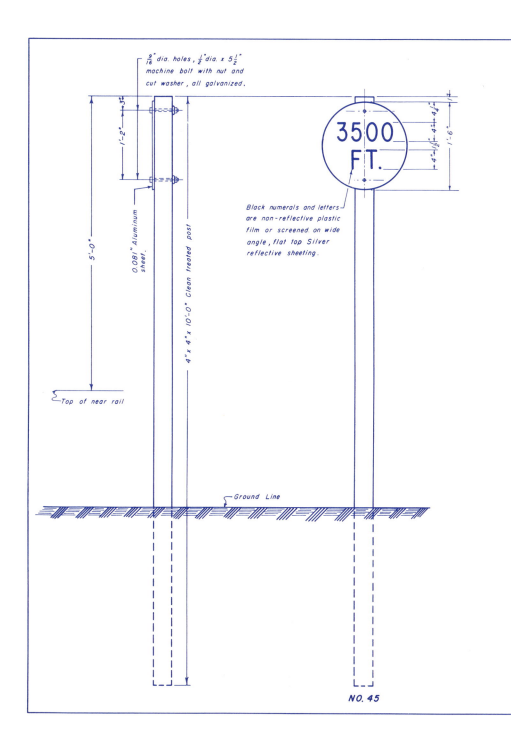

NOTES
No. 45 - LENGTH OF TRAIN (IN FEET) SIGNS:

Signs are to be set at right angles to the track, not less than 7'-6" from the near rail to the side of post, at locations designated by the General Managers.
"Signs available are 0 FT., 500 FT., 1000 FT., 1500 FT., 2000 FT., 2500 FT., 3000 FT., 3500 FT., 4000 FT., 4500 FT., 5000 FT., 5500 FT., 6000 FT., 6500 FT., 7000 FT., 7500 FT. Each installation will require the 0 FT. sign. The remaining signs are placed at 500-ft. intervals, using 0 FT. as the reference point. If it is desired to measure trains ranging in length from 4000-ft. to 7500-ft., signs labeled 0 FT. and 4000 FT. to 7500 FT. inclusive must be requisitioned.

BILL OF MATERIAL	
No. REQ'D	ITEM
	No. 45-LENGTH OF TRAIN (in feet) SIGNS-COMPLETE
1	No. 45 Sign Panel; Specify Marking, such as 0 FT., 4000 FT., etc.
1	4"x 4"x 10'-0" "Clean" treated timber post for No. 45 Sign.
2	$\frac{1}{2}$" dia. x $5\frac{1}{2}$" galvanized machine bolts.
2	Galvanized hexagon nuts $\frac{1}{2}$" dia. tap.
2	Galvanized cut washer for $\frac{1}{2}$" dia. bolts.

THE A.T. & S.F. RY. SYSTEM
STANDARD SIGNS
CHICAGO, FEB. 1973

APPROVED L. Cena VICE PRESIDENT
APPROVED W.S. Autrey CHIEF ENGINEER SYSTEM

BILL OF FASTENINGS FOR SIGN No. 55

Qty.	Description	Remarks
3	3/4" x 10 3/4" (Min.) x 20 ga. (0.036") Hanger straps	Galv. or cad. plated
3	No. 10 x 2 1/2" Rd. hd. slotted mach. screws with sq. nuts	" " " "
3	No. 10 x 3/4" " " " " " " " "	" " " "
9	No. 10 Plain washers	" " " "
3	No. 10 Shakeproof washers	" " " "

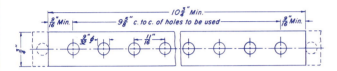

No. 55 - DETAIL of 3/4" x 20 ga. (0.036") galv. HANGER STRAP

No. 53

No. 54

NOTES

No. 53 - STATION GROUND BOUNDARY AND RIGHT-OF-WAY POST:
To be made of scrap rail of any weight, showing at least two feet of sound base at one end. Rail may have any defects as to head, web or base on the remaining three feet. A variation of 6 inches in length of rail is permissible. Upper two feet of post to be painted white.

The initials of the legal name of owning Railway Company and the words "PROPERTY LINE" to be painted in black on the rail base. Post to be set at all corners or angles on boundary line of station grounds, right-of-way or detached tracts of Railway Company's property not marked by fence. Base of rail to be set at the property line.

Where above placing is impracticable, post will be set in boundary line, distance to corner in feet to be painted in black on rail head. Base of rail to face the corner.

No. 54 - SUPERELEVATION MARKER FOR CURVES: Plates to be cut from 20 gage copper. Figures to be clearly impressed to preserve legibility. Plates to be stamped 0", 1/2", 1", 1 1/2", 2", 2 1/2", 3", 3 1/2", 4", 4 1/2", 5", 5 1/2" and 6". Star following figures indicates full elevation. Star to be punched in field as required. Plates to be set in center of track on tie nearest to points of 1/2" variation in superelevation, beginning with 0" at P.S. Plates to be fastened to tie with two old dating nails.

No. 55 - STOCK YARD SIGN: To be placed as detailed on Standard 12 ft. iron gate of stock yards per C.E.S. 5138, sheet 4, where required to deter illegal use of the pens and with the approval of the General Manager.

Where placement other than on field gate is considered to be more effective, subject to approval of General Manager, sign may be mounted adjacent to truck chute or other conspicuous location.

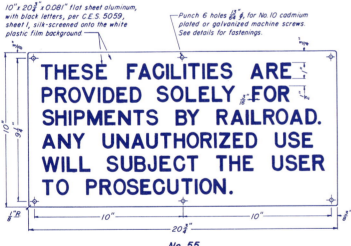

No. 55

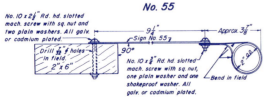

No. 55 - SECTION A-A

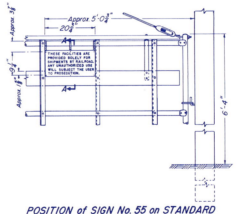

POSITION of SIGN No. 55 on STANDARD 12 ft. IRON GATE per C.E.S. 5138, SHEET 4

REVISIONS OR ADDITIONS

Date	Changed Items	Approved
2-1960	Reference note under Sign No. 51. Sign No. 55 deleted.	R+B
5-1962	Signs Nos. 51, 52 and 56 deleted. Sign No. 55 added.	R+B
5-1963	Addition to note, Sign No. 55	R+B

THE A. T. & S. F. RY. SYSTEM
STANDARD SIGNS

CHICAGO, JULY 1951

APPROVED: _____ VICE PRESIDENT

APPROVED: _____ CHIEF ENG'R SYSTEM

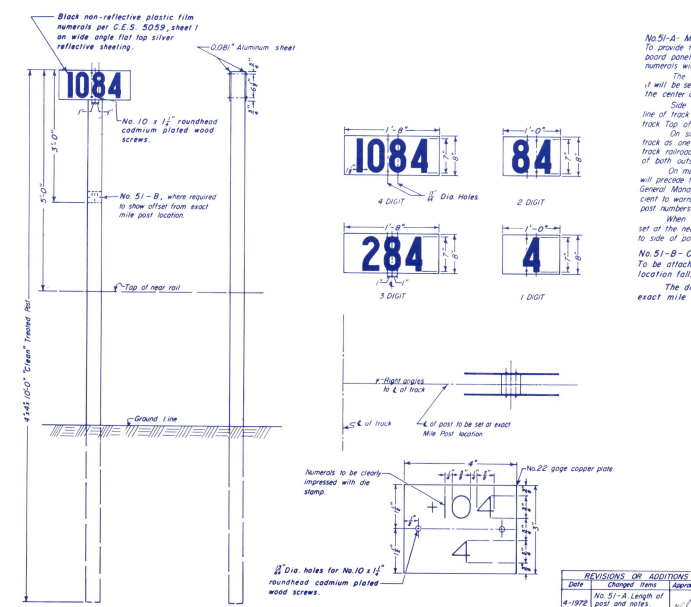

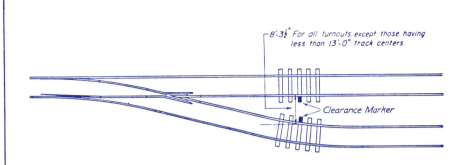

NO. 57.
CLEARANCE MARKER IN UNBONDED TERRITORY

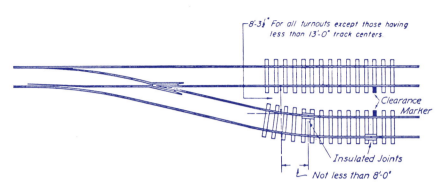

NO. 58.
CLEARANCE MARKER IN BONDED TERRITORY

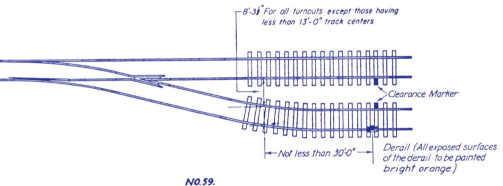

NO. 59.
CLEARANCE MARKER WITH DERAIL IN BONDED OR UNBONDED TERRITORY

DETAIL OF CLEARANCE MARKER

NOTES

No. 57, 58, AND 59- CLEARANCE MARKERS: Outside of rails and tops of ends of ties to be painted bright orange as indicated; the paint to be renewed whenever it becomes so indistinct that it cannot be readily seen by train and yard men. The distance 8'-3½" is between gage lines of the near rails of the turnouts.

No. 60- CLEARANCE SIGN: When approved by General Manager, this sign may be used in addition to markers No. 57, 58 or 59, and in other special locations.

Sign to be set at right angles to the track, 7 feet 6 inches from the near rail to the side of post, at clearance point conforming to No. 57, 58 or 59, with message side of sign facing away from the switch.

Lumber dimensions on this plan are standard sizes, board measure; not dressed dimensions.

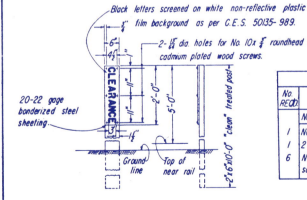

NO. 60.

BILL OF MATERIAL	
No. REQ'D	ITEM
1	No. 60- CLEARANCE SIGN-COMPLETE
1	No. 60 overlay sign panel
1	2"x 6"x 10'-0" "clean" treated timber post
6	No. 10 x ⅝" roundhead cadmium plated wood screws

REVISIONS OR ADDITIONS		
Date	Item	Approved
8-1942	No. 60 added.	
10-1948	Derail and Clearance Marker; Color Changed	
7-1951	Sheet number changed	
8-1958	Clearance, increased.	
10-1963	Clearance, increased from 8'-0" to 8'-3½".	
1-1972	No. 60 Revised	

THE A. T. & S. F. RY. SYSTEM
STANDARD SIGNS
CLEARANCE MARKER
CHICAGO, FEB. 1929.

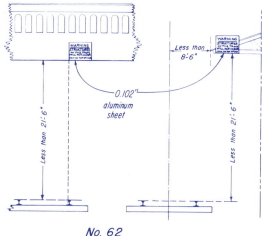

For use only in
STATE OF ILLINOIS

No. 62

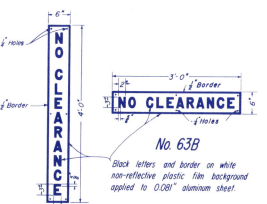

No. 63B

No. 63A

Black letters and border on white non-reflective plastic film background applied to 0.081" aluminum sheet.

NOTES
NON-CLEARANCE WARNING SIGNS:

No. 61 - Sign to be set with face facing away from the structure to be protected, at a distance of 8'-6" from near rail to side of post. Sign to be set 100 feet in advance of the ends of buildings or other structures which are less than 8'-6" from the center line of any track.

Where there is more than one building or structure along such track, one sign will be set for the first building only, as one approaches from the turnout. If track is accessible from either end, or extends a working distance beyond building or other structure which is less than 8'-6" from center line of track, two signs will be set, each 100 feet in advance of building or structure to be protected, as one approaches from either direction.

When sign cannot be set exactly in accordance with above instructions, the most suitable location will be selected, in no case placing the sign post closer than 8'-6" to the near rail.

No. 62 - FOR ILLINOIS; Illinois Commerce Commission, General Order 22, October 14, 1920. To be placed in a conspicuous position "at all overhead freight loading platforms, awnings, canopies, coal chutes, ore tipples, entrances to warehouses, shop buildings and similar structures, where the vertical clearance is less than twenty-one feet six inches." Sign to be same size as Sign No. 61 with black letters on white non-reflective plastic film background. The message is the same as No. 61 except for the word "SIDE", which should be replaced by the word "TOP."

Sign to be placed above track to be protected, with near edge above gage side of right hand rail as one faces in the direction of the structure.

When sign cannot be placed exactly in accordance with above instructions, the most suitable location will be selected.

Nos. 63A and 63B - FOR IOWA; Iowa State Commerce Commission, Docket K-1281, December 10, 1935. No. 63A to be used for side clearance less than 8'-6" and No. 63B for vertical clearance less than 22'-0".

GENERAL NOTES

For grades and species of lumber see C.E.S. 5783.

Lumber dimensions on this plan are standard sizes, board measure; not dressed dimensions.

When signs Nos. 62, 63A and 63B are attached to steel structures, plastic tape shall be applied between contact surfaces.

BILL OF MATERIAL	
No. REQ'D	ITEM
	No. 61 WARNING SIGN-COMPLETE
1	No. 61 sign panel
1	4"x 4"x 10'-0" "Clean" treated timber post for No. 61 sign
2	½" dia. x 5½" galvanized machine bolts
2	Galvanized hexagon nuts, ½" dia. tap
2	Galvanized cut washers for ½" dia. bolts

REVISIONS OR ADDITIONS		
Date	Item	Approved
4-1938	Nº 63A and 63B added	
7-1951	Sheet number changed	
7-1968	Design Signs Nos. 61,62, 63A and 63B. Notes.	
4-1972	Sign Nos. 61, 62, 63A and 63B and notes revised.	

THE A. T. & S. F. Ry. SYSTEM
STANDARD SIGNS
CHICAGO. JAN. 1923

APPROVED
VICE PRESIDENT

APPROVED
CHIEF ENGINEER SYSTEM

Revised: May 1924. C.F.W.F.

CLEARANCE 14 FT. 6 IN.
No. 64

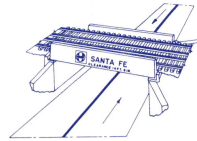

**TYPICAL UNDIVIDED UNDERPASS
TWO LANE HIGHWAY**

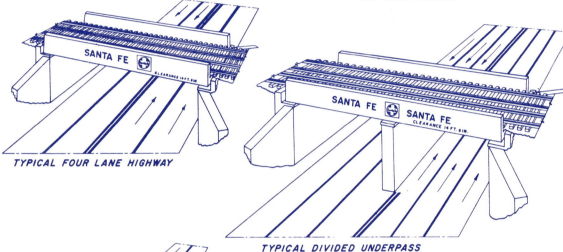

TYPICAL FOUR LANE HIGHWAY

**TYPICAL DIVIDED UNDERPASS
SIX LANE HIGHWAY**

**TYPICAL DIVIDED UNDERPASS
TWO LANE HIGHWAY**

NOTES
No. 64 – CLEARANCE SIGN FOR UNDERPASSES: Sign shall be painted on both sides of underpass structures, over center of traffic lanes for multilanes and divided underpass two lane highways, over center of structure for undivided underpass two lane highways, stating correctly in feet and inches the shortest distance from top of pavement to underside of structure.

Signs are to be painted only when the clearance is less than the minimum required in the states shown below:

Kansas		
Louisiana	Iowa	
Nebraska } 14'-0"	Missouri } 15'-0"	
New Mexico	California	
Arizona		
Illinois } 14'-6"	Colorado – 16'-0"	
Texas		

Oklahoma – All structures regardless of vertical clearance.

**THE A. T. & S. F. RY. SYSTEM
STANDARD SIGNS**
CHICAGO, JAN. 1955

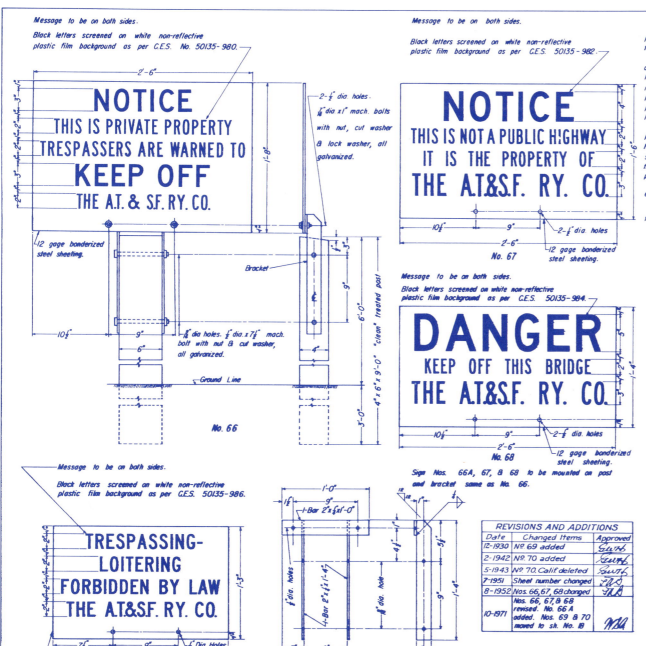

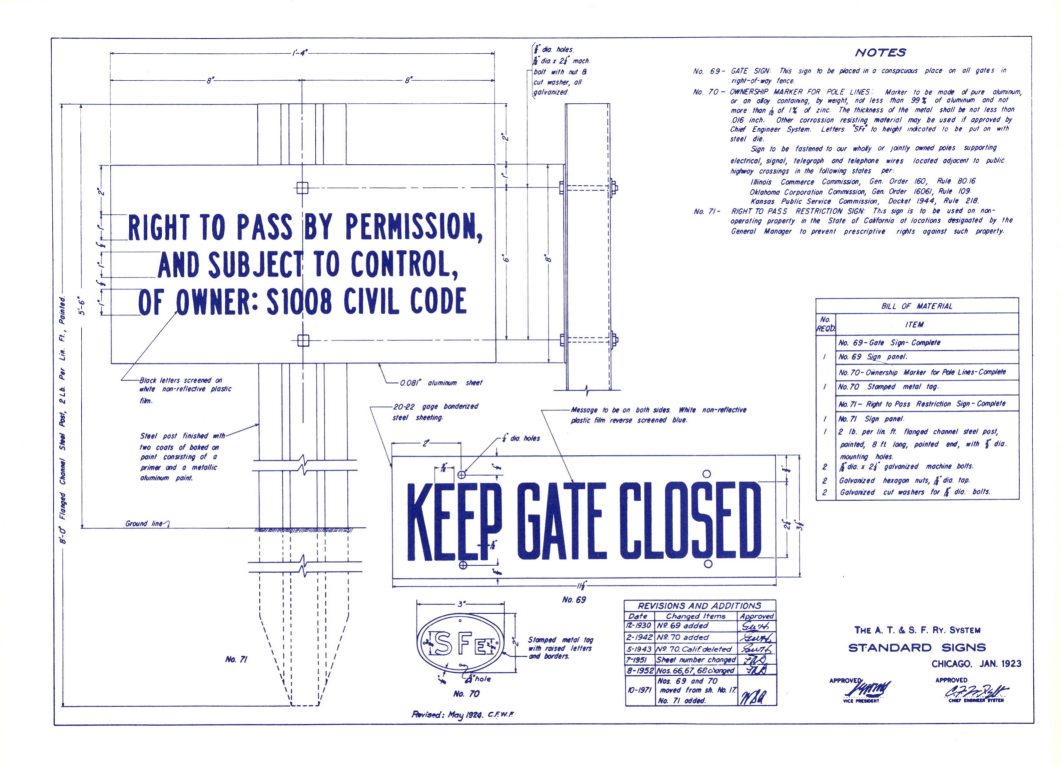

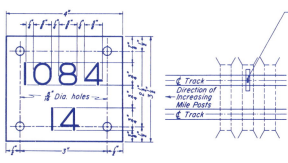

No. 72

LOCATION OF BRIDGE NUMBER TAG FOR ARCHES, BOXES, PIPES, ETC.

One Bridge No. Tag shall be placed in the center of the track and in the center of the track tie nearest the center of the structure.

In multiple main track territory, one Bridge No. Tag shall be placed in the center of the right hand main track when facing the direction of increasing mile posts.

LOCATION OF BRIDGE NUMBER TAG FOR BRIDGES LESS THAN 200 FEET LONG

In multiple main track territory, one Bridge No. Tag shall be placed in the center of the first tie on the approach end of the bridge (when facing the direction of increasing mile posts) and in the center of the right hand main track (when facing the direction of increasing mile posts).

In single main track territory, one Bridge No. Tag shall be placed in the center of the first tie on the approach end of the bridge (when facing the direction of increasing mile posts) and in the center of the main track.

LOCATION OF BRIDGE NUMBER TAGS FOR BRIDGES MORE THAN 200 FEET LONG

In multiple main track territory, two Bridge No. Tags shall be used, one Bridge No. Tag shall be placed in the center of the first tie on the approach end of the bridge (when facing the direction of increasing mile posts) and in the center of the right hand main track (when facing the direction of increasing mile posts); likewise one Bridge No. Tag shall also be placed in the center of the first tie on the leaving end of the bridge (when facing the direction of increasing mile posts) and in the center of the left hand main track (when facing the direction of increasing mile posts).

In single main track territory, two Bridge No. Tags shall be used, a Bridge No. Tag shall be placed in the center of the first tie on each end of the bridge and in the center of the main track.

INSTRUCTIONS FOR NUMBERING BRIDGES

1.- BRIDGE STRUCTURES TO BE NUMBERED:

Numbers shall be assigned to all Bridge Structures (bridges, arches, culverts, pipes, stock passes, structures over irrigation ditches, undergrade railway and highway crossings and overhead railway and highway crossings) carrying fluid under or traffic under or over a track or tracks. Small "track" boxes and small pipes carrying drainage through the ballast from between the tracks shall not be numbered. Crossings which may be classified as "Pipe Lines" such as pipes or conduits carrying oil, gas, water, steam, air, sewage or electric, telephone, telegraph wires, etc. shall not be numbered.

Bridge Structures, on Highways, Roads, Farm Crossings and Sidewalks, which are located on Company Property, but not crossing the track, shall not be numbered.

2.- BRIDGE STRUCTURES TO BE LISTED IN "BRIDGE LIST":

All Bridge Structures, whether numbered or not, will be listed in the "Bridge List".

Bridge Structures on Highways, Roads, Farm Crossings and Sidewalks, which are located on Company Property, but not crossing the track, will be described (not numbered) in the "Bridge List" opposite the proper mile post location, showing the nature of the structure in the usual manner with such explanations under the column of Remarks as "75 foot Wooden Truss on Piles over Clear Creek on North side of track" or "4'x 4'x 28' Treated Wooden Box under Highway, South side of track", also by whom maintained. Such structures to be listed only when owned by the Company.

Signal Bridges are not to be considered in this connection. (See sheet 30 of C.E.S. No. 5059.)

3.- BRIDGE NUMBERING UNITS:

For the purpose of numbering, each individual bridge structure, without regard to the number of tracks carried, is considered to be a unit and only one number will be given to it. Thus, a multiple track bridge is a unit if any of the parts of the structure, (such as abutments, caps, dump boards, etc.) are common to the whole structure.

4.- METHOD OF NUMBERING (DECIMAL SYSTEM):

Main Track Bridge Numbers are determined by the mile post location of the bridge opening and the Bridge Number (location) is expressed by the mile post number and the decimal fraction of a mile.

The upper line numerals on the Bridge Number Tag indicate the mile post location of the bridge; the lower line numerals indicate the location in decimal fractions of a mile, from the mile post. The decimal fraction of a mile is expressed to the nearest tenth of a mile, except that where two or more structures are located within the same tenth of a mile, these structures shall be numbered to the nearest hundredth of a mile. In the same manner, the decimal fraction should be extended to thousandths of a mile, etc. where it is necessary to avoid duplication of bridge numbers.

For example, when only one bridge is located anywhere between Mile Post 9.95 and Mile Post 10.0499, it should be numbered 10.0; however, should there be a bridge at Mile Post 9+5174 and another at Mile Post 10+0106, the first shall be numbered 9.98 and the second 10.02.

For miles longer than 5280 feet, the decimal number of the bridge shall be calculated by dividing the mile post plus by the actual length of the mile. For standard 5280 feet miles or shorter, the decimal number of the bridge shall be calculated by dividing the mile post plus by 5280.

When additional bridges are placed, the existing bridges shall maintain their number and the new bridge shall be assigned the appropriate decimal fraction of a mile to avoid duplication of bridge numbers, even though the final bridge numbers are out of consecutive order.

For example, when a bridge at Mile Post 10+0794 bears the number 10.2 and a new bridge is placed at Mile Post 10+1003, the old bridge will maintain 10.2 and the new bridge shall be 10.19, even though it is out of consecutive order.

5.- SPREAD DOUBLE TRACKS:

On Double Track territory where the tracks are separated considerably, the bridges will be numbered as on independent lines except that the Mile Post number used in determining the bridge number on the newer track will be preceded by the letter "X".

6.- SIDE AND CONNECTING TRACKS:

On Side and Connecting Tracks, where the same drainage is handled as on the Main Track, bridge number tags will not be set for the Side Track structure, but in the "Bridge List" the number of the Main Track structure will be assigned in accordance with paragraph 4. Where spurs lead off at a considerable angle so that the rule outlined above becomes impracticable, the structure should be shown in the "Bridge List" in the same manner as though it were on an independent Main Track whose initial head block is at Mile Post naught.

7.- BRIDGES REMOVED OR FILLED IN:

Whenever a bridge is removed or filled in it will continue to carry its original number, thus identifying it for permanent record, and its number will not be used for any other bridge opening.

REVISIONS OR ADDITIONS		
Date	Items Changed	Approved
Aug. 1970	Bridge No. Tag size & location	RHB

GENERAL INSTRUCTIONS

1.- Bridge Number Tags shall be cut from No. 22 gage copper plate. Numerals shall be clearly impressed with a die stamp as shown on this plan.
2.- The upper line numerals on the Bridge Number Tag shall indicate the mile post location of the bridge; the lower line numerals, the location in decimal fractions of a mile from the mile post.
3.- Bridge Number Tag shall be fastened to the tie with four 2"x#16 galvanized flat head drive screws.
4.- When a tie bearing a Bridge Number Tag is removed from the track, the Tag shall be attached to the new tie.
5.- Bridge Number Tags shall be placed for main track bridges only, where there are no side tracks on the bridge, or where the side tracks are adjacent and parallel to the main track. Bridges on spur tracks out of the main track and which diverge considerably from the main track shall have Bridge Number Tags.
6.- Bridge Number Tags shall be set in accordance with the location sketches shown on this plan.
7.- On non-parallel or spread multiple main tracks, Bridge Number Tags shall be located for the bridges as on single track.
8.- Where center of the tie is covered, Bridge Number Tag will be placed on end of the tie outside of rail.

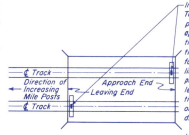

FLAT HEAD DRIVE SCREW
2"x#16 Galvanized
Wt. Per 100 = 2.4#

THE A.T. & S.F. RY. SYSTEM
STANDARD SIGNS
BRIDGE NUMBERING

CHICAGO, MAY 1963.

APPROVED:
R.D. Shelton
VICE PRESIDENT

APPROVED:
R.H. Beeder
CHIEF ENG'R. SYSTEM

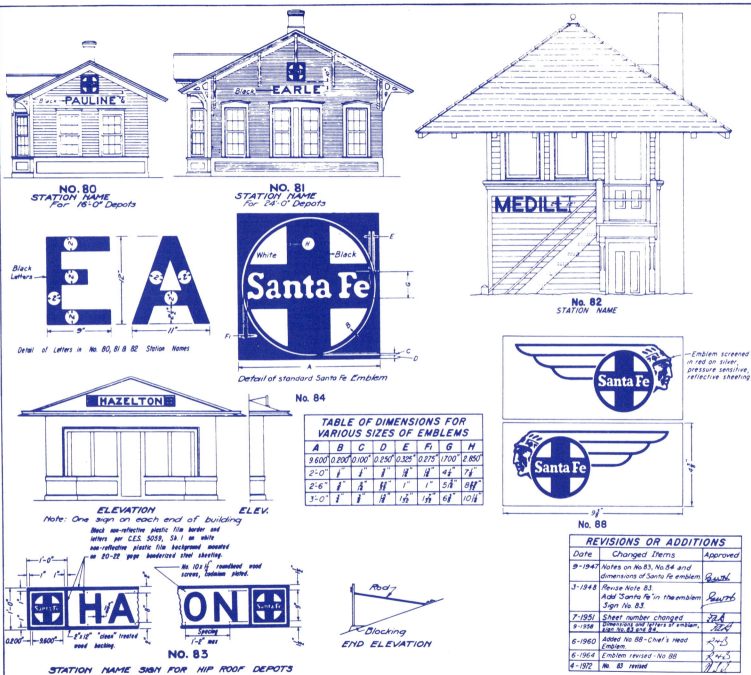

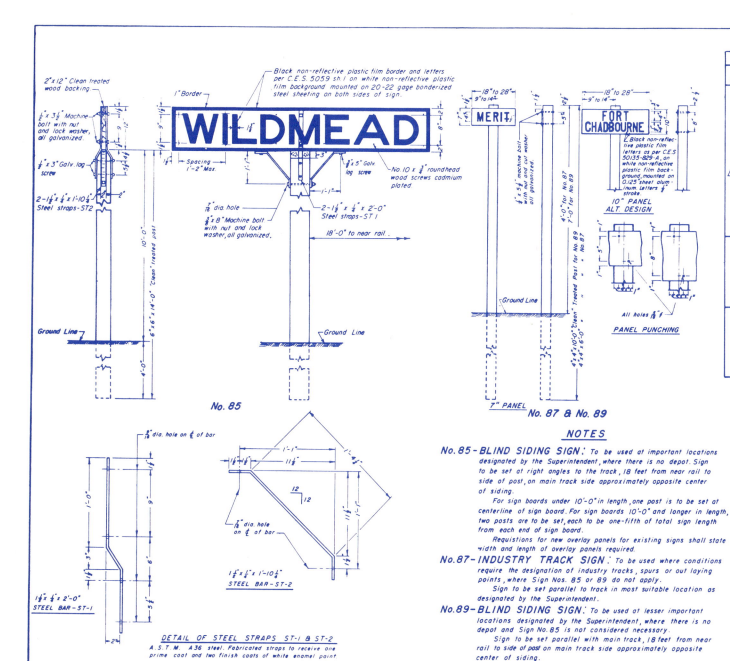

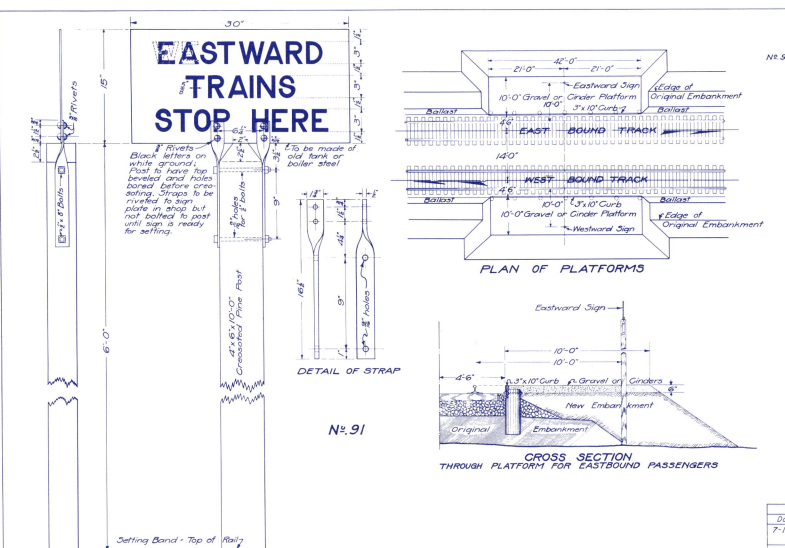

NOTES

No. 65 - SWITCHING LIMITS, SIGN: To be used at the limits of yard engine service.

Sign to be set at right angles to the track, 8'-6" from the near rail to the side of the post, 1'-8" above top of ground, on the right hand side of the track, when facing the yard. Face of sign to be set facing yard.

Where yard limits and switching limits are coincidental, the switching limits sign shall be fastened to the yard limits sign post, 1'-8" above the top of ground.

Superintendent shall designate stations and locations for the signs.

No. 143 - MEN AT WORK, SIGN: For protection of Store Department employes, when working in, or around cars.

Sign to be displayed by workmen at such points as may be necessary to give proper protection, and same are alone authorized to remove them.

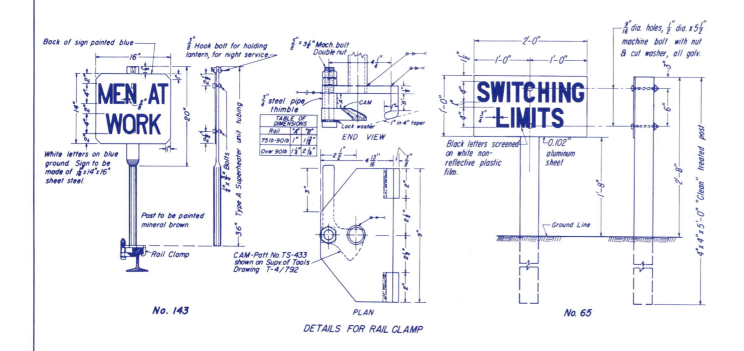

BILL OF MATERIAL	
NO. REQ'D.	ITEM
	No. 65 - SWITCHING LIMITS SIGN - COMPLETE
1	No. 65 Sign panel.
1	4"x 4"x 5'-0" "Clean" treated timber post for No. 65 sign.
2	½" dia. x 5½" galvanized machine bolts.
2	Galvanized hexagon nuts, ½" dia. tap.
2	Galvanized cut washers for ½" dia. bolts.

REVISIONS OR ADDITIONS		
Date	Changed item	Approved
11-1954	Sign No. 65 added.	
8-1957	Revision note, Sign No. 65.	
5-1965	Alternate design, Signs Nos. 87, 91 and 126A deleted. Sign No. 65, post and note.	
4-1972	Revised sign No. 65	

THE A. T. & S. F. RY. SYSTEM
STANDARD SIGNS

CHICAGO, JULY 1951

APPROVED:
VICE PRESIDENT

APPROVED:
CHIEF ENG'R SYSTEM

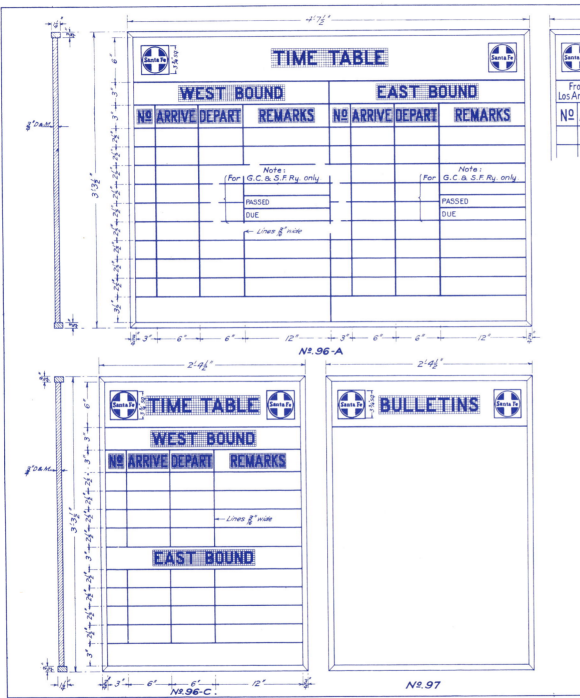

NOTES.

MATERIAL :— Standard Bulletin Boards to be made of dry Red Cypress, Clear Yellow Pine, Redwood or Oregon Fir.

PAINTING :— All Bulletin and Sign Boards to be painted on front side with 3 coats of genuine lamp black in oil or the Sherwin-Williams Stencil Black. For lettering, striping and trade mark the S.W. Standard Depot Paint #2500 is used.

Where necessary, the words "North Bound" and "South Bound" may be substituted for the words "East Bound" and "West Bound" shown on these signs.

EMBLEM :— Standard "Santa Fe" emblem has $3\frac{3}{4}"$ x $3\frac{3}{4}"$ white field. For details see C.E.S. 5059, sheet 1A.

REVISIONS OR ADDITIONS		
Date	Changed Items	Approved
7-1951	Sheet number changed	
9-1958	Sign Nos. 96-A, 96-B, 96-C and 97: Lettering of "Santa Fe" Emblem note added.	

THE A.T. & S.F. RY. SYSTEM.

STANDARD SIGNS

TOPEKA, MARCH, 1911

Revised, Jan. 1923. A.G.W.

No. 101-BAGGAGE ROOM SIGN and No. 102-A-WAITING ROOM SIGN: To be made of a dry Red Cypress, Redwood, or Oregon Fir board ¾" x 9" x 2'-5¼" long, with 1⅛" x 1¾" frame on three edges and two strips ½ x 1⅛ attached to the board to complete the frame. The 3½" projection left to be used for fastening sign to door jamb.
  Signs to be painted on both sides with three coats of gloss white. Signs to be lettered on both sides, letters 2¾" high, ⅜" width of stroke. Frame and letters to be painted black.

No. 103-NUMBER BOARD FOR STATION BUILDINGS, ETC.: To be made of untreated pine, S4S, ⅞ x 5¾ x 0'-9" long. Figures, 5 inches high, ¾ inch width of stroke, to be painted black on white ground. Edges of board to be painted white.

No.104-"POSITIVELY NO ADMITTANCE" SIGN:
  Sign to be made of a No.18 gage steel plate, 4" x 14", porcelain enameled.
  Face of sign to have white letters on a red field, as shown on plan. Back to be enameled black.
  Sign to be provided with four ¼" holes as shown, for attachment.
  Sign to be used at all points required by Current Fire Rules, and elsewhere as designated by Division Superintendent.

REVISIONS OR ADDITIONS		
Date	Changed Items	Approved
7-1951	Sheet number changed	
3-1961	Signs Nos. 102-D, E, and F deleted.	
4-1972	Signs Nos. 102-B and C deleted. Notes.	

The A. T. & S. F. Ry. System
STANDARD SIGNS
CHICAGO, JAN. 1923

APPROVED — VICE PRESIDENT
APPROVED — CHIEF ENGINEER SYSTEM

Revised: Mar., 1926. A.G.W.

GENERAL LAYOUT OF SIGN

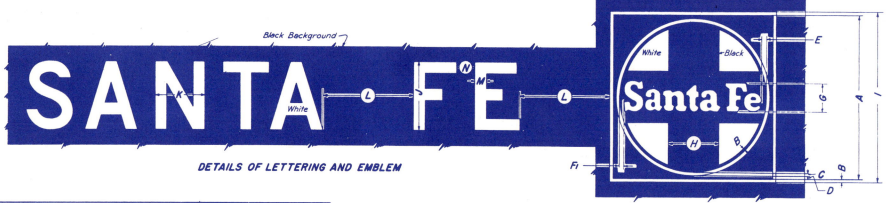

DETAILS OF LETTERING AND EMBLEM

TABLE OF DIMENSIONS FOR VARIOUS SIZES OF SIGNS

A	B	C	D	E	F₁	G	H	I	J	K	L	M	N	O
2'-0"	1/2"	1/4"	5/8"	13/16"	13/16"	4 1/4"	7 7/8"	2'-1"	10"	7 1/2"	10"	1 3/4"	2 1/4"	12'-0"
3'-0"	3/4"	3/8"	15/16"	1 7/32"	1 7/32"	6 3/8"	10 11/16"	3'-1 1/2"	1'-3"	11 1/4"	1'-3"	2 5/8"	3 3/8"	18'-0"
4'-0"	1"	1/2"	1 1/4"	1 5/8"	1 5/8"	8 1/2"	14 1/4"	4'-2"	1'-8"	1'-3"	1'-8"	3 1/2"	4 1/2"	23'-11"
5'-0"	1 1/4"	5/8"	1 9/16"	2 1/32"	2 1/32"	10 5/8"	17 13/16"	5'-2 1/2"	2'-1"	1'-6 3/4"	2'-1"	4 3/8"	5 5/8"	29'-11"
6'-0"	1 1/2"	3/4"	1 7/8"	2 7/16"	2 7/16"	12 3/4"	21 3/8"	6'-3"	2'-6"	1'-10 1/2"	2'-6"	5 1/4"	6 3/4"	35'-10"
7'-0"	1 3/4"	7/8"	2 3/16"	2 27/32"	2 27/32"	14 7/8"	2'-0 15/16"	7'-3 1/2"	2'-11"	2'-2 1/4"	2'-11"	6 1/8"	7 7/8"	41'-10"
8'-0"	2"	1"	2 1/2"	3 1/4"	3 1/4"	17"	2'-4 1/2"	8'-4"	3'-4"	2'-6"	3'-4"	7"	9"	47'-9"

NOTES

№ 121 – "SANTA FE" ADVERTISEMENT SIGN

1- This sign to be stenciled or painted on steel girder and concrete bridges when same are adaptable to its use and only in such locations as are plainly visible to the public from highways, streets, electric lines, steam roads etc. General Managers will designate such locations.

2- In painting this sign each location should be handled as an individual problem but in so far as possible this plan should be followed. In general the largest size practicable as determined by the ruling dimensions "I" or "O" should be used. The style and proportion of the letters to one another, other than the lettering in the emblems, should conform to C.E.S. 5059, sheet No. 1. Lettering in emblems should conform to sheet No. 1A.

3- As it is desirable to place the emblems squarely within the panels between stiffeners on the side of plate girder bridges the distance of the lettering "Santa Fe" from the emblems, indicated by "L" in the table may be considered as a variable. Thus the length of the sign, "O" will also be affected. However, the distance between the words "Santa" and "Fe", which also equals "L", should be maintained as shown in the table.

4- Where sign is placed on a concrete structure the background should first be painted black and then the sign best suited as to dimensions as determined from the table should be painted thereon.

REVISIONS OR ADDITIONS		
Date	Changed Items	Approved
7-1951	Sheet number changed	
9-1958	Dimensions and letters of emblem.	

THE A. T. & S. F. RY. SYSTEM
STANDARD SIGNS
CHICAGO, NOV. 1945

APPROVED:
VICE PRESIDENT

APPROVED:
CHIEF ENG'R. SYSTEM

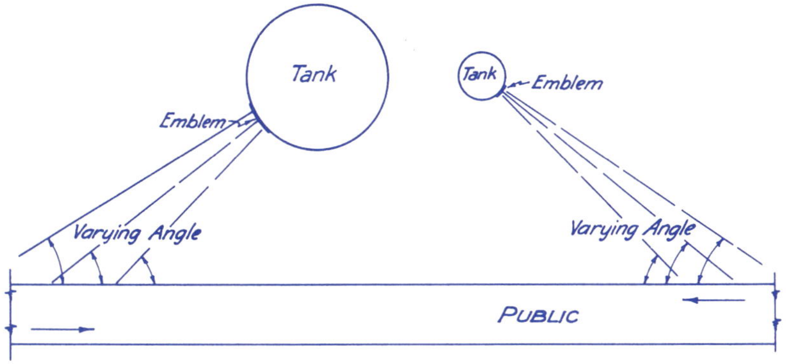

Optional Method of showing emblems on two tanks close together.

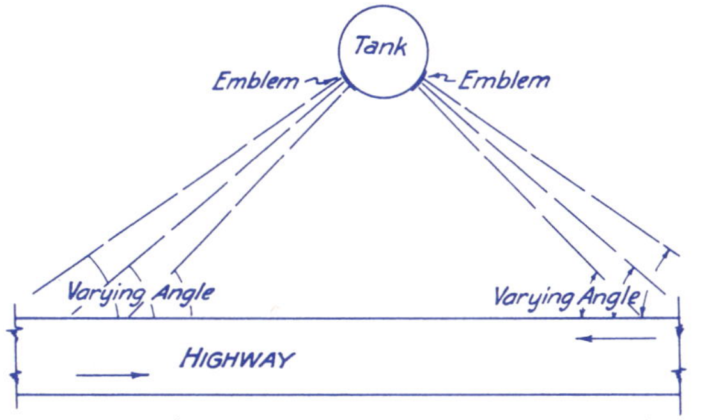

Optional Method of showing Emblem when one sign does not show up well from both directions, as when tank is close to road.

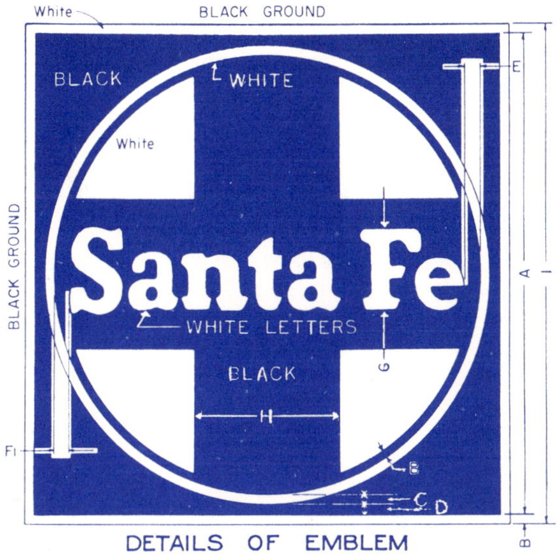

DETAILS OF EMBLEM

SIGN No. 136

TABLE OF DIMENSIONS								
A	B	C	D	E	F1	G	H	I
4'-0"	1"	1/2"	1 1/4"	1 5/8"	1 5/8"	8 1/2"	14 1/4"	4'-2"
6'-0"	1 1/2"	3/4"	1 7/8"	2 7/16"	2 7/16"	12 3/4"	21 3/8"	6'-3"
8'-0"	2"	1"	2 1/2"	3 1/4"	3 1/4"	17"	2'-4 1/2"	8'-4"

NOTES

Sign to be stencilled or painted on steel tanks in such locations as are plainly visible to the public from highways, streets, electric lines, steam roads, etc. In general, one emblem shall be painted on the side of tank facing the highway or railway, but in cases where one sign cannot be plainly seen from vehicles approaching from either direction, two signs, as shown in sketch, may be used.

In painting the sign, each location should be handled as an individual problem, depending upon distance of tank from highway or railway, and upon existence of obstructions such as trees and buildings, but in general, the largest size practicable should be used. General Manager will designate location and size of emblem and height above ground.

On the standard 55,000 barrel oil tank, 8' emblem may be used.

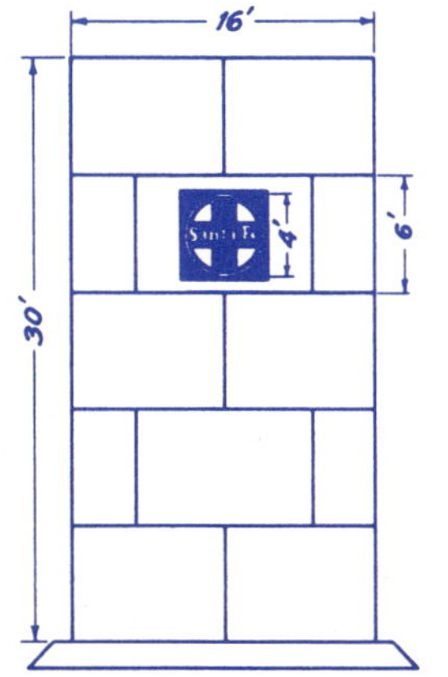

4' EMBLEM ON 16'x30' TANK

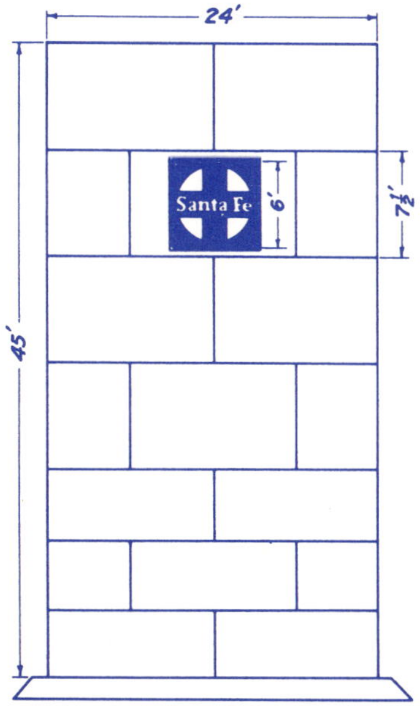

6' EMBLEM ON 24'x45' TANK

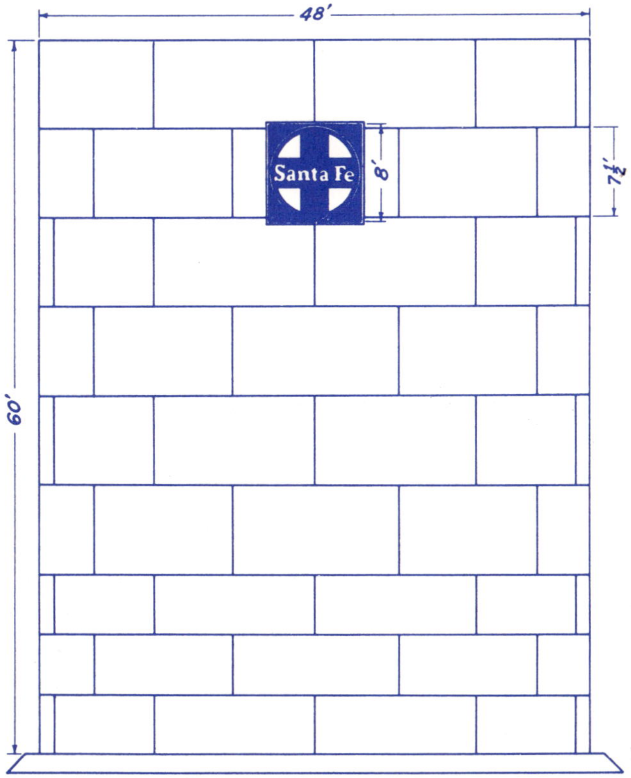

8' EMBLEM ON 48'x60' TANK

REVISIONS OR ADDITIONS		
Date	Changed Items	Approved
7-1951	Sheet number changed	[signature]
9-1958	Dimensions and letters of emblem.	[signature]

THE A. T. & S. F. RY. SYSTEM

STANDARD SIGNS

"SANTA FE" EMBLEM ON STEEL TANKS

CHICAGO, SEPT. 1928.

APPROVED: [signature] VICE PRESIDENT

APPROVED: [signature] CHIEF ENG'R. SYSTEM

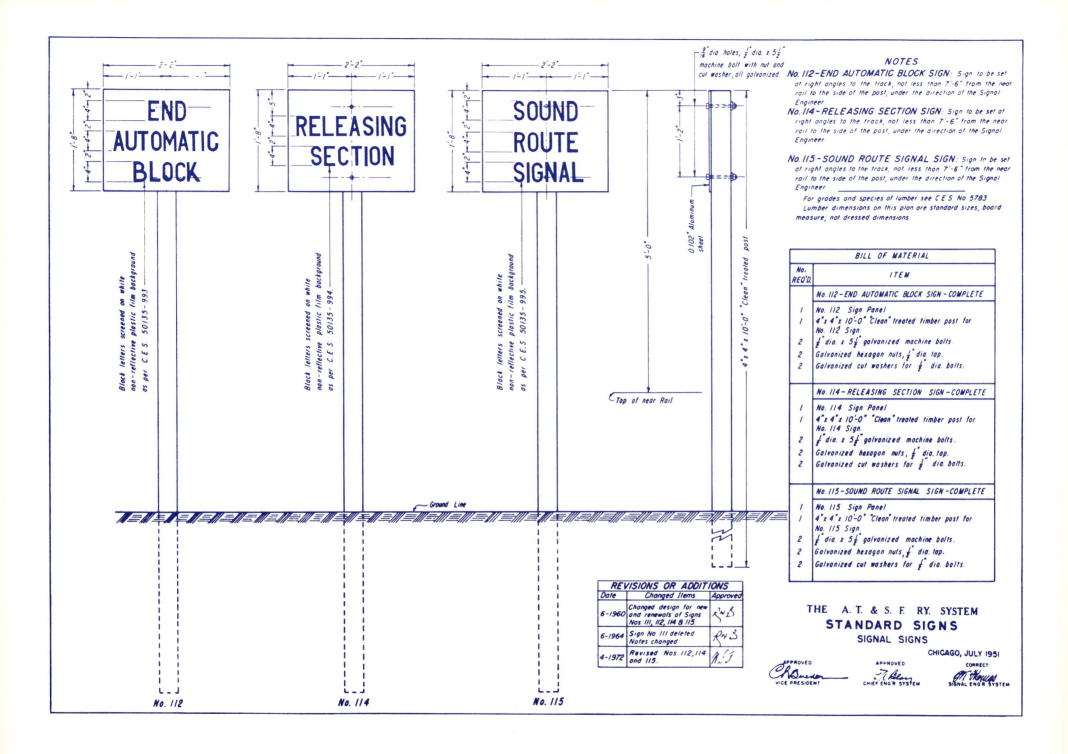

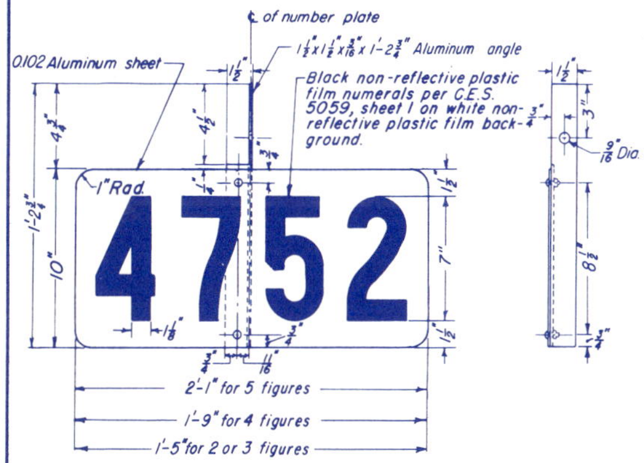

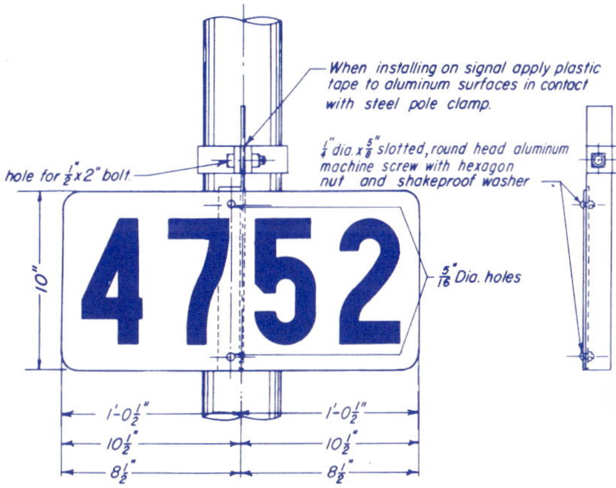

METHOD OF FASTENING NUMBER PLATE TO SIGNAL MAST

No. 113

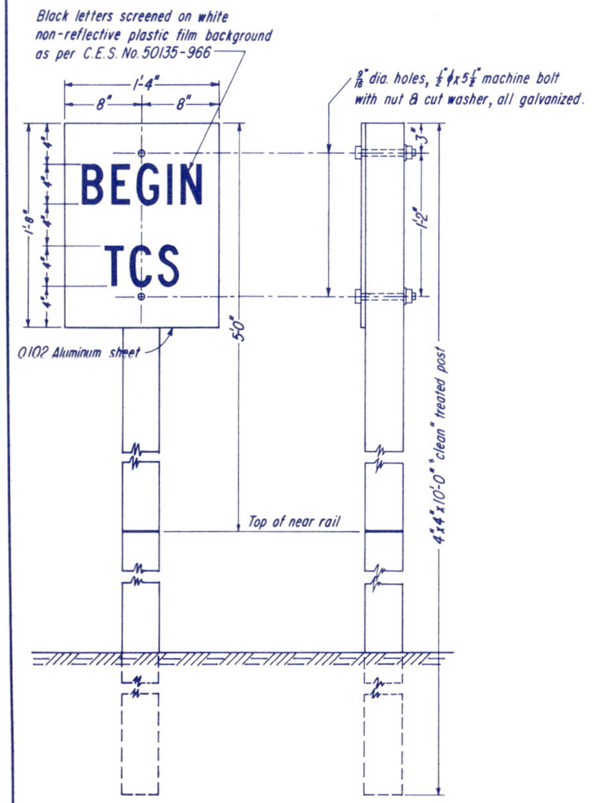

No. 116

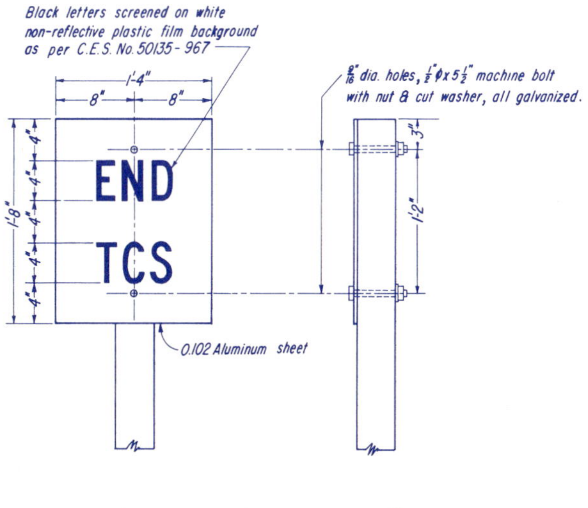

Sign to be mounted on post same as No. 116.

No. 117

NOTES

No. 113-SIGNAL NUMBER PLATE: Plate to be in accordance with Signal Engineer System specifications.

Signal numbers are determined by their mile post location and the direction of traffic governed. The mile post is the base to which is added, an odd figure for a westward, and an even figure for an eastward signal.

The first westward signal west of M.P. 34, for example, is 341, the second 343; the first eastward signal west of M.P. 34 is 342, the second 344.

No. 116-BEGIN T.C.S. SIGN: Sign to be set at right angles to the track, not less than 7'-6" from the near rail to the side of post, under direction of the Signal Engineer.

No. 117-END T.C.S. SIGN: Sign to be set at right angles to the track, not less than 7'-6" from the near rail to the side of the post, under the direction of the Signal Engineer.

Sign to be mounted on post same as Sign No. 116.

BILL OF MATERIAL	
No. REQ'D.	ITEM
	No. 113-SIGNAL NUMBER PLATE-COMPLETE
1	No. 113 Number Plate
1	$1\frac{1}{2}$" x $1\frac{1}{2}$" x $\frac{3}{16}$" x 1'-$2\frac{3}{4}$" Aluminum Angle for No. 113 Sign.
2	$\frac{1}{4}$" dia. x $\frac{3}{8}$" slotted, round head aluminum machine screws.
2	Aluminum hexagon nuts for $\frac{1}{4}$" dia. aluminum machine screws.
2	Aluminum shakeproof washers for $\frac{1}{4}$" dia. aluminum machine screws.
	No. 116-BEGIN T.C.S. SIGN-COMPLETE
1	No. 116 Sign Panel
1	4" x 4" x 10'-0" "clean" treated timber post for No. 116 Sign.
2	$\frac{1}{2}$" dia. x $5\frac{1}{2}$" galvanized machine bolts
2	Galvanized hexagon nuts, $\frac{1}{2}$" dia. tap.
2	Galvanized cut washers for $\frac{1}{2}$" dia. bolts.
	No. 117-END T.C.S. SIGN-COMPLETE
1	No. 117 Sign Panel
1	4" x 4" x 10'-0" "clean" treated timber post for No. 117 Sign.
2	$\frac{1}{2}$" dia. x $5\frac{1}{2}$" galvanized machine bolts.
2	Galvanized hexagon nuts, $\frac{1}{2}$" dia. tap.
2	Galvanized cut washers for $\frac{1}{2}$" dia. bolts.

REVISIONS OR ADDITIONS		
Date	Changed Items	Approved
Aug. 1957	Sign No. 113 changed	[signature]
Nov. 1959	Signs Nos. 116, Alt. 116 & 117, also note on renewals	RHB
May 1965	Sign No. Alt. 116 deleted Notes revised	RHB
Aug. 1970	Change to Aluminum Metal Signs, Notes revised	RHB

THE A. T. & S. F. RY. SYSTEM

STANDARD SIGNS

SIGNAL SIGNS

CHICAGO, JULY 1951.

APPROVED: VICE PRESIDENT — APPROVED: CHIEF ENG'R SYSTEM — CORRECT: SIGNAL ENG'R SYSTEM

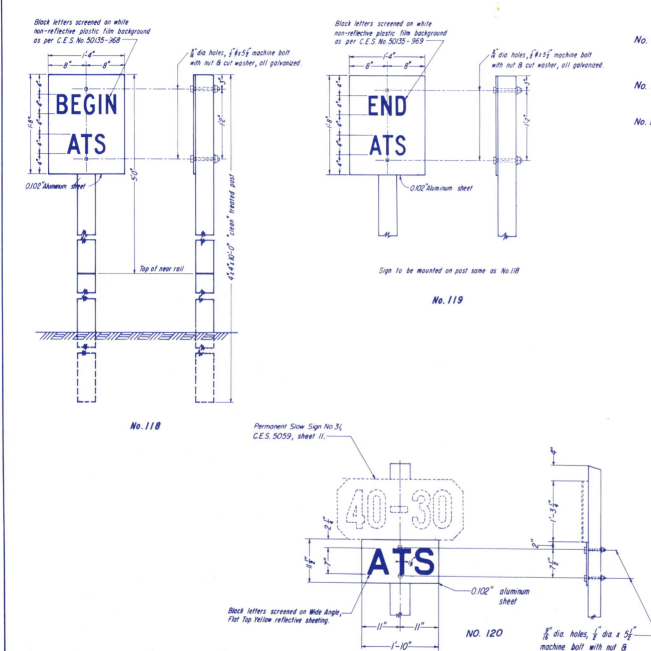

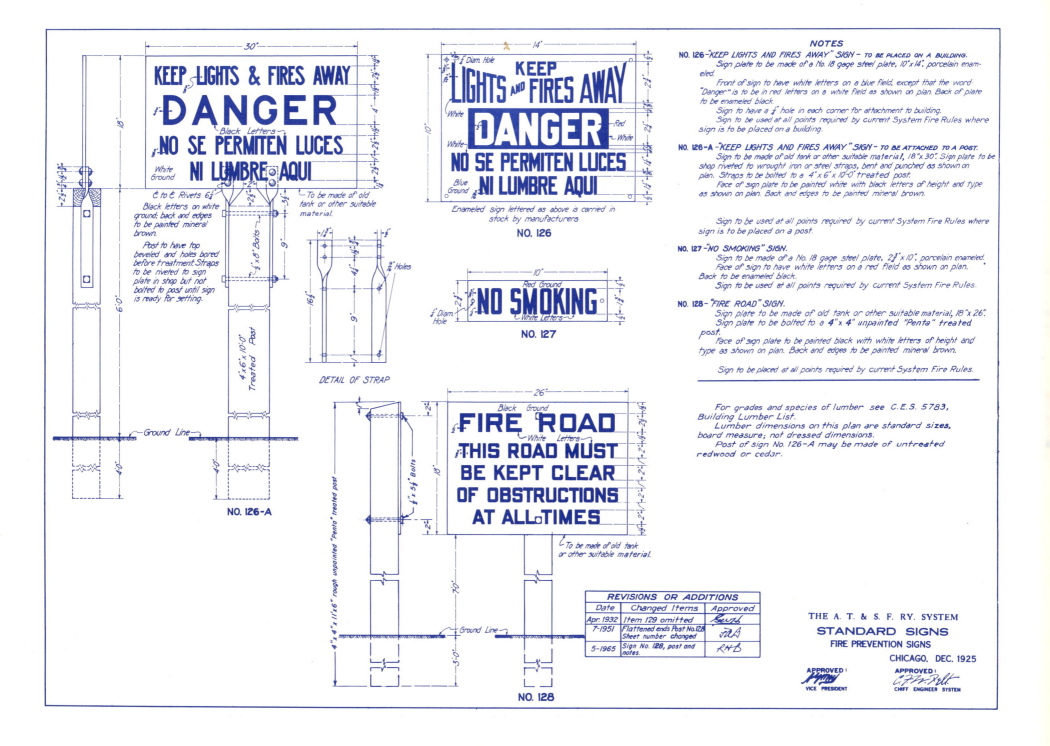

Sign No. 140

All letters black, except in words "FOR FIRE ONLY" which are to be mineral brown; all on white ground.

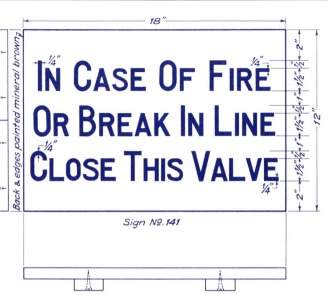

Sign No. 141

All letters black, except in word "FIRE" which are to be mineral brown; all on white ground.

Sign No. 142

All letters mineral brown, on white ground.

No. 140 – "PLACE NO OBSTRUCTION" SIGN
  This sign to be made of 1" (b.m.) lumber, S.4 S., painted as indicated and placed as required by Current Fire Rules.

No. 141 – "CLOSE THIS VALVE" SIGN
  This sign to be made of 1" (b.m.) lumber, S.4 S., painted as indicated and placed as required by Current Fire Rules.

No. 142 – "BREAK GLASS" SIGN
  This sign to be made of 1" (b.m.) lumber, S.4 S., painted as indicated and placed as required by Current Fire Rules.

REVISIONS OR ADDITIONS		
Date	Changed Items	Approved
12-1931	No. 142 added	
7-1951	Sheet number changed	

THE A. T. & S. F. RY. SYSTEM
STANDARD SIGNS
FIRE PREVENTION SIGNS
CHICAGO, SEPT., 1928.

APPROVED: _____ VICE PRESIDENT.
APPROVED: _____ CHIEF ENGINEER SYSTEM.

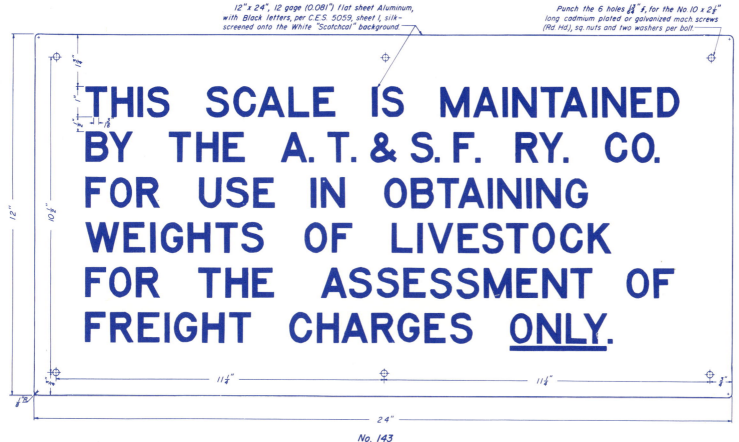

12" x 24", 12 gage (0.081") flat sheet Aluminum, with Black letters, per C.E.S. 5059, sheet I, silk-screened onto the White "Scotchcal" background.

Punch the 6 holes $\frac{13}{64}$" ∮, for the No. 10 x 2½" long cadmium plated or galvanized mach. screws (Rd. Hd.), sq. nuts and two washers per bolt.

NOTES

1.— Sign No. 143, STOCK SCALE SIGN, shall be placed on the "Beam Box for Stock Scales", C.E.S. No. 5758, dated November 1930, where required, and with the approval of the General Manager.

2.— On System Lines other than the Atchison, Topeka and Santa Fe Railway Company, substitute the initials of such company in lieu of the "A.T. & S.F. RY. CO.", i.e., "G.C. & S.F. RY. CO." or "P. & S.F. RY. CO." When ordering, requisitions should show the company involved.

THIS SCALE IS MAINTAINED BY THE A.T. & S.F. RY. CO. FOR USE IN OBTAINING WEIGHTS OF LIVESTOCK FOR THE ASSESSMENT OF FREIGHT CHARGES ONLY.

No. 143

After fastening Sign No. 143 upset ends of machine screws.

POSITION OF SIGN No. 143

REVISIONS OR ADDITIONS		
Date	Changed Items	Approved
8-1960	Method of fastening Sign No. 143.	

THE A. T. & S. F. RY. SYSTEM
STANDARD SIGNS
STOCK SCALE SIGN

CHICAGO, MARCH 1960.

APPROVED: VICE PRESIDENT
APPROVED: CHIEF ENG'R. SYSTEM

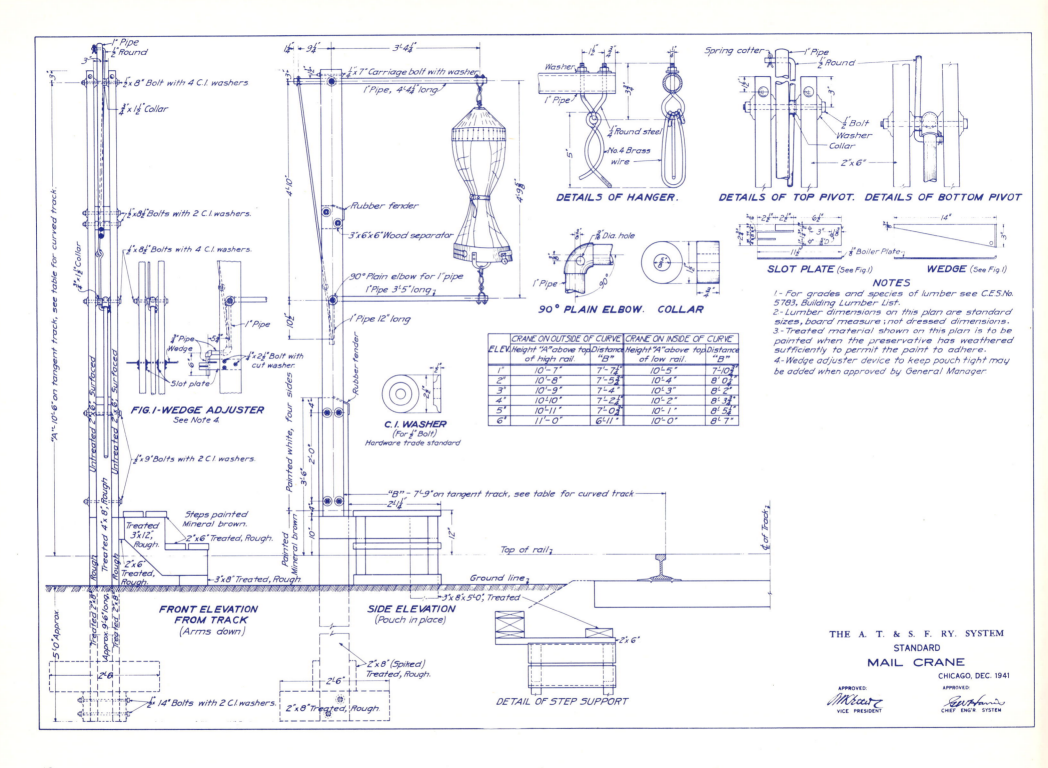

NOTES
Spikes shall conform to the current A.R.E.A. specifications for reinforced throat track spikes.

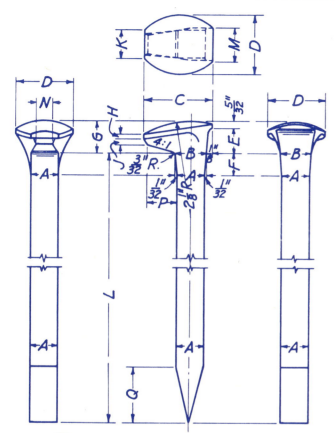

$\frac{5}{8}" \times 6"$ for 85 lb. and heavier rail.
$\frac{9}{16}" \times 5\frac{1}{2}"$, for lighter than 85 lb. rail.

TABLE OF DIMENSIONS

Size	A	B	C	D	E	F	G	H	J	K	L	M	N	P	Q	No. per 200 lb. Keg
5/8"×6"	5/8	11/16	9/16	15/16	17/32	1/2	11/16	3/32	1/8	5/8	6	3/4	3/8	11/16	1 1/4	240
9/16"×5 1/2"	9/16	5/8	1 1/2	1 1/4	15/32	7/16	5/8	3/32	3/32	9/16	5 1/2	11/16	5/16	5/8	1 1/8	315

REVISIONS OR ADDITIONS

Date	Changed Item	Approved
1-1950	A.R.E.A. Standard for 5/8"×6 1/2" Spikes.	JAB
5-1959	Drawing and data for 5/8" × 6 1/2" spike removed.	RHD

THE A. T. & S. F. RY. SYSTEM
STANDARD
CUT TRACK SPIKES
CHICAGO, MAR. 1939

APPROVED:
VICE PRESIDENT

APPROVED:
CHIEF ENG'R. SYSTEM

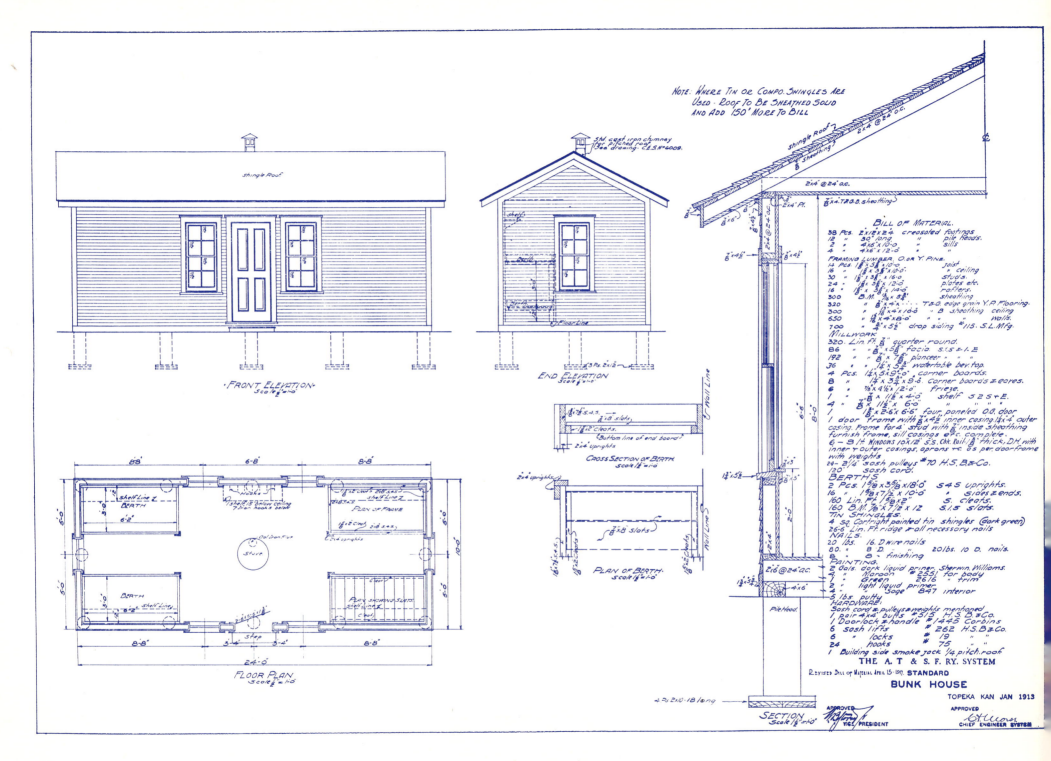

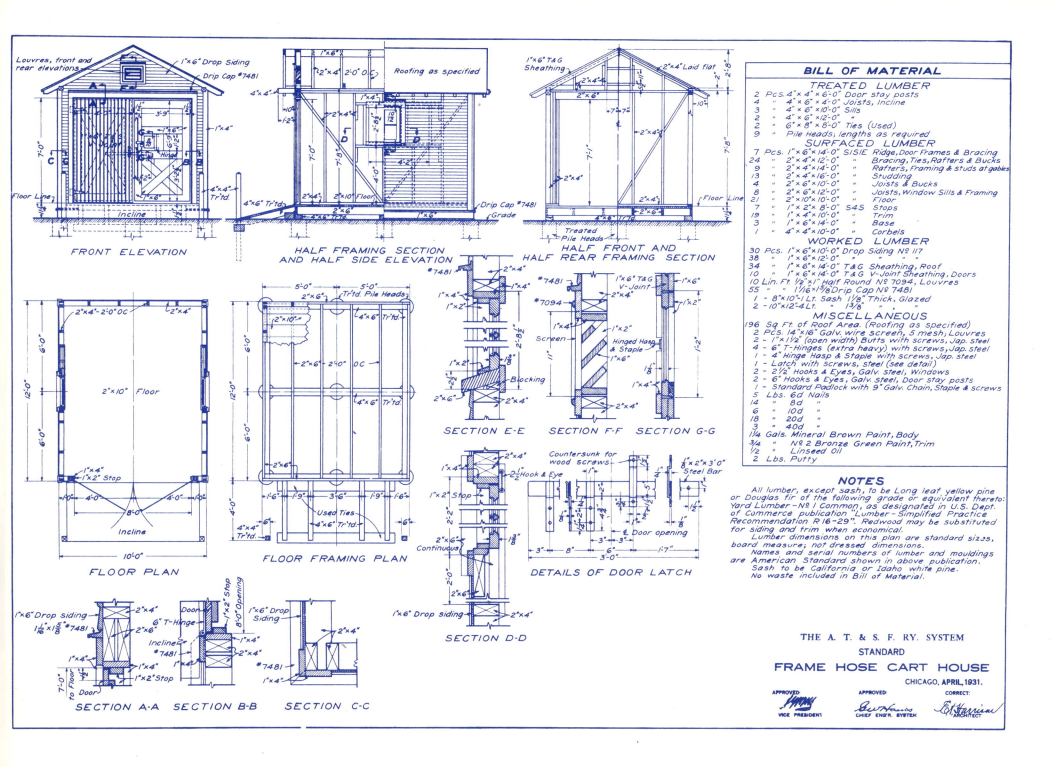

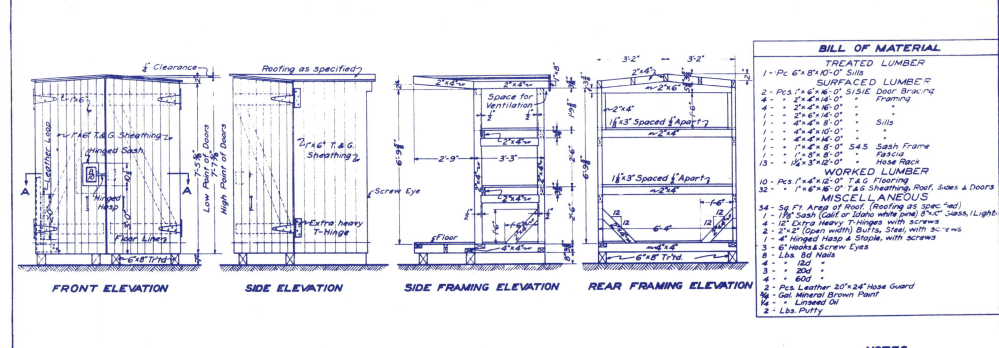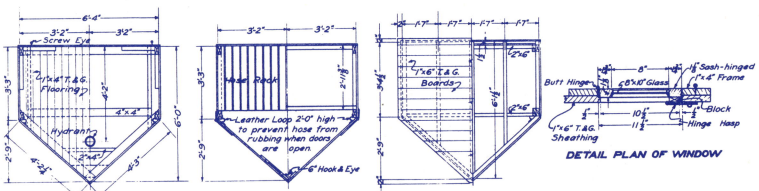

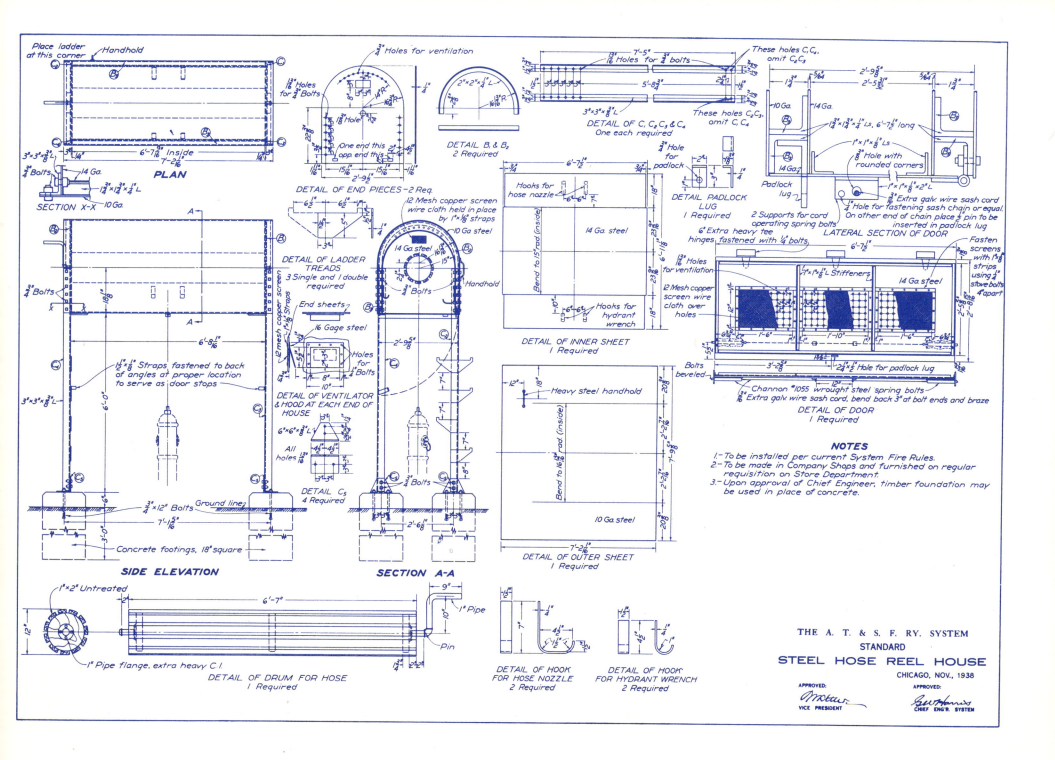

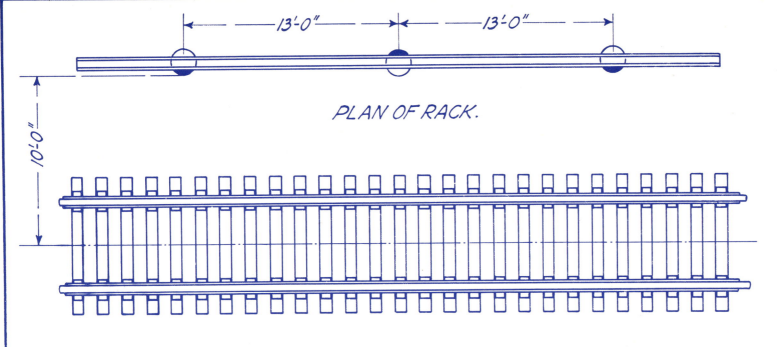
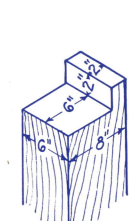

PLAN OF RACK.

NOTES:
Posts to be butt ends of treated piles; old bridge ties may be used when pile butts are not available.
Posts must be set firm with a minimum penetration of 18", Rail Seat 2'-2" above top of ground.
For locating rail racks see "Rules and Regulations for the Maintenance of Way and Structures."

REVISIONS OR ADDITIONS		
Date	Changed Items	Approved
12-1932	Height and notch	*signature*

The A.T. & S.F. Ry. System
STANDARD
RAIL RACK

Chicago, Jan. 1928
Approved:

signature
Vice President.

signature
Acting Chief Engr. System.

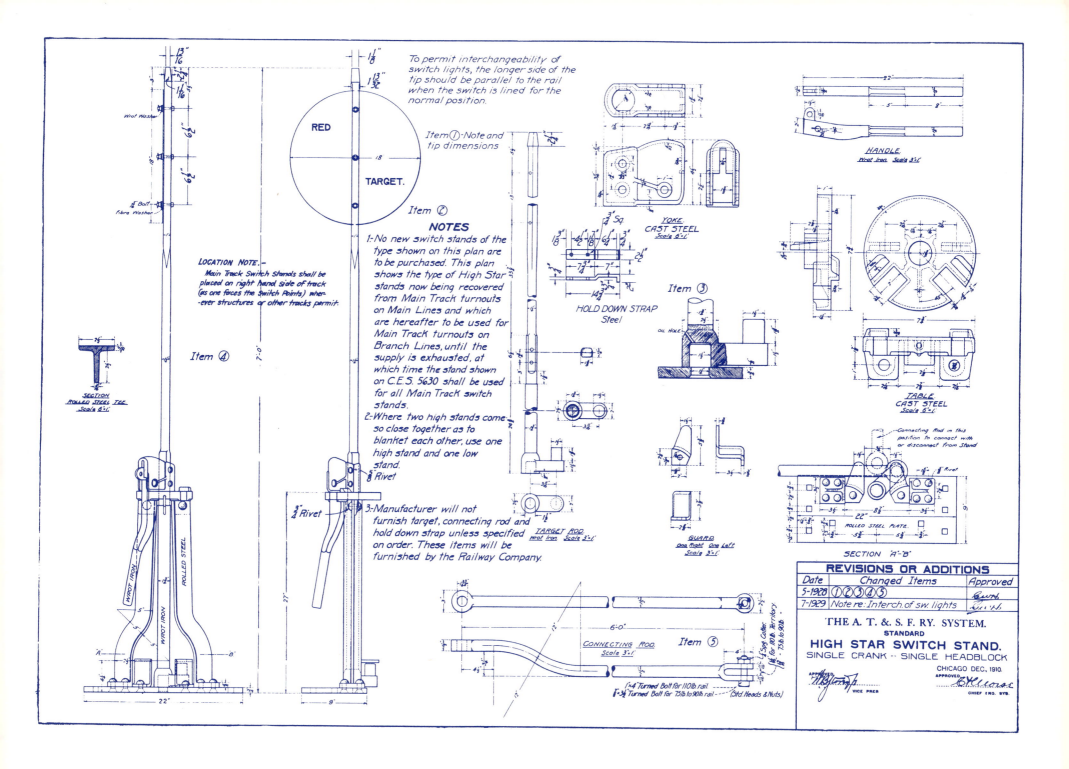

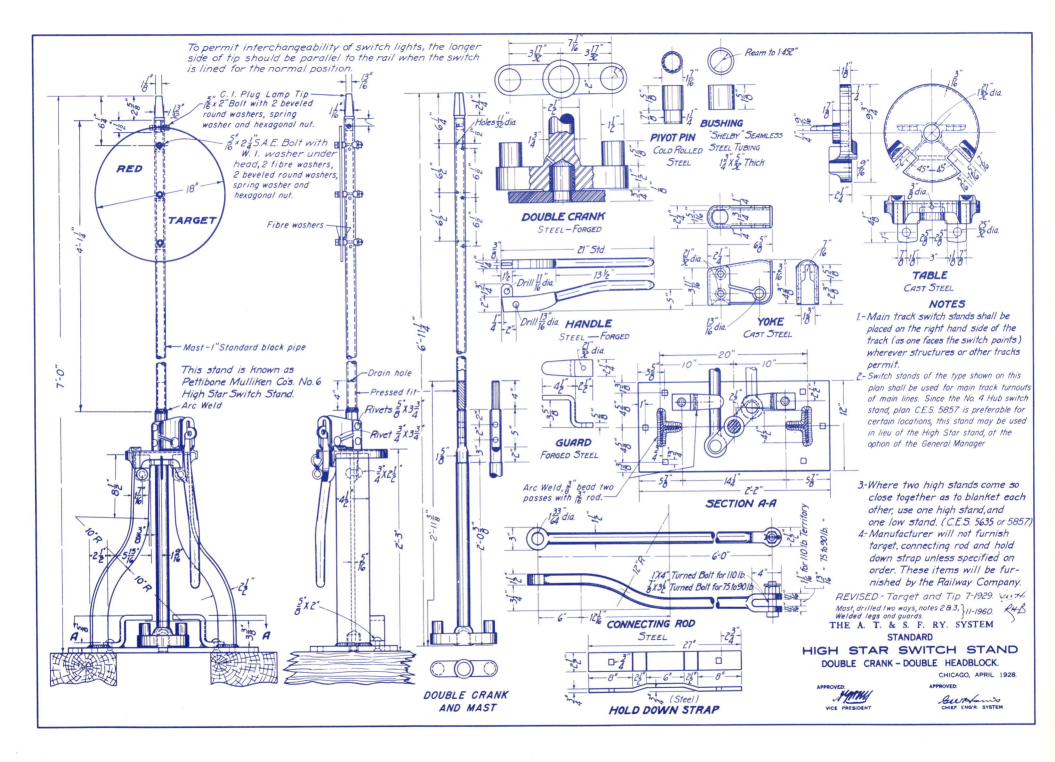

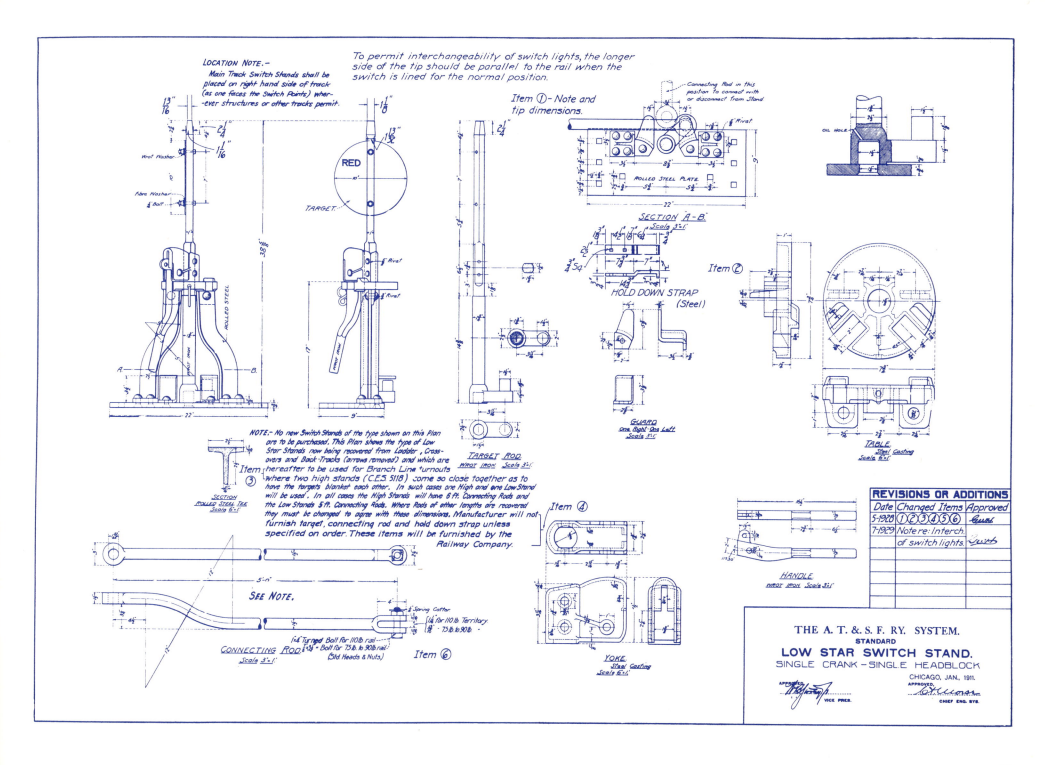

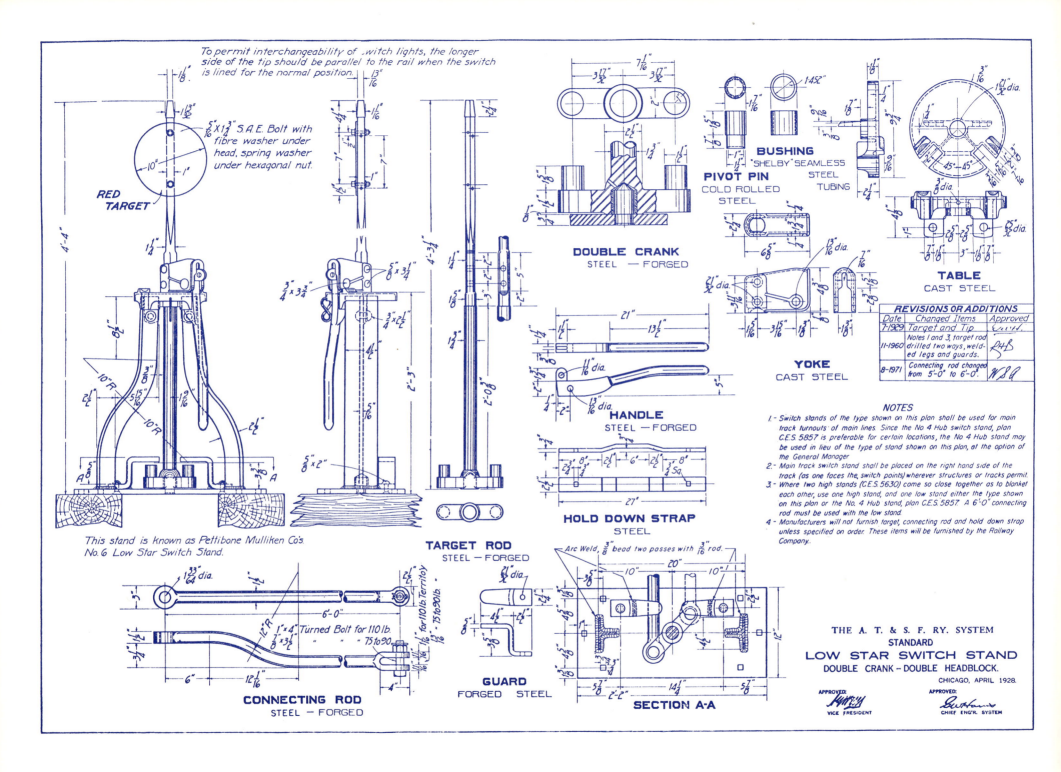

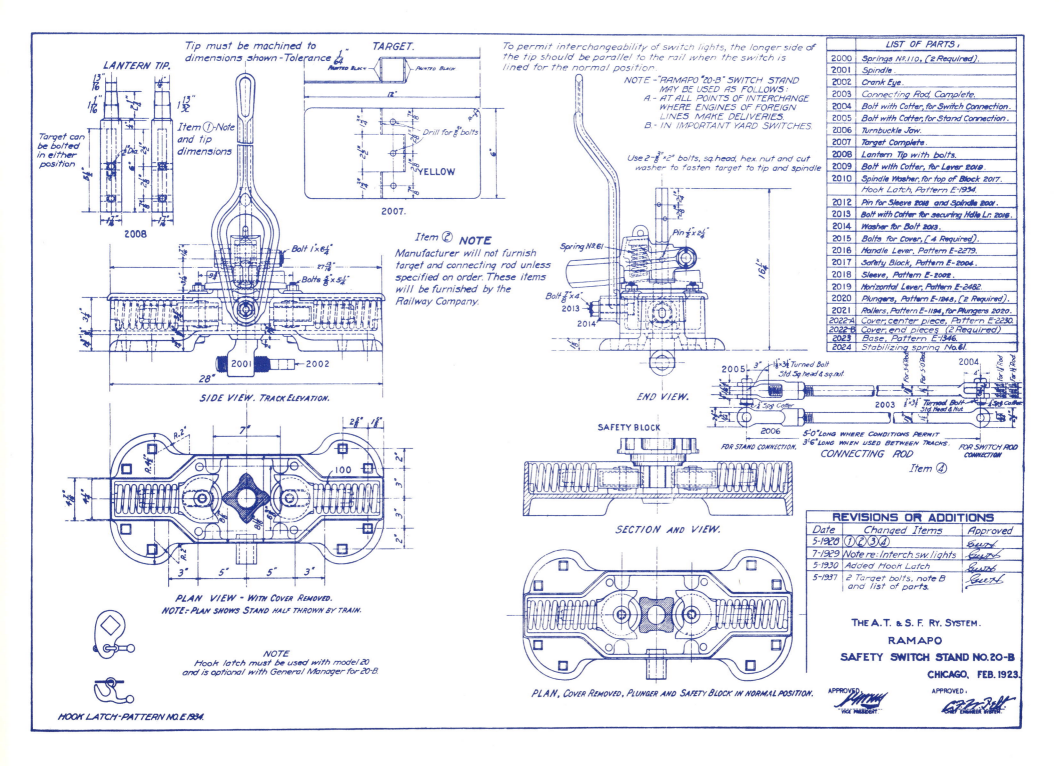

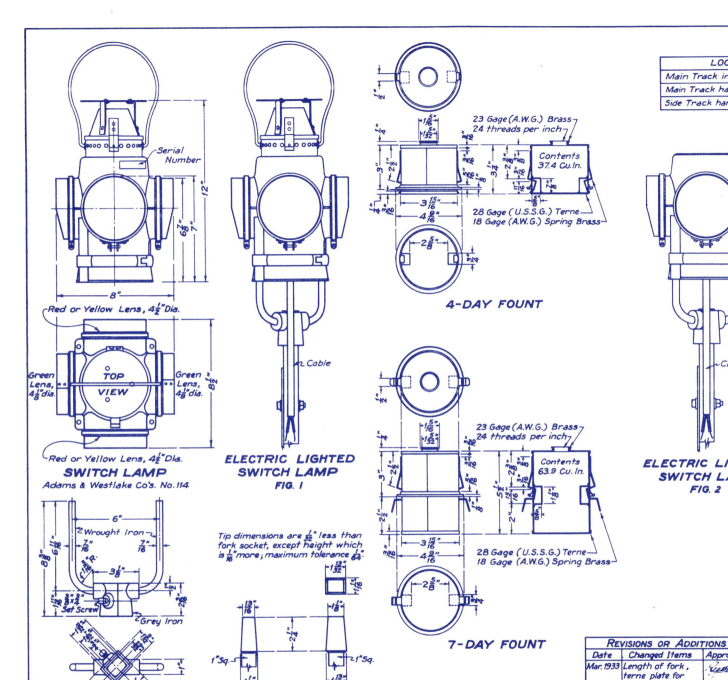

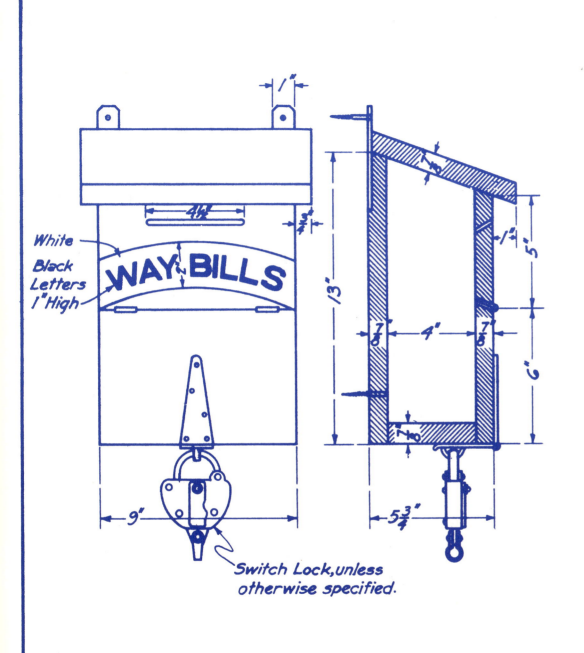

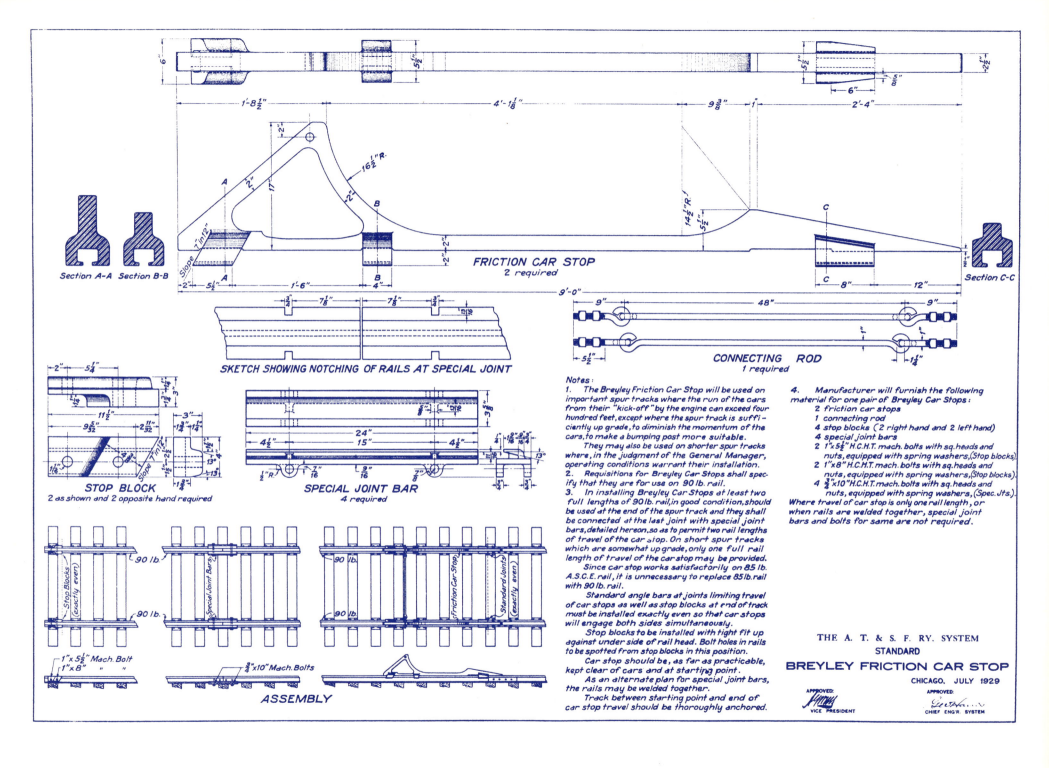

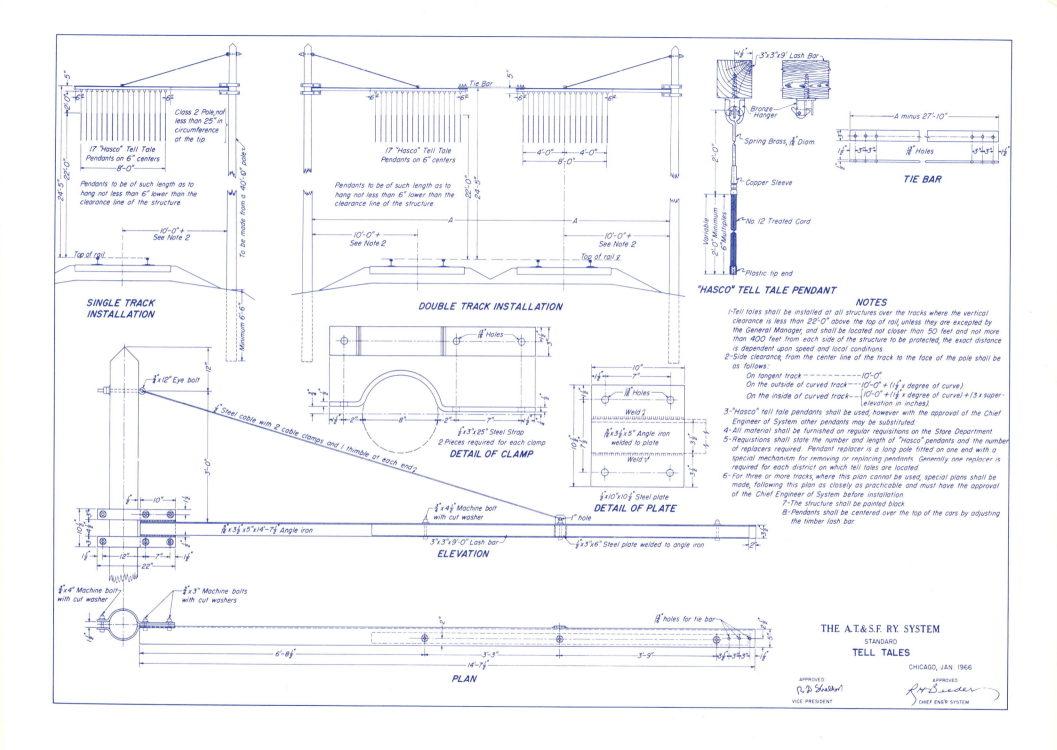

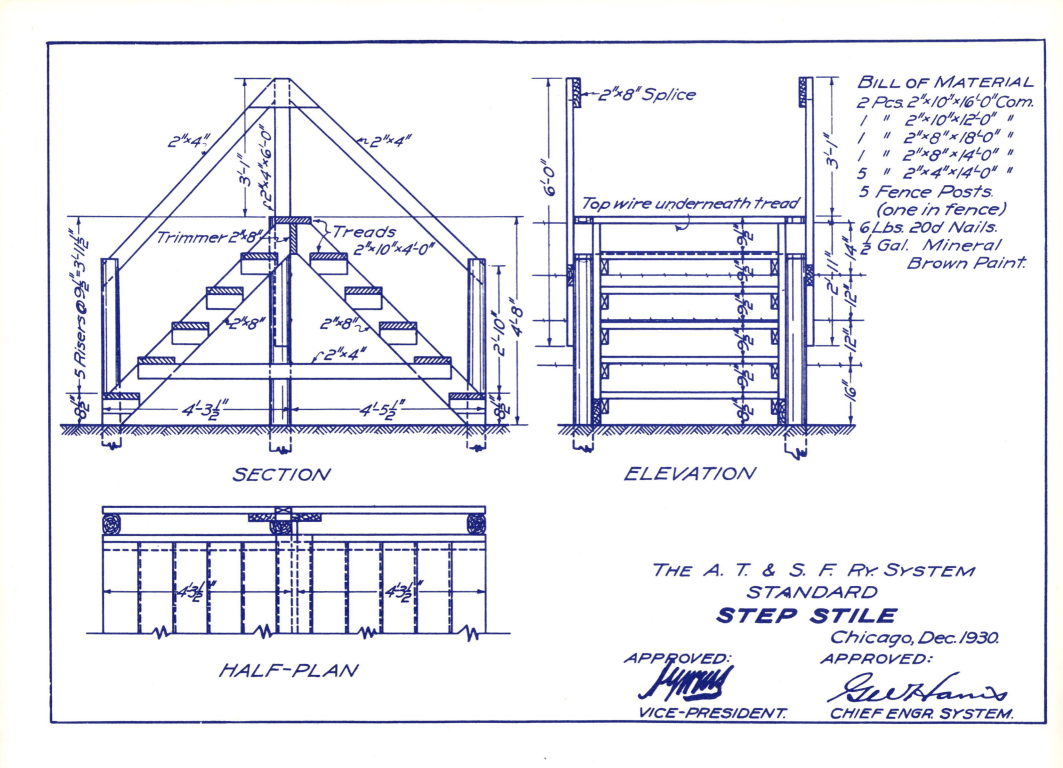

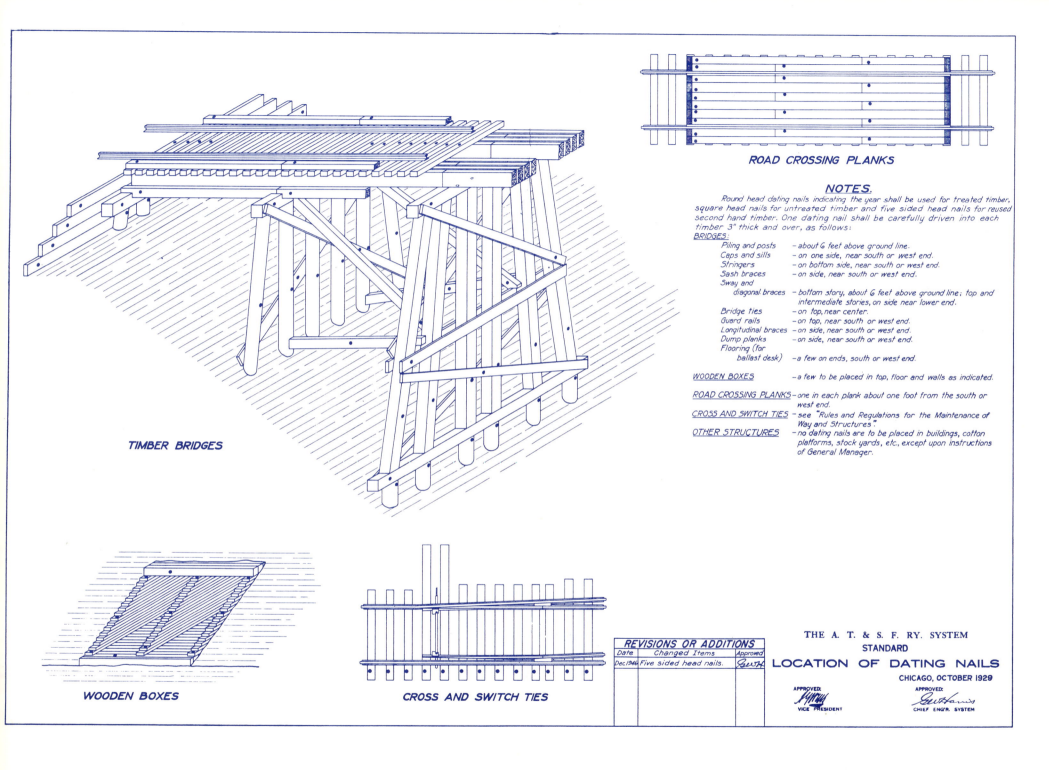

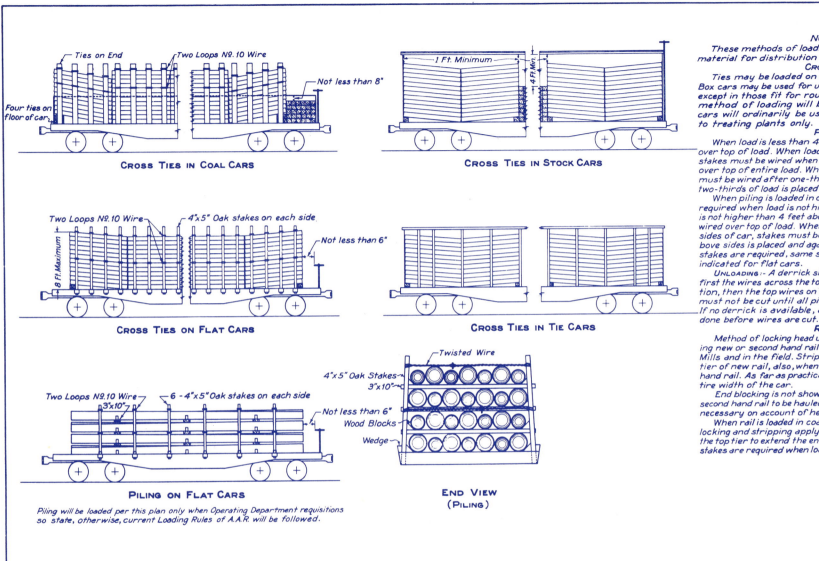

NOTES

These methods of loading apply to this Company's material for distribution to the line.

CROSS TIES

Ties may be loaded on flat cars for short hauls only. Box cars may be used for untreated but not for treated ties, except in those fit for rough freight only, and same method of loading will be used as for stock cars. Tie cars will ordinarily be used for shipment from woods to treating plants only.

PILING

When load is less than 4 feet high, stakes must be wired over top of load. When load is between 4 feet and 8 feet high, stakes must be wired when half of load is placed and again over top of entire load. When load is over 8 feet high, stakes must be wired after one-third of load is placed; again after two-thirds of load is placed and again over top of entire load.

When piling is loaded in coal cars, stakes or wires are not required when load is not higher than sides of car. When load is not higher than 4 feet above top of car sides, stakes must be wired over top of load. When load is more than 4 feet above sides of car, stakes must be wired when one-half of load above sides is placed and again over top of entire load. When stakes are required, same size and number to be used as indicated for flat cars.

UNLOADING:— A derrick should be used when available. Cut first the wires across the top of the load for the center portion, then the top wires on the end stakes. The lower wires must not be cut until all piling above them has been unloaded. If no derrick is available, any notching of stakes must be done before wires are cut.

RAIL

Method of locking head up and base up to be used for loading new or second hand rail and is to be followed by the Steel Mills and in the field. Strips should be placed between each tier of new rail, also, when available, between tiers of second hand rail. As far as practicable, tiers should extend the entire width of the car.

End blocking is not shown, but may be provided for new or second hand rail to be hauled long distances or when deemed necessary on account of heavy grades.

When rail is loaded in coal cars, above requirements for locking and stripping apply, except it is not so important for the top tier to extend the entire width of the car, also no stakes are required when load is not higher than sides of car.

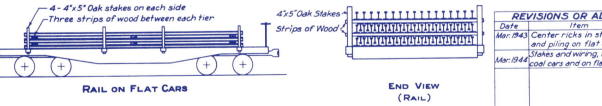

REVISIONS OR ADDITIONS		
Date	Item	Approved
Mar. 1943	Center ricks in stock cars and piling on flat cars.	
Mar. 1944	Stakes and wiring, ties in coal cars and on flat cars.	

THE A. T. & S. F. RY. SYSTEM
STANDARD
LOADING OF CROSS TIES, PILING AND RAIL
CHICAGO, APRIL, 1931.

APPROVED: VICE PRESIDENT
APPROVED: CHIEF ENG'R. SYSTEM

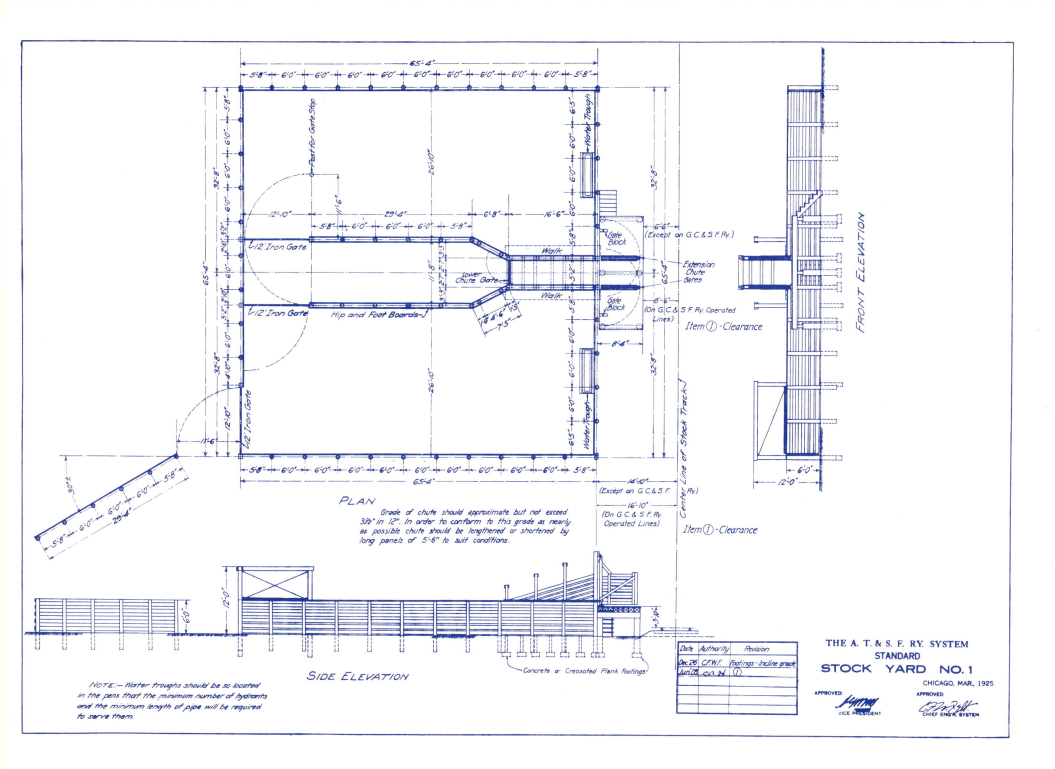

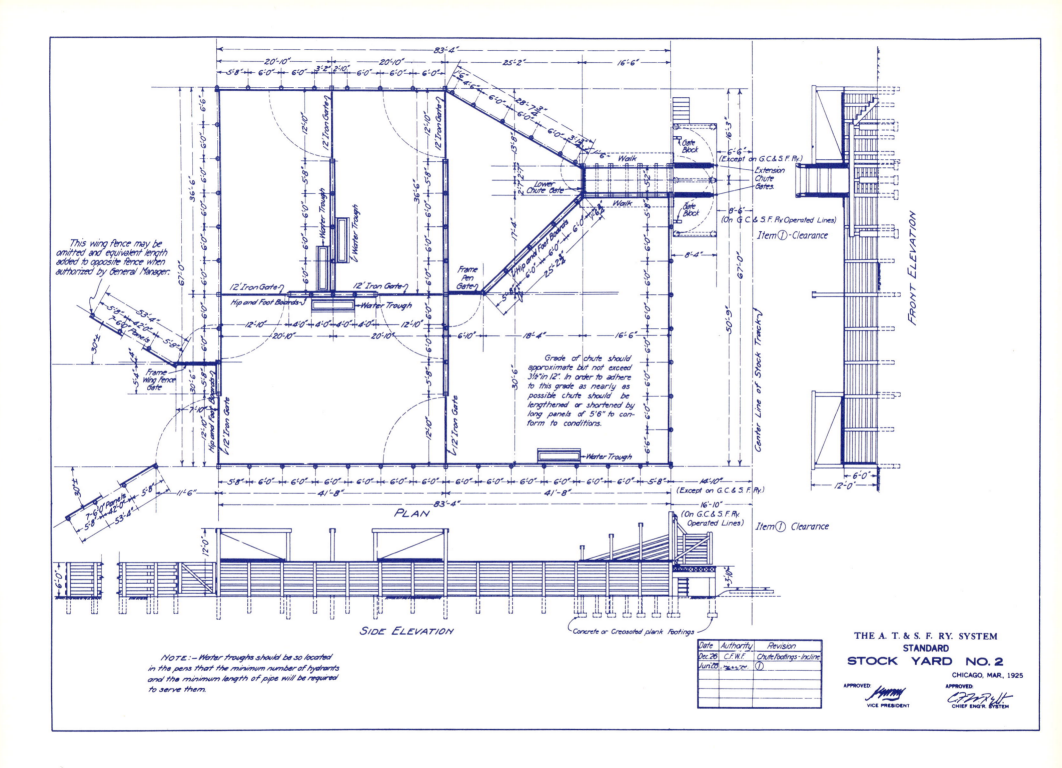

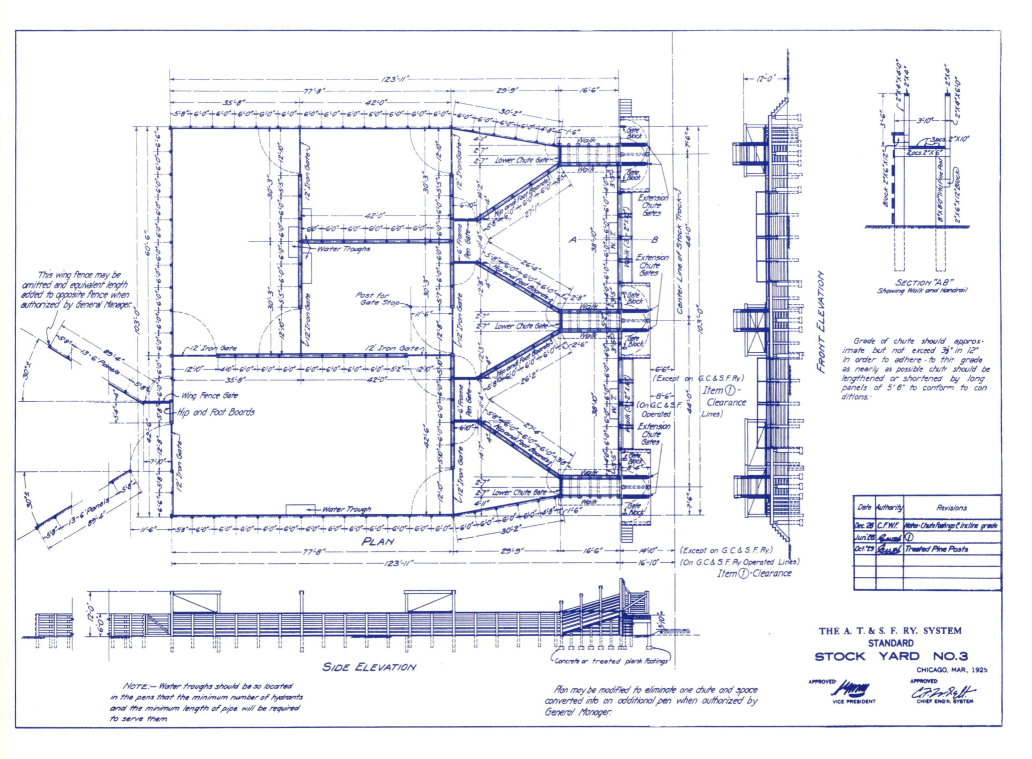

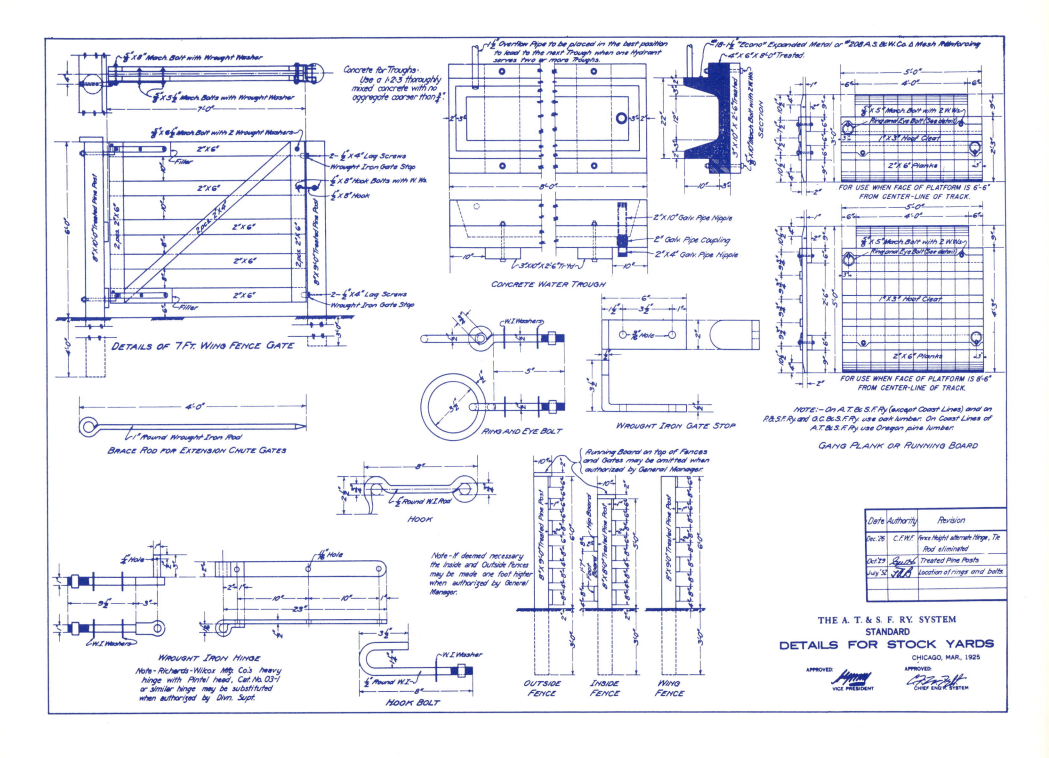

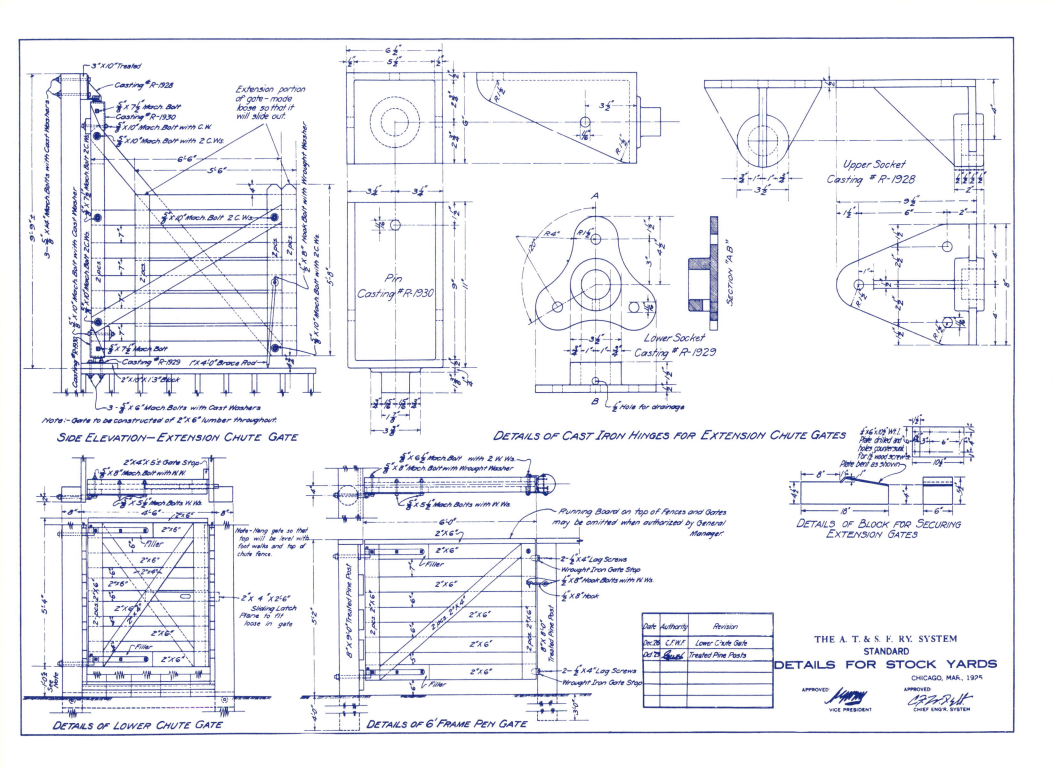

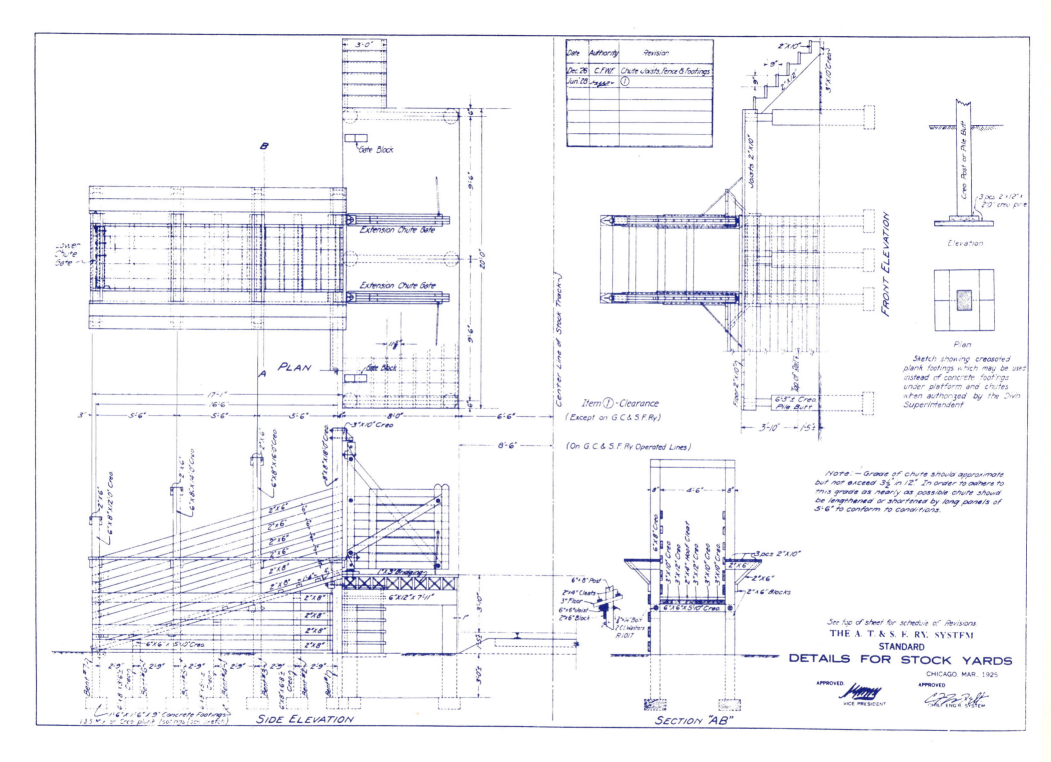

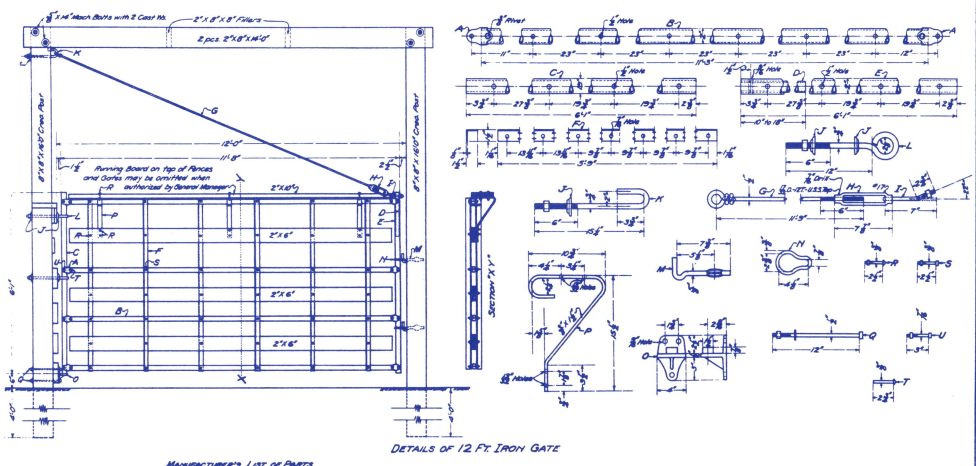

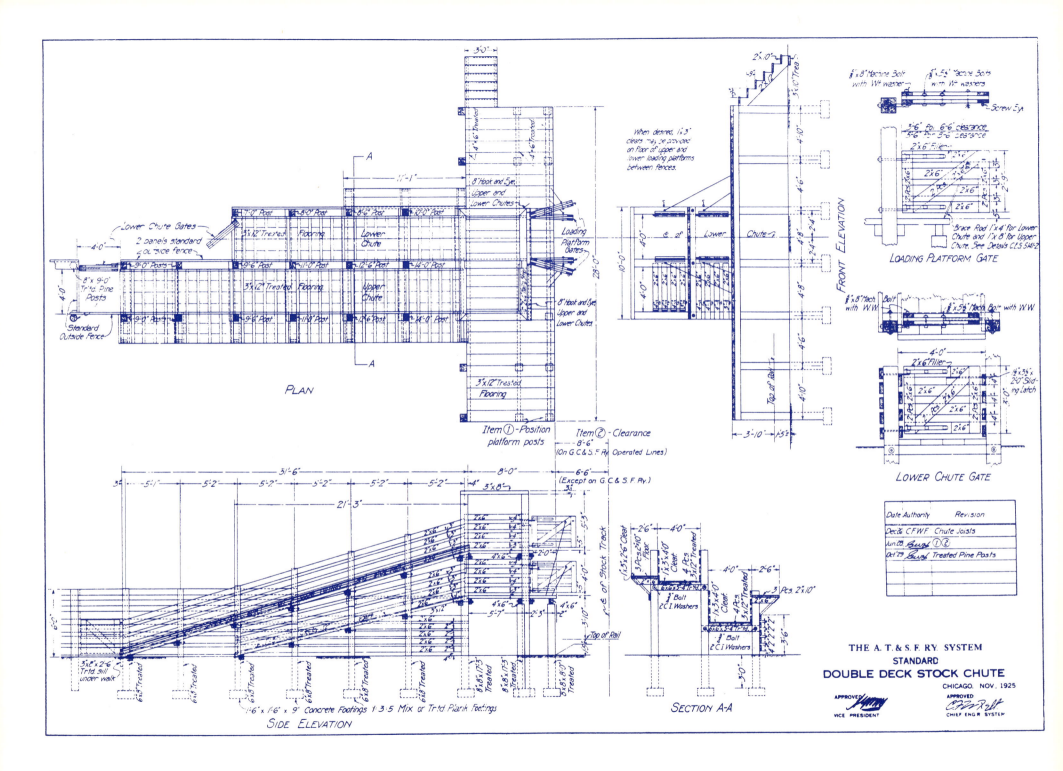

BILL OF MATERIAL

7 Pcs. 2"x 6"—16' R. Fencing.
6 " 2"x 8"—16' "
7 " 1"x 6"—12' "
2 — 8"x 9'-0" Treated Pine Posts.
11 Pcs. 2"x 6"—16' R. Runway, Lower chute, Inside fence.
8 " 3"x12"—12' Treated Floor, "
7 " 1"x 3"—12' R. Floor cleats "
2 " 6"x 6"—16' Trtd. Floor joists "
1 — 6"x 8"—7' Treated Post.
1 — 6"x 8"—8' "
1 — 6"x 8"—8'-6" "
1 — 6"x 8"—10' "
3 Pcs. 2"x10"—12' R. Sidewalk
2 " 2"x 6"—12' " Brackets
7 " 4"x 6"—14' Trtd. Floor joists, platform
14 " 3"x12"—16' Treated Floor, "
15 — 8"x 8"—8' Posts,
16 Pcs. 2"x 6"—16' Runway, Upper chute, Inside fence.
8 " 3"x12"—16' Treated Floor
11 " 1"x 3"—12' Floor cleats
2 " 6"x 6"—16' Floor joists · Treated.
4 — 6"x 8"—9' Treated Posts,
2 — 6"x 8"—9'-6" "
2 — 6"x 8"—11'-0" "
2 — 6"x 8"—12'-6" "
2 — 6"x 8"—14'-0" "
6 — 8"x 6"—8'-0" "
6 Pcs. 2"x10"—16'-0" R. Inclined sidewalk, Upper chute.
5 " 2"x 6"—12'-0" " Sidewalk brackets,
3 " 4"x 6"—12'-0" Floor joists, Upper platform,
5 " 3"x12"—12'-0" Floor,
12 " 2"x 6"—12'-0" Platform fence, upper and lower.
4 " 3"x 8"—12'-0" Trtd. Top bracing over platform.
4 " 2"x 6"—12'-0" R. 2 Lower chute gates.
2 " 2"x 6"—14'-0" "

16 Pcs. 2"x 6"—12' R. 4 Upper loading gates. } For use when face of platform
1 " 2"x 6"—16' " } is 8'-6" from ℄ of track.

12 Pcs. 2"x 6"—12' R. 4 Upper loading gates. } For use when face of platform
1 " 2"x 6"—16' " } is 6'-6" from ℄ of track.

12 Pcs. 2"x 6"—12' Oak, 2 Gang planks. } For use when face of
5 " 1"x 3"—16' Pine, Hoof cleats for gang planks. } platform is 8'-6" from ℄ of track.

10 Pcs. 2"x 6"—10' Oak, 2 Gang planks. } For use when face of
3 " 1"x 3"—16' Pine, Hoof cleats for gang planks. } platform is 6'-6" from ℄ of track.
*Use Oregon Pine on Coast L.

1 Pc. 2"x12"—14' R. Runners, stairs.
2 Pcs. 2"x10"—12' " Treads,
1 Pc. 3"x10"—3' Treated Footing, "

HARDWARE

60 Lbs. 60 d. Wire nails.
75 " 30 d.
30 " 10 d.
20 — 3/4"x 13" Mach. Bolts (nut and 2 cast washers).
4 — 3/4"x 15" Mach. Bolts (With nut and 2 cast washers) Platform floor joists.
14 — 3/4"x 19" " (With nut and 2 cast washers) "
12 Wrought Iron Hinges (With nut and 2 Wt. washers) 6 Gates. C.E.S. 5138-1.
24 — 5/8"x 5½" Mach. Bolts (With nut and 1 Wt. washer) "
12 — 5/8"x 8" " (With nut and 1 Wt. washer) "
4 Rings and Eye-bolts (With nut and 2 Wt. washers) 2 Gang planks. C.E.S. 5138-1.
2 — 5/8"x 5" Mach. Bolts (With nut and 1 Wt. washer) "
2 — 1"x 8'-0" Wt. I. Brace Rods, Upper Chute Gates. See Details, this sheet.
2 — 1"x 4'-0" " Lower "
4 — 1/2"x 8" Hook Bolts, Brace Rods for Chute Gates. See Details, C.E.S. 5138-1.
4 — 3" Screw Eyes, Chute Gates. See Details, this sheet.
4 — 8" Hooks (with 1 Screw Eye), Chute Gates. See Details, this sheet.

CONCRETE MATERIALS

14 Sacks Portland Cement, Footings under Posts. ⎫ If treated Footings are used
1.5 Cu. Yd. Sand, " ⎬ omit Concrete Materials and sub-
3 Cu. Yds. Crushed Stone, " ⎭ stitute 111 pcs. 2"x12"x2' Treated.

Extra Material needed when cleats are used on floors of loading platforms.

6 Pcs. 1"x 3"—12'
3 Lbs. 10 d. Wire Nails.

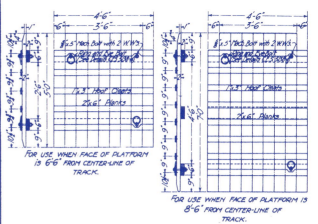

FOR USE WHEN FACE OF PLATFORM IS 6'-6" FROM CENTER-LINE OF TRACK.

FOR USE WHEN FACE OF PLATFORM IS 8'-6" FROM CENTER-LINE OF TRACK.

GANG-PLANK OR RUNNING-BOARD FOR UPPER LOADING CHUTE OF STANDARD DOUBLE DECK STOCK CHUTE

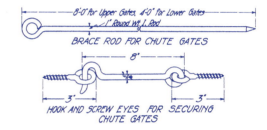

BRACE ROD FOR CHUTE GATES

HOOK AND SCREW EYES FOR SECURING CHUTE GATES

Date	Authority	Revision
Dec 26	C.F.W.F.	Chute Joists
Oct 29		Treated Pine Posts

THE A. T. & S. F. RY. SYSTEM
STANDARD
DOUBLE DECK STOCK CHUTE
CHICAGO, NOV., 1925

APPROVED: _____ VICE PRESIDENT
APPROVED: _____ CHIEF ENG'R SYSTEM

ADJUSTMENTS IN MATERIAL WHEN NEW STOCK YARDS ARE BUILT WITH DOUBLE DECK CHUTE

To Be Deducted from Bill of Material for No. 1 Stock Yard when Double Deck Chute is Used.   See C.E.S. 5134-2.

- 9 – 8"x 9'-0" Treated Pine Posts, Outside Fence.
- 12 Pcs. 2"x 8"-12' R.   "   "
- 6   "   1"x 6"-12'   "   "
- 2   "   2"x10"-12'   "   "
- Hardware – 5 Lbs. 30 d. Wire Nails.

To Be Deducted from Bill of Material for No. 2 Stock Yard when Double Deck Chute is Used.   See C.E.S. 5135-2.

- 9 – 8"x 9'-0" Treated Pine Posts, Outside Fence.
- 10 Pcs. 2"x 8"-12' R.   "   "
- 6   "   1"x 6"-12'   "   "
- 3   "   2"x10"-12'   "   "
- Hardware – 5 Lbs. 30 d. Wire Nails.

To Be Deducted from Bill of Material for Double Deck Chute when Used with No. 2 Stock Yard.   See C.E.S. 5141-2.

- 2 – 8"x 9'-0" Treated Pine Posts, Outside Fence, 4"x 4" Pocket.
- 3 Pcs. 2"x 8"-16' R.   "   "
- 2 Pcs. 1"x 6"-12'   "   "
- Hardware – 2 Lbs. 30 d. Wire Nails.

To Be Deducted from Bill of Material for No. 3 Stock Yard when Double Deck Chute is Used.   See C.E.S. 5136-2.

- 5 – 8"x 9'-0" Treated Pine Posts, Outside Fence.
- 1 – 8"x 8'-0"   "   "   "   Inside Fence.
- 1 Pcs. 2"x10"-12' R. Outside Fence, Top Board.
- 2 "   2"x 8"-16'   "   "
- 2 "   2"x 8"-12'   "   "
- 1 "   1"x 6"-16'   "   "
- 1 "   1"x 6"-12'   "   "
- 6 "   2"x 8"-12'   Outside Fence Boards, Chute.
- 9 "   2"x10"-12'   Foot Walks.
- 4 "   2"x 6"-12'   Brackets.
- 3 "   2"x 6"-12'   Chords across Posts.
- 3 "   2"x10"-12'   Inside Fencing.
- 3 "   2"x 8"-12'   "   "
- 15 "   2"x 6"-12'   "   "
- 3 "   2"x 4"-18'   Hoof Cleats.
- 2 "   3"x12"-18'   Treated Floor.
- 3 "   3"x10"-18'   "   "
- 2 "   8"x 8"-18'   Posts, Bent 1.
- 2 "   6"x 8"-16'   "   "   3.
- 2 "   6"x 8"-14'   "   "   5.
- 2 "   6"x 8"-12'   "   "   7.
- 1 "   6"x 8"-14'   "   "   2.
- 2 "   6"x 8"-10'   "   "   4 and 6, Chute.
- 1 "   6"x 6"-18'   Joists   2, 4 and 6.
- 2 "   6"x 6"-14'   "   1, 3, 5 and 7.
- 1 "   3"x10"-6'   Top Chord, Bent No. 1.
- 1 "   2"x 6"-14' R. Horizontals, Lower Gate.
- 1 "   2"x 6"-16'   Verticals,   "   "
- 1 "   2"x 4"-18'   Braces, Stops and Latch, Lower Gate, Chute.
- 2 "   2"x 6"-18'   Verticals, hinge end, Extension Gates.
- 6 "   2"x 6"-12'   Other Verticals,   "   "
- 10 "   2"x 6"-12'   Horizontals,   "   "
- 2 "   2"x 6"-12'   Long Braces,   "   "

(Continued next column)

- 1 Pc. 2"x 6"-16' R. Short Braces, Extension Gates.
- 3 Pcs. 6"x12"-8'   Sills, Platform.
- 9   "   2"x10"-20'   Joists,   "
- 13 "   2"x10"-16'   Floor,   "
- 6   "   1"x 3"-12'   Bridging, "
- 6   "   6'-3" Pile Butts.
- 1 Pc. 2"x12"-14' R. Stairs, Runners.
- 1 "   2"x10"-2'   "   Treads.
- 1 "   3"x10"-3' Tr't'd   Footing.
- 2 Pcs. 2"x 6"-8' Oak* Gang Plank, 3'-0". } For use when face of platform is
- 1 "   2"x 6"-12' Oak*   "   "   } 6'-6" from ℄ of track.
- 1 "   1"x 3"-16' Pine,   "   Hoof Cleats.   *Oregon Pine on Coast Lines.
- 6 Pcs. 2"x 6"-10' Oak, Gang Plank, 5'-0". } For use when face of platform is
- 2 "   1"x 3"-16' Pine,   "   Hoof Cleats.   } 8'-6" from ℄ of track.

Hardware

- 20 Lbs. 60 d Wire Nails.
- 75   "   30 d   "   "
- 6   "   10 d   "   "

- 2 – 1"x 4'-0" Brace Rods, Extension Gates. See details.
- 2 – ½"x 8" Hook Bolts (with 1 nut and 1 Wt. washer) Extension Gates. See details.
- 6 – ⅝"x 6" Mach. Bolts (with 1 nut and 1 cast washer)   "   "   "   "
- 4 – ⅝"x 7½"   (with 1 nut.)   "   "   "   "
- 2 – ⅝"x 7½"   (with 1 nut and 2 cast washers) "   "   "   "
- 4 – ⅝"x 10"   (with 1 nut and 1 cast washer) "   "   "   "
- 8 – ⅝"x 10"   (with 1 nut and 2 cast washers) "   "   "   "
- 6 – ⅝"x 14"   (with 1 nut and 1 cast washer) "   "   "   "
- 2 Upper Sockets, Casting No. R 1928.
- 2 Lower   "   "   "   R 1929.
- 4 Pins   R 1930.
- 2 Wt. I. Hinges (with 1 nut and 2 Wt. washers) Lower Chute Gate. See details.
- 2 – ⅝"x 8" Mach. Bolts (with nut and 1 Wt. washer)   "   "   "   "   "
- 4 – ⅝"x 5½"   (with nut and 1 Wt. washer)   "   "   "   "   "
- 2 Rings and Eye-bolts (with nut and 2 Wt. washers) Gang Plank.
- 1 – ⅝"x 5" Mach. Bolt (with nut and 2 Wt. washers)   "   "

Concrete

- 12 Sacks Portland Cement. Footings.
- 1 Cu. Yd. Sand.
- 2 Cu. Yds. Crushed Stone.

To Be Deducted from Bill of Material for Double Deck Chute when Used with No. 3 Stock Yard.   See C.E.S. 5141-2.

- 2 – 8"x 9'-0" Treated Pine Post, Outside Fence, 4"x 4" Pocket.
- 3 Pcs. 2"x 8"-16' R.   "   "   "   "
- 2 Pcs. 1"x 6"-12'   "   "   "   "
- Hardware – 2 Lbs. 30 d Wire Nails.

LOCATION PLAN
DOUBLE DECK STOCK CHUTE
FOR NO'S. 1, 2 AND 3 STOCK YARDS

Date	Authority	Revision
Jun 20		①
Oct. 29		Treated Pine Posts

DOUBLE DECK CHUTE USED WITH STANDARD NO. 1 STOCK YARD

DOUBLE DECK CHUTE USED WITH STANDARD NO. 2 STOCK YARD

Item ① - Clearance

DOUBLE DECK CHUTE USED WITH STANDARD NO. 3 STOCK YARD

See top of sheet for schedule of revisions.

THE A. T. & S. F. RY. SYSTEM
STANDARD
DOUBLE DECK STOCK CHUTE

CHICAGO, NOV., 1925

APPROVED
VICE PRESIDENT

APPROVED
CHIEF ENG'R. SYSTEM

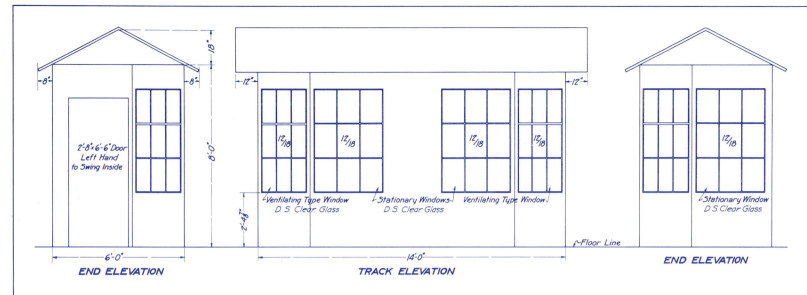
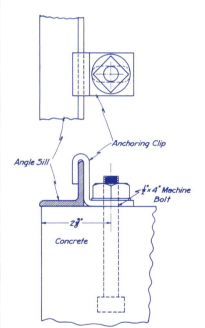
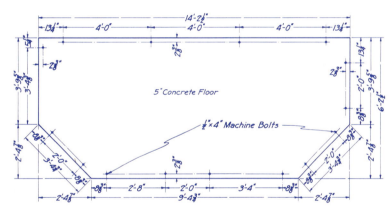

NOTES.
1. Walls, roof and ceiling to be 20 gage, or heavier (as specified), copper bearing steel, copper content not less than 0.20%.
2. Walls to be lined with approved type of wall board.
3. Anchor bolt locations as shown on floor plan must be adhered to.
4. Outside of building to be painted in conformance with current System standard painting instructions.
5. Type of building shown is manufactured by the Butler Mfg. Co., upon approval of Chief Engineer System other types may be substituted.
6. No openings in rear wall.
7. This building to be used with following track scales:-
   46 Ft. 100 Ton
   50 Ft. 150 Ton

REVISIONS OR ADDITIONS		
Date	Changed Items	Approved
2-1951	Sheet 1 of 2	JLB

THE A. T. & S. F. RY. SYSTEM
STANDARD
SCALE HOUSE
FOR TRACK SCALES

CHICAGO, JULY, 1930.

APPROVED: VICE PRESIDENT
APPROVED: CHIEF ENG'R. SYSTEM

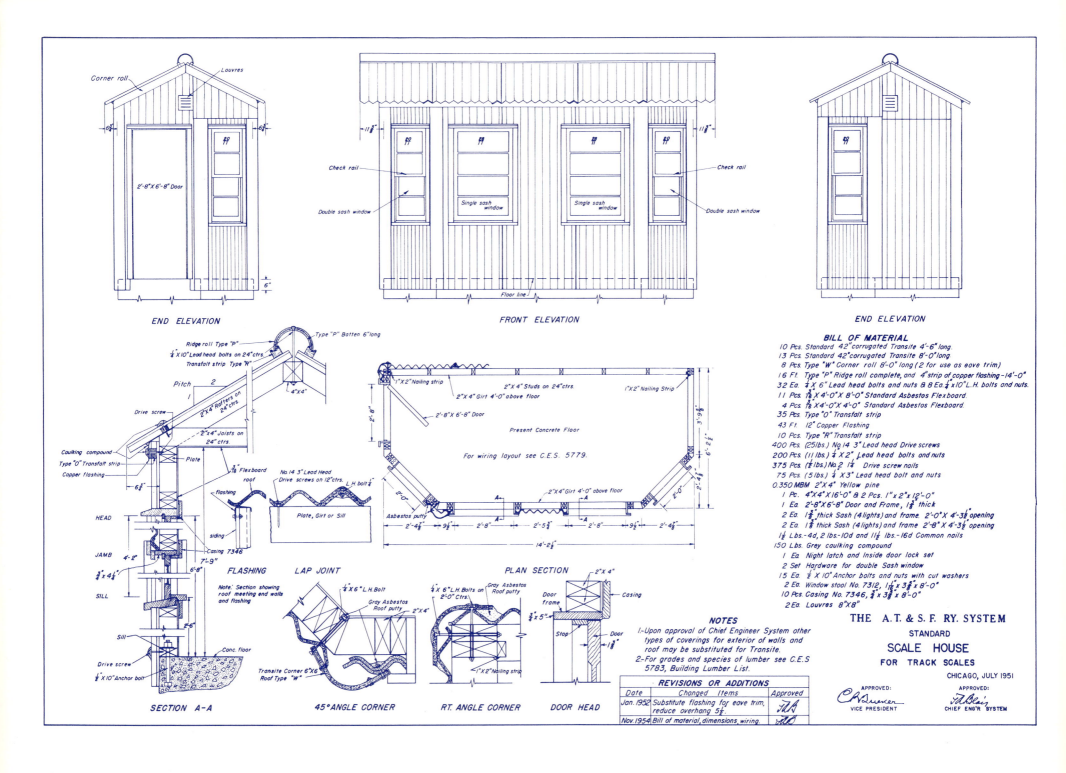

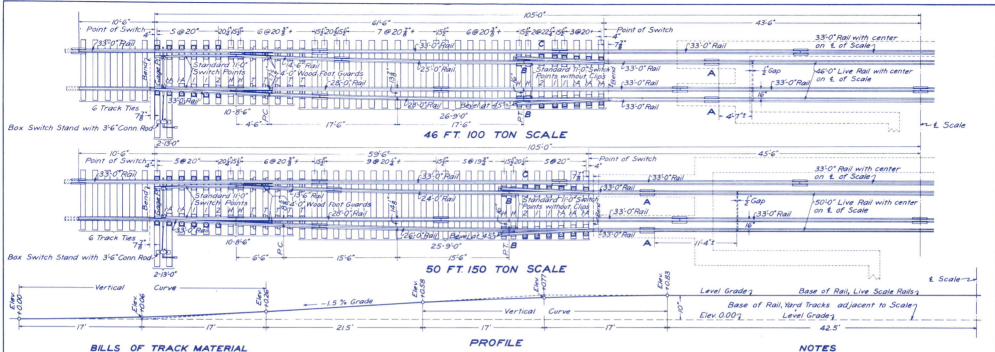

46 FT. 100 TON SCALE

50 FT. 150 TON SCALE

PROFILE

BILLS OF TRACK MATERIAL

The following bills include all track material for 231 ft. of the dead track and all of the live track except such special timbers, plates and fastenings as are included in bills of material for scale decks. All material is for 90 lb. rail and standard unless otherwise shown.

Scale		Description of Material
100 Ton	150 Ton	
12	12	Track Ties
20	20	7"x 9"x 8'-6" Switch Ties 3622.5 ft. BM-100 Ton Scale
52	50	7"x 9"x 9'-0" " 3528 ft. BM-150 "
4	4	7"x 9"x 13'-0" "
	2	50'-0" Rails
2		46'-0" "
17	17	33'-0" "
1		29'-0" " (To be cut on center)
4	2	28'-0" "
	1	27'-0" " (To be cut on center)
2		26'-0" "
	2	25'-0" "
2		24'-0" "
4 Prs.	4 Prs.	11'-0" Switch Points (2 prs. without clips)
2	2	No.1 Switch Rods for 11'-0" Switch
4	4	Bent & Planed Angle Bars (2 Right hand & 2 Left hand)
4	4	Pipe Thimbles
8	8	Heel Blocks for 11'-0" Switch Points (2 grooved for Right hand & 2 for Left hand points as detailed)
4	4	Switch Heel Straps
23 Prs.	23 Prs.	Slotted Angle Bars
84	84	15/16"x 5" Track Bolts
16	16	7/8"x 10 1/4" Switch Heel Bolts
16	16	7/8"x 8" Machine Bolts with sq. heads, sq. nuts
116	116	Spring Washers for 7/8" Bolts
2	2	Gage Plates
20	20	#1-A Switch Plates
16	16	#1 " "
8	8	#2 " "
16	16	"H" (Switch Heel) Plates
20 Prs.	20 Prs.	"T" (Twin Turnout) "
48	48	Rail Braces
8	8	4'-0" Wood Foot Guards with bolts (if required)
2	2	"Box" Switch Stands with 3'-6" Conn. rods
343	264	Tie Plates (2 trimmed 3/4" on inside edge)
4 1/2 Kegs	3 1/2 Kegs	Track Spikes

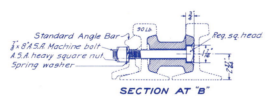

SECTION AT "B"
Showing grooved Heel Block

ELEVATION OF WOOD FOOT GUARD
Untreated Oak

NOTES

Track layouts are to be symmetrical about centers of scales and are based on use of 90 lb. 33 ft. rails, preferably first class relayer.
Live rails to be 46 ft. or 50 ft. in length and may be made from two shorter rails heavily welded together and used without angle bars.
Other rails may be of lengths other than shown but switch point locations must be maintained.
Gaps at ends of live rails must be not less than 1/4" nor more than 3/4".
At points "A", slotted angle bars to be placed on unbroken rails and slot spiked to prevent rails from creeping.
Slotted angle bars, if procurable, to be used at all joints and slot spiked.
At points "B", heel blocks to be grooved as detailed to provide head room for 7/8" machine bolts and standard angle bars used. Bent and planed angle bars and pipe thimbles are not required on the expansion points.
At points "C", standard tie plates to have 3/4" sheared from inside edge.
Ties not shown on this drawing are specially milled at treating plants and are included in bills of material for scale decks. For 46 ft., 100 ton and 50 ft., 150 ton scales see drawings C.E.S. No. 5707, Sheet 3, and No. 5743, Sheet 3, respectively.
Standard tie plates to be used where special plates are not indicated on this drawing and as provided for on scale deck plans.
Ties under switch plates of expansion points to be adzed 5/16" and swabbed with hot preservative.
Ends of stock rails, near heels of expansion points, to be beveled at 45°.
Use of foot guards behind heels of switches is required by law in the States of Missouri and Kansas; in other States their use is optional with General Manager.
Where automatic weighing recorder is used dead track to be offset instead of live track.

REVISIONS OR ADDITIONS

Date	Changed Items	Approved
11-1954	Grip nuts omitted. Added wood foot guard details.	

THE A. T. & S. F. RY. SYSTEM
STANDARD
TRACK LAYOUTS FOR SCALES
CHICAGO, NOV., 1930.

APPROVED: VICE PRESIDENT
APPROVED: CHIEF ENG'R. SYSTEM

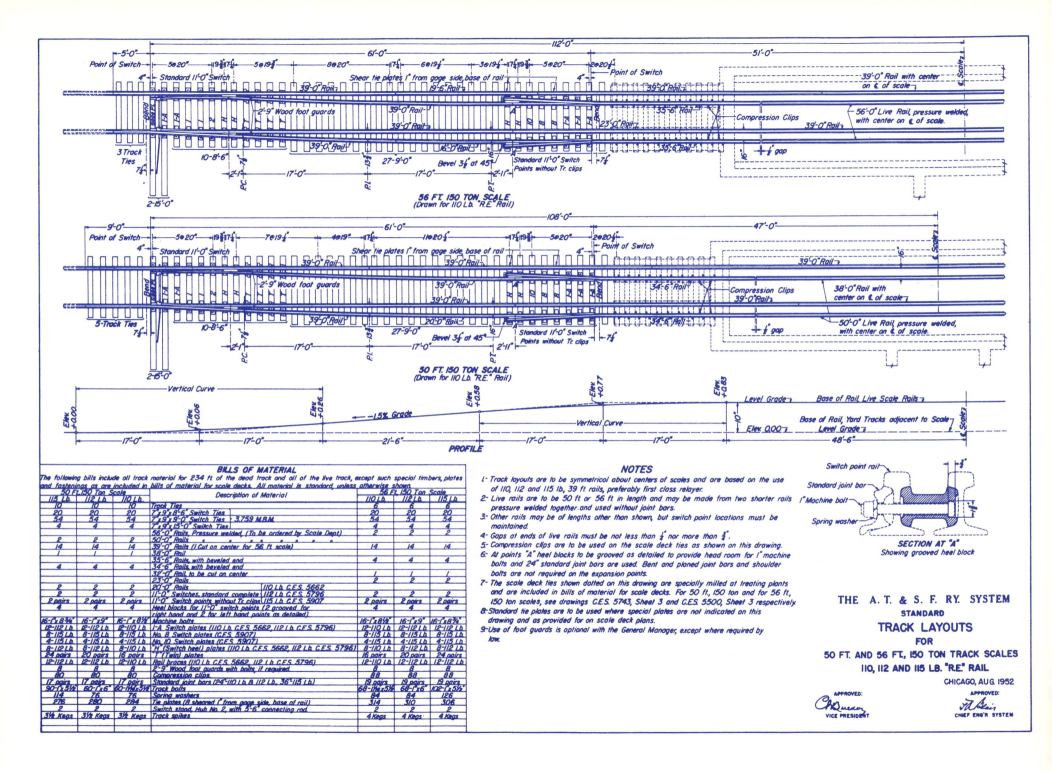

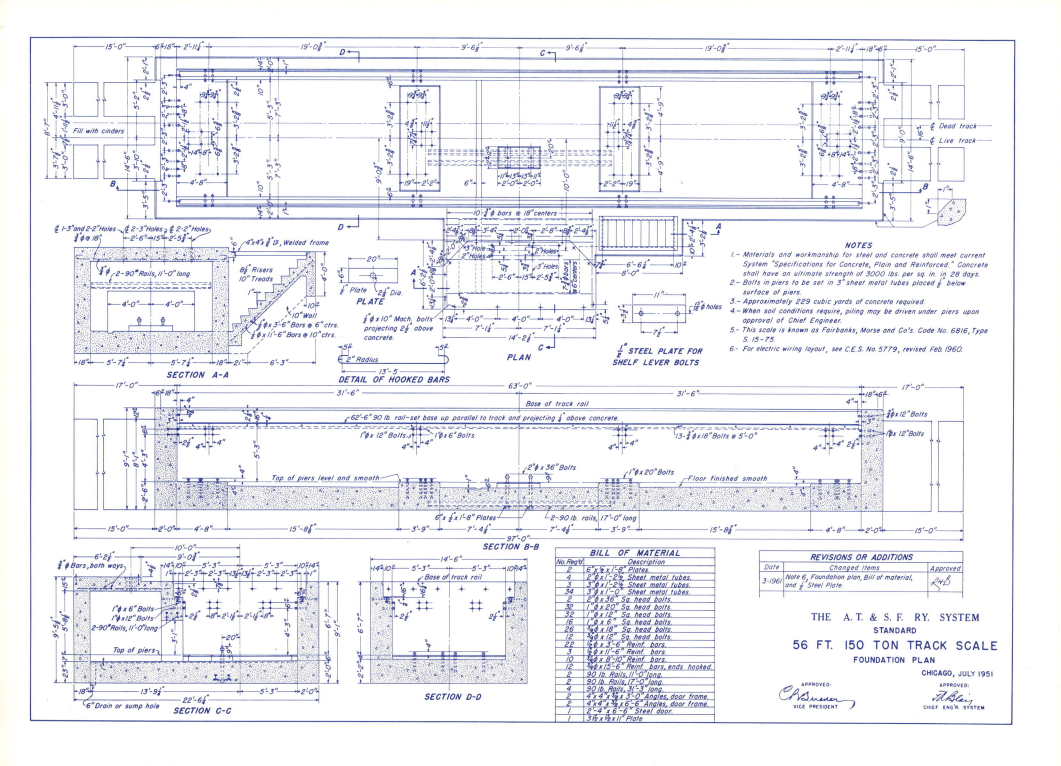

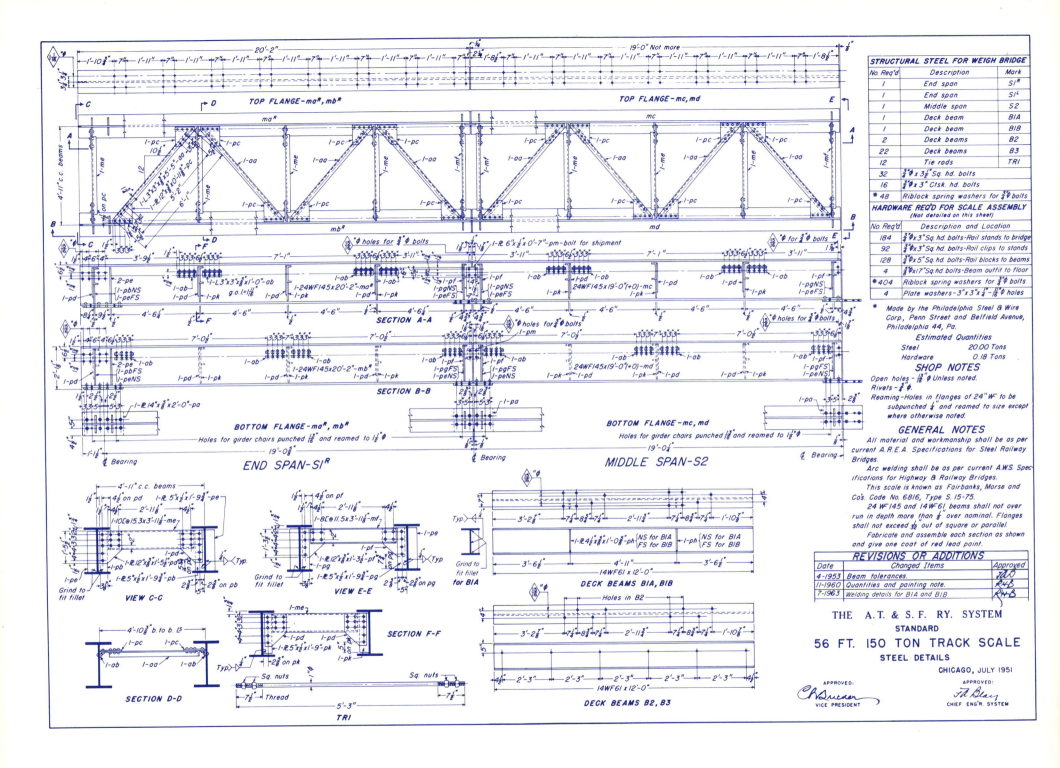

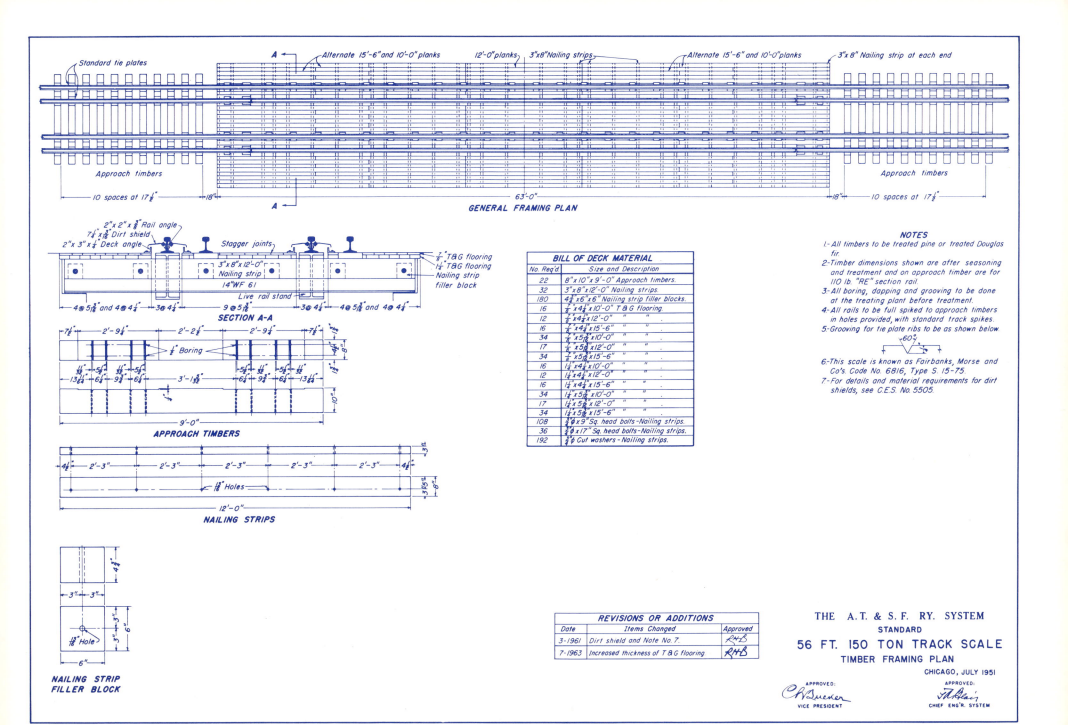

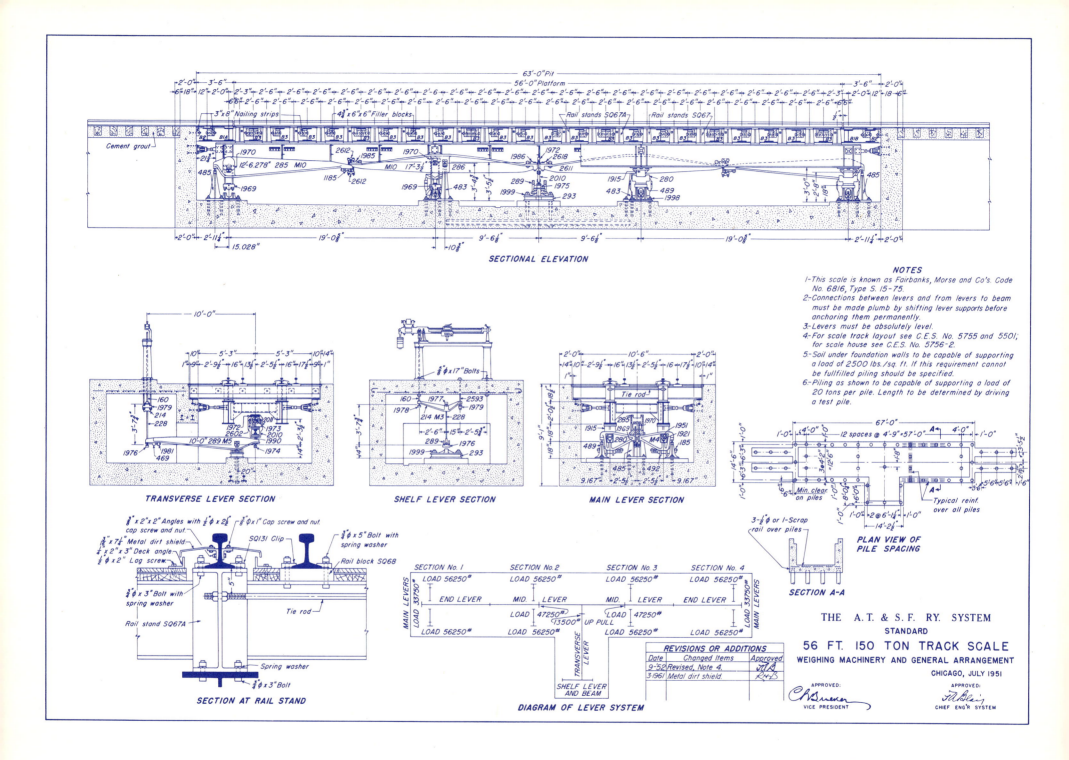

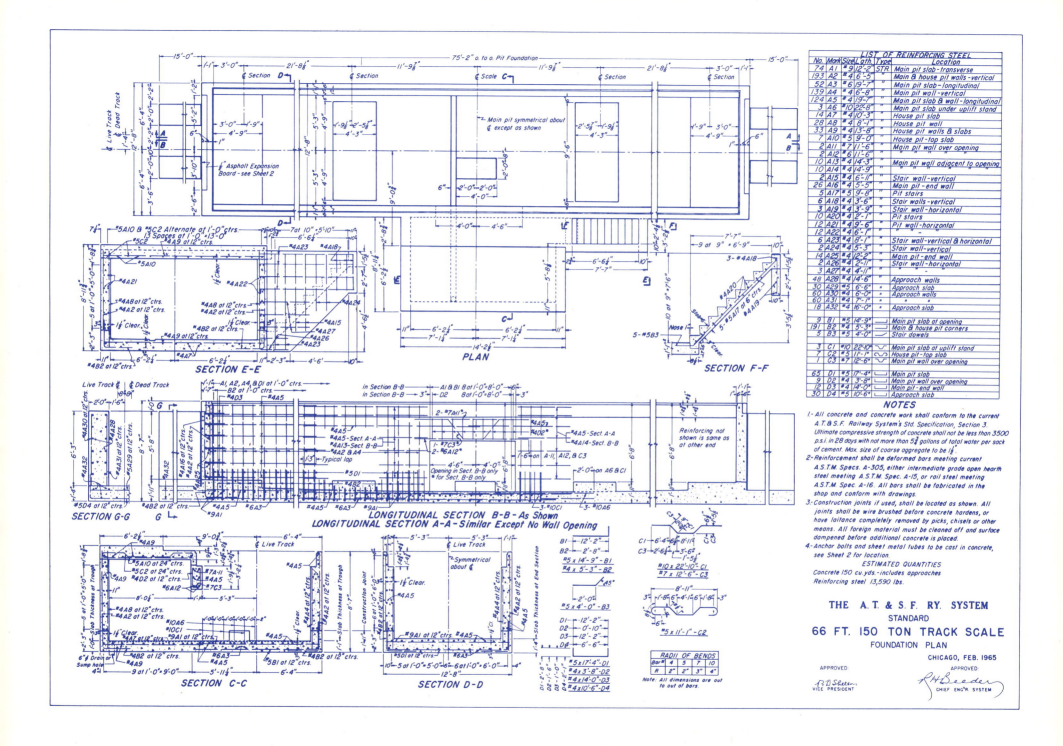

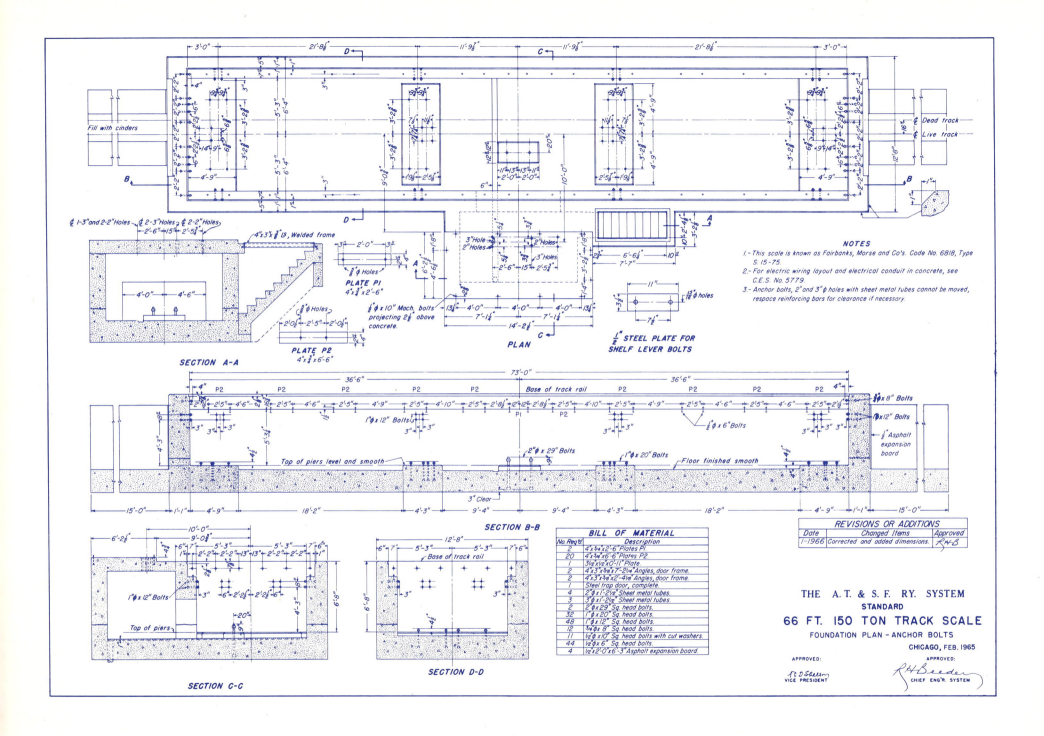

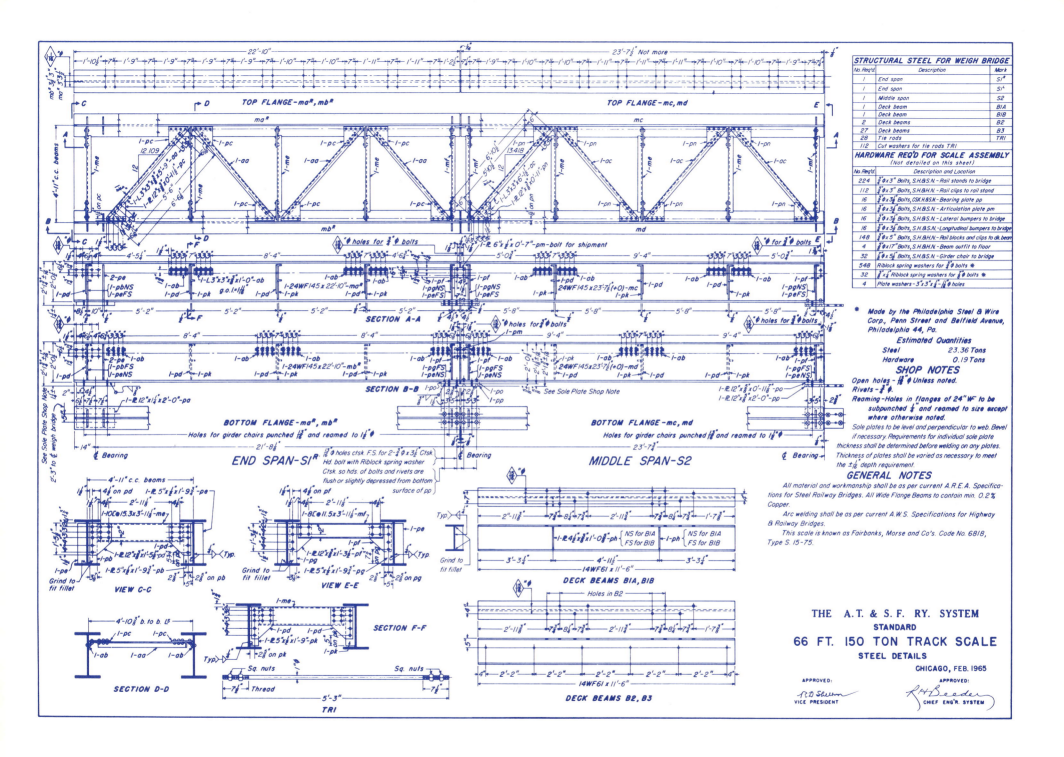

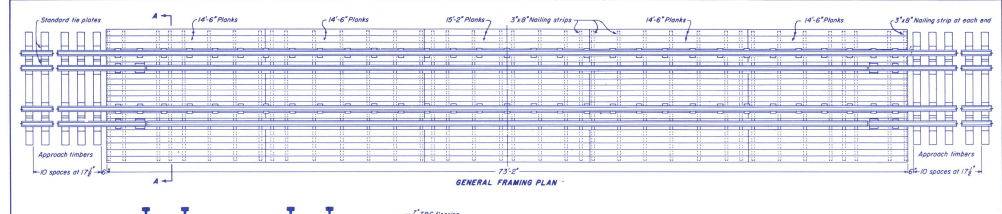

GENERAL FRAMING PLAN

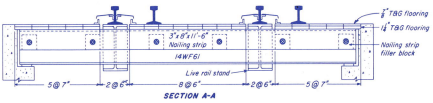

SECTION A-A

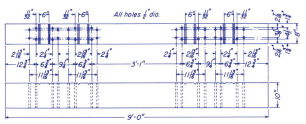

APPROACH TIMBERS

NAILING STRIPS

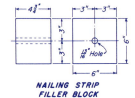

NAILING STRIP FILLER BLOCK

BILL OF DECK MATERIAL	
No. Req'd.	Size and Description
22	8"x10"x9'-0" Approach timbers.
38	3"x8"x11'-6" Nailing strips.
216	4¾"x6"x6" Nailing strip filler blocks.
34	⅞"x6"x14'-6" T & G flooring.
8	⅞"x6"x15'-2" " "
40	⅞"x7"x14'-6" " "
10	⅞"x7"x15'-2" " "
34	1¼"x6"x14'-6" " "
8	1¼"x6"x15'-2" " "
40	1¼"x7"x14'-6" " "
10	1¼"x7"x15'-2" " "
132	¾"Ø x 9" Sq. head bolts - Nailing strips.
42	¾"Ø x 17" Sq. head bolts - Nailing strips.
228	¾"Ø Cut washers - Nailing strips.

NOTES

1.- All timbers to be treated pine or treated Douglas fir.
2.- Timber dimensions shown are after seasoning and treatment and on approach timber are for 131 lb. "R.E." section rail.
3.- All boring and grooving to be done at the treating plant before treatment.
4.- All rails to be full spiked to approach timbers in holes provided, with standard track spikes.
5.- Grooving for tie plate ribs to be as shown below.

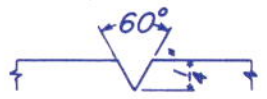

6.- This scale is known as Fairbanks, Morse and Co's. Code No. 6818, Type S. 15-75.

THE A.T. & S.F. RY. SYSTEM
STANDARD
66 FT. 150 TON TRACK SCALE
TIMBER FRAMING PLAN
CHICAGO, FEB. 1965

APPROVED:
R.D. Shelton
VICE PRESIDENT

APPROVED:
R.H. Beeder
CHIEF ENG'R. SYSTEM

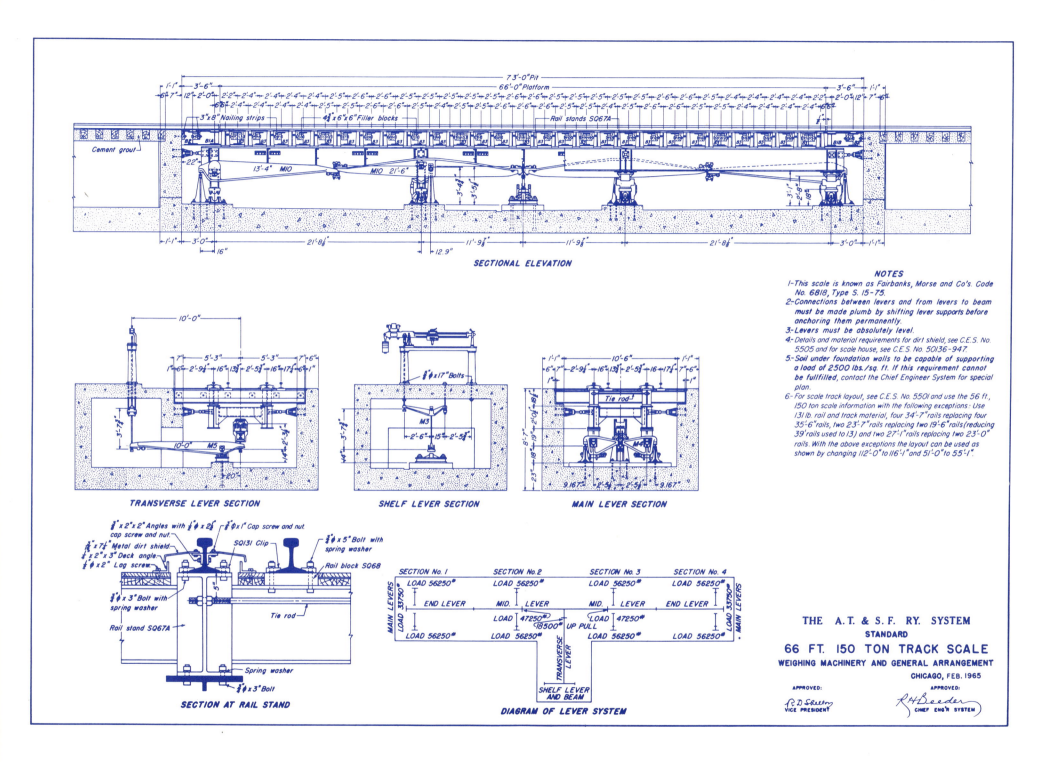

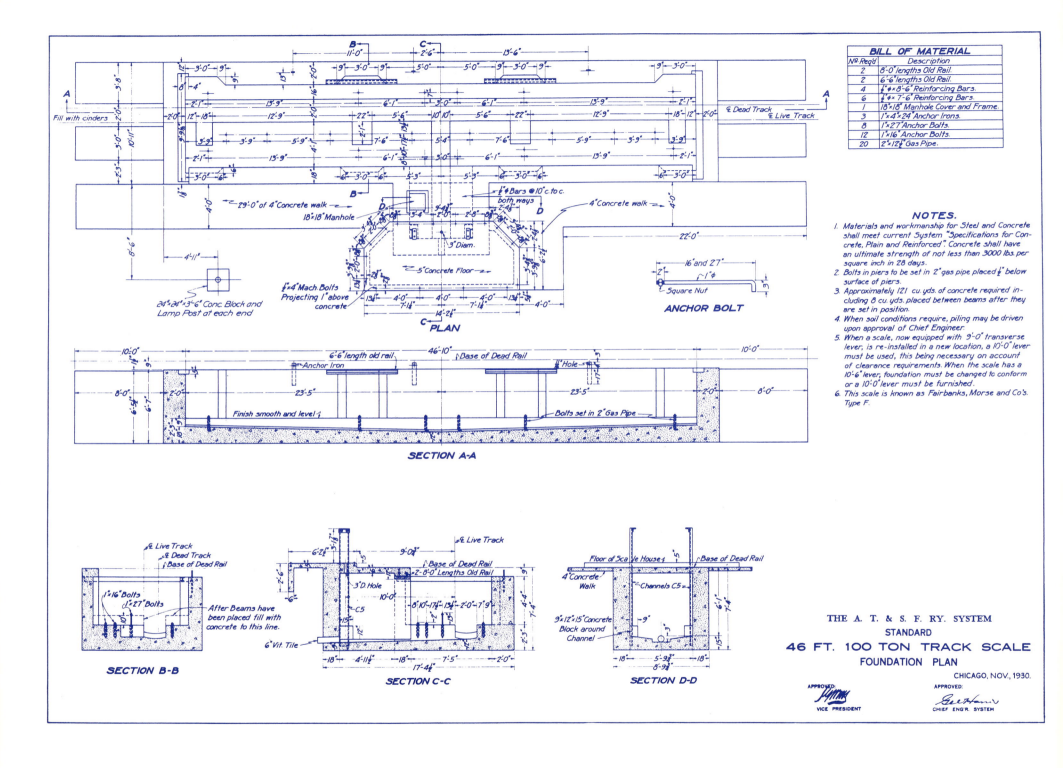

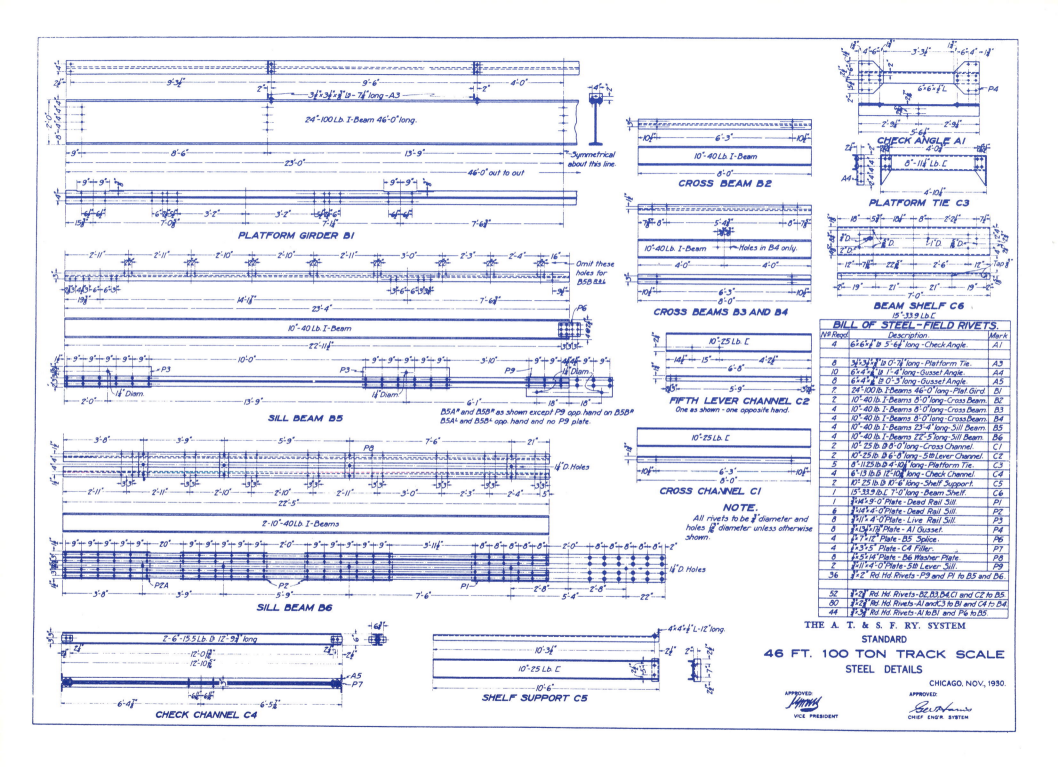

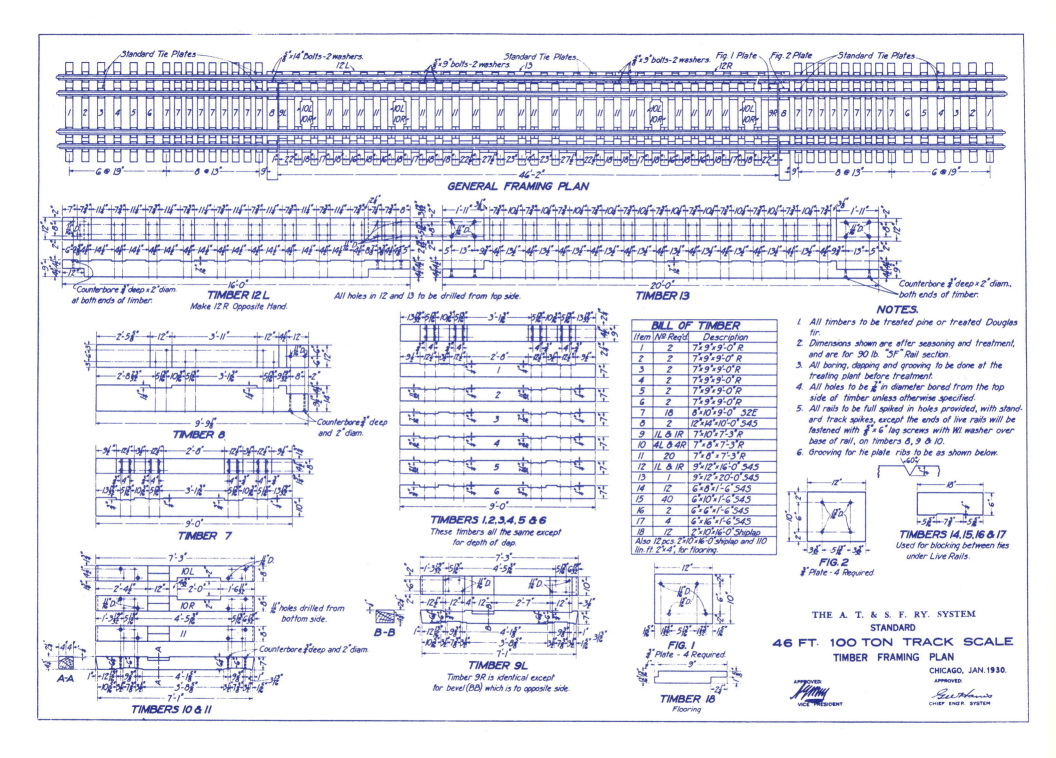

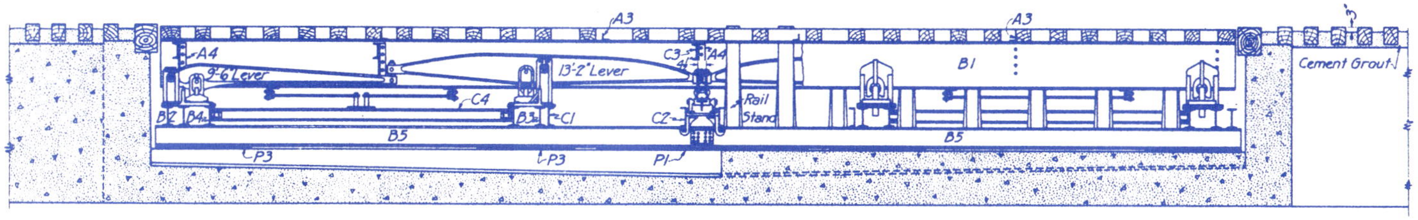

SECTIONAL ELEVATION

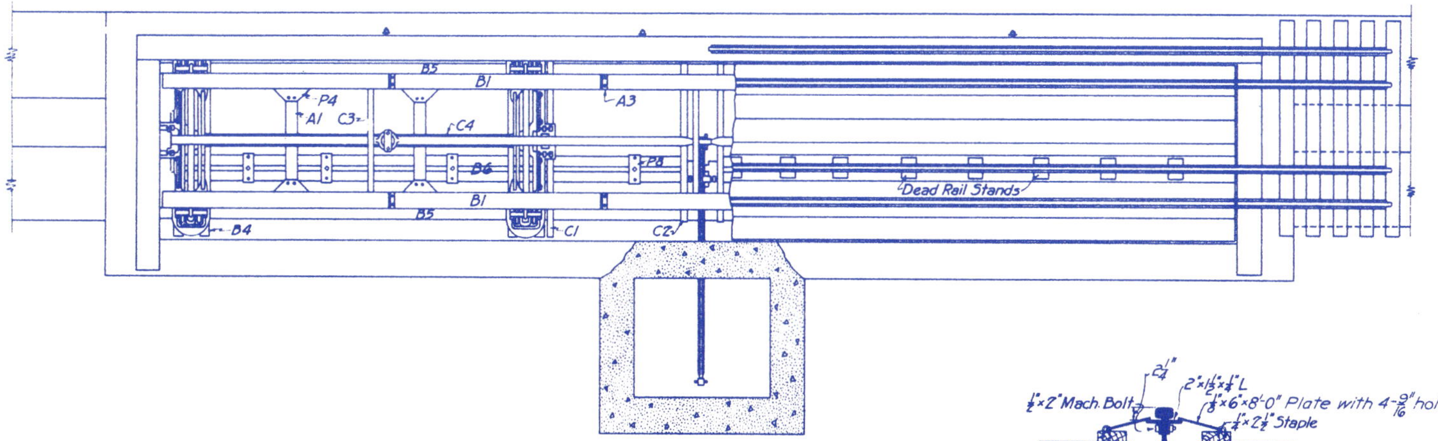

PLAN

BILL OF MATERIAL	
No. Req'd.	Description.
16	Dead Rail Stands - W3881.
32	Dead Rail Clips - WM31.
106	Tie Clips - W3880.
176	Beveled Washers - WM30.
96	Cast Washers - CM268.
24	$\frac{1}{8}$"×6"×8'-0" Plates - Dirt Guards.
92	Lin. Ft. 2"×$1\frac{1}{2}$"×$\frac{1}{4}$" Ls - Dirt Guard Stops.
20	$\frac{1}{4}$"×2" Machine Bolts - Stop Ls.
4	$\frac{3}{4}$"×10"×12" Plates - Sheet 3 Fig. 1.
4	$\frac{3}{4}$"×10"×12" Plates - Sheet 3 Fig. 2.
100	$\frac{1}{4}$"×$2\frac{1}{2}$" Staples - Dirt Guards.
24	$\frac{5}{8}$"×6" Lag Screws.
24	$\frac{3}{4}$" Cut Washers - Lag Screws.
24	$1\frac{1}{4}$" Cut Washers - Lag Screws.
120	$\frac{5}{8}$"×7" Sq. Hd. Bolts - Ties to B1.
4	$\frac{5}{8}$"×9" Sq. Hd. Bolts - Ties to A3.
8	$\frac{5}{8}$"×9" Sq. Hd. Bolts - Splice Timbers 12 and 13.
4	$\frac{5}{8}$"×12" Sq. Hd. Bolts - Ties to A3.
4	$\frac{5}{8}$"×14" Sq. Hd. Bolts - Splice Timbers 8 and 12.
3	$\frac{5}{8}$"×16" Sq. Hd. Bolts - Timbers 12 and 13 to Anchor Irons.
96	$\frac{3}{4}$"×$3\frac{1}{2}$" Sq. Hd. Bolts - Rail Stands to B5 and B6.
32	$\frac{3}{4}$"×4" Sq. Hd. Bolts - Dead Rail to Stands.
4	$\frac{3}{4}$"×2" Sq. Hd. Bolts - C6 to C5.
155	$\frac{5}{8}$" Cut Washers.

NOTES.

1. This scale is known as Fairbanks, Morse and Co's. Type F.
2. Connections between levers and from levers to beam must be made plumb by shifting lever supports before anchoring them permanently.
3. Levers must be absolutely level.

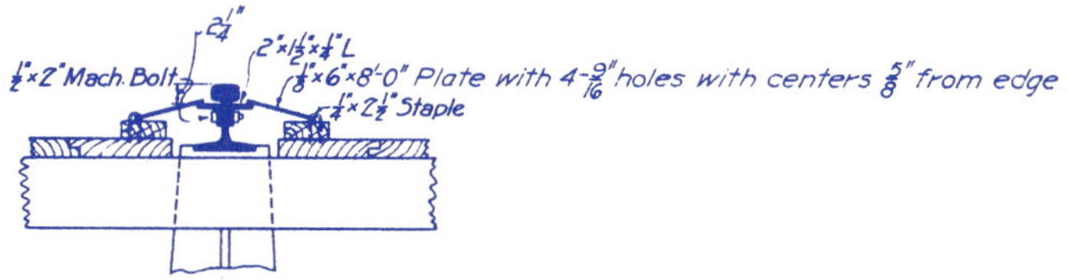

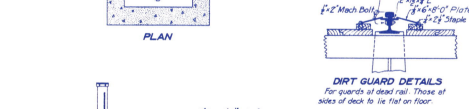

DIRT GUARD DETAILS

For guards at dead rail. Those at sides of deck to lie flat on floor.

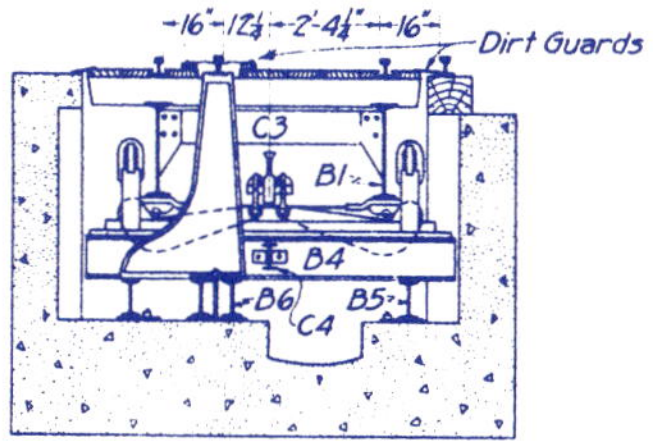

MAIN LEVER SECTION

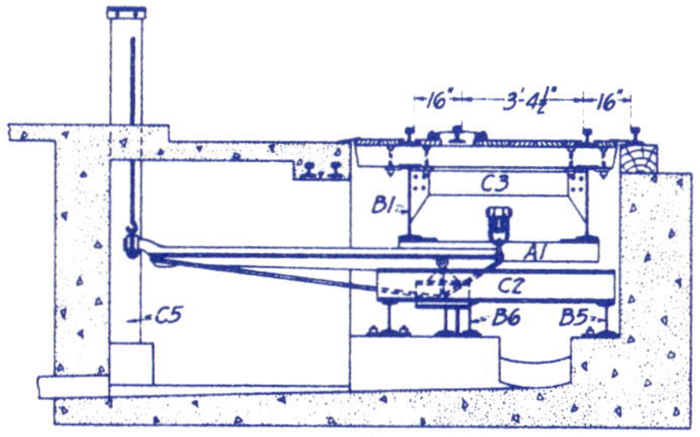

TRANSVERSE (FIFTH) LEVER SECTION

THE A. T. & S. F. RY. SYSTEM

STANDARD

46 FT. 100 TON TRACK SCALE

WEIGHING MACHINERY AND GENERAL ARRANGEMENT

CHICAGO. NOV., 1930.

APPROVED: VICE PRESIDENT

APPROVED: CHIEF ENG'R SYSTEM

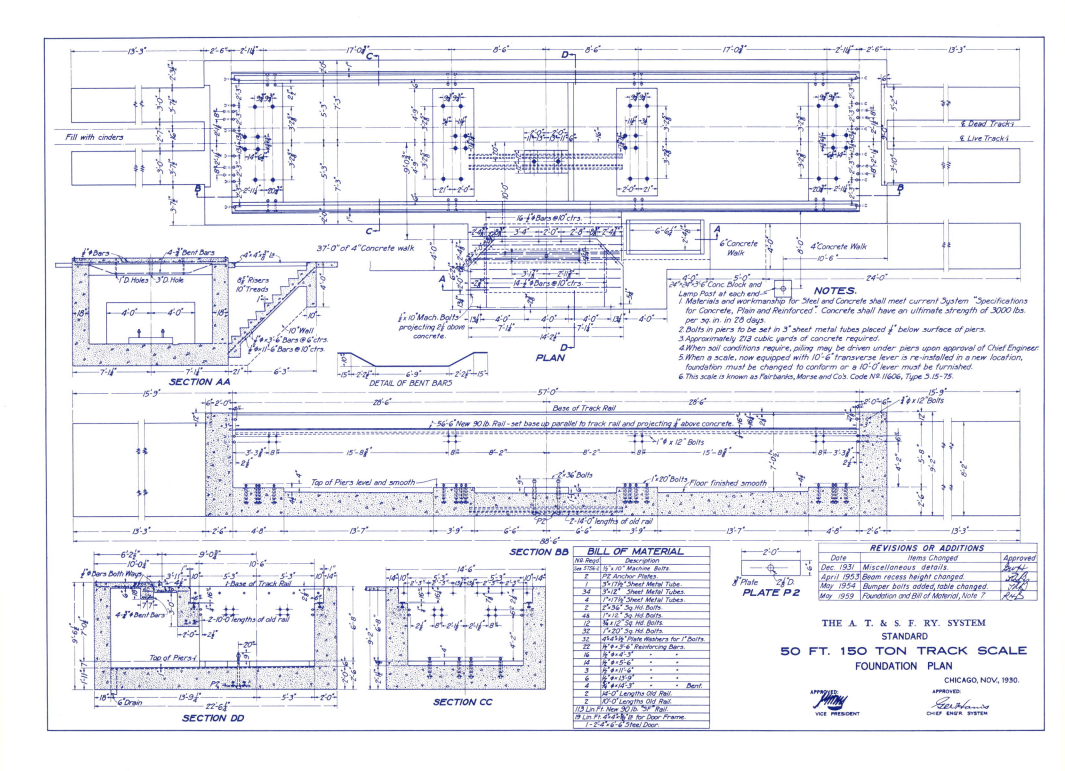

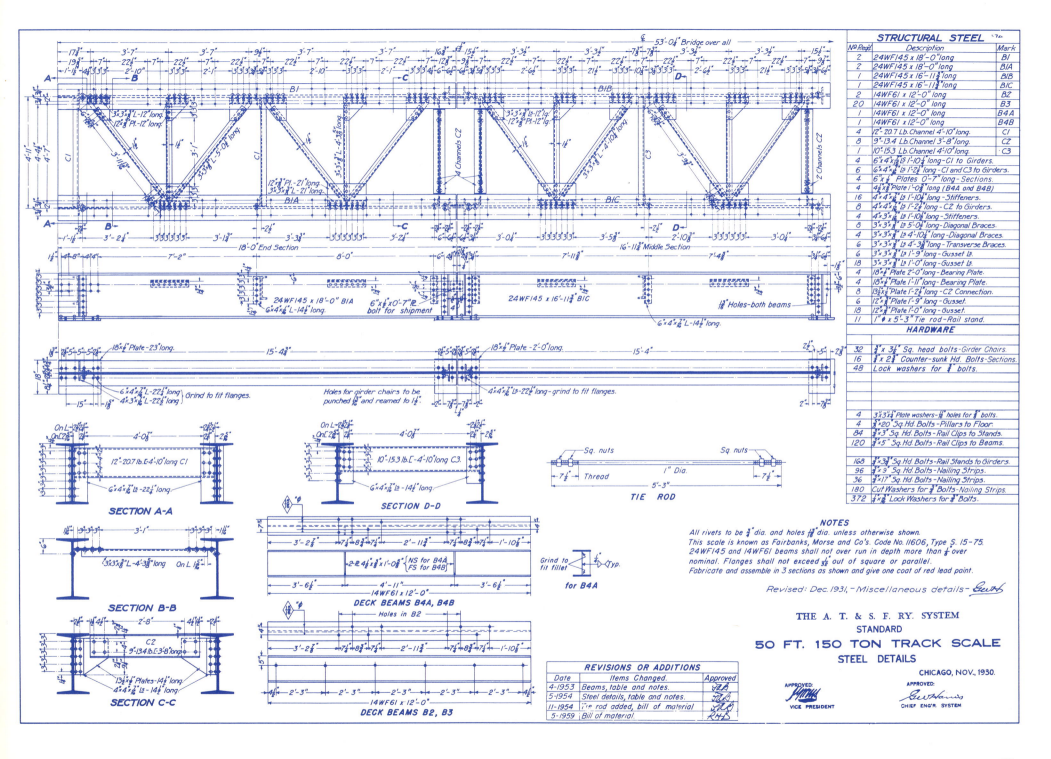

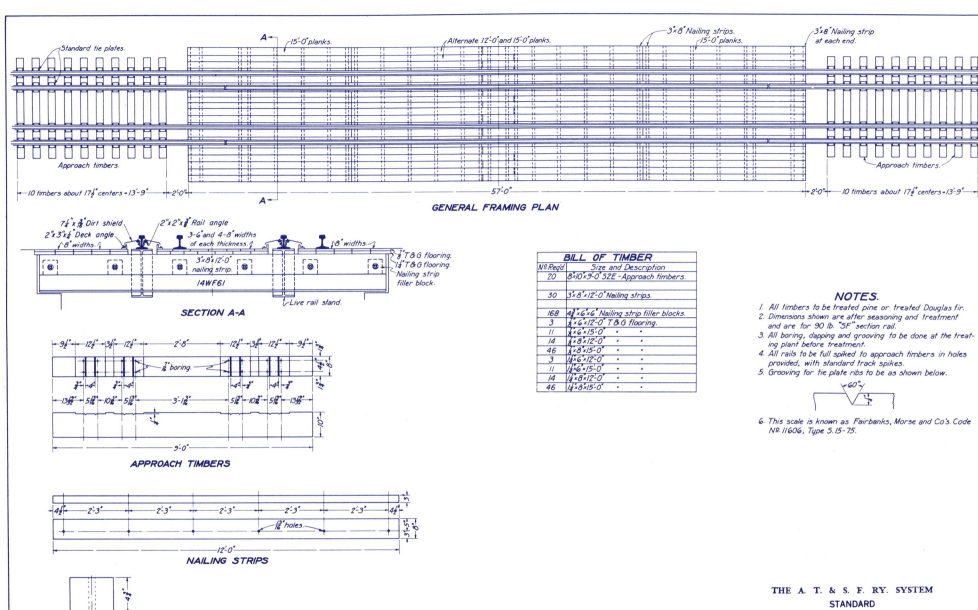

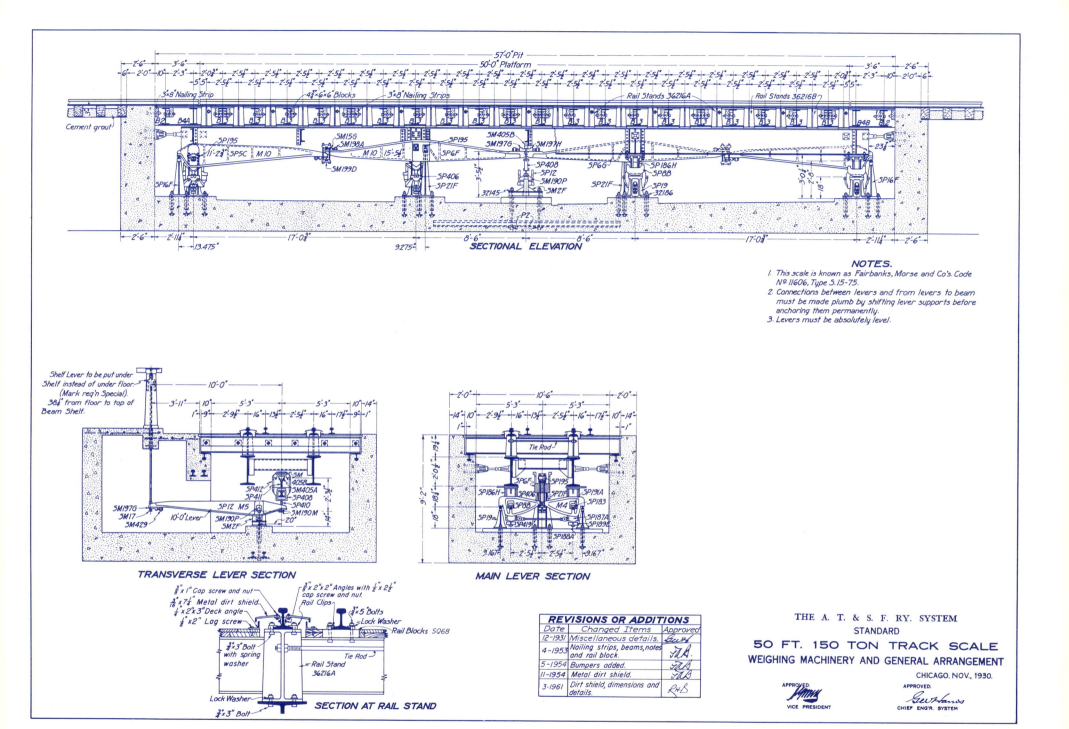

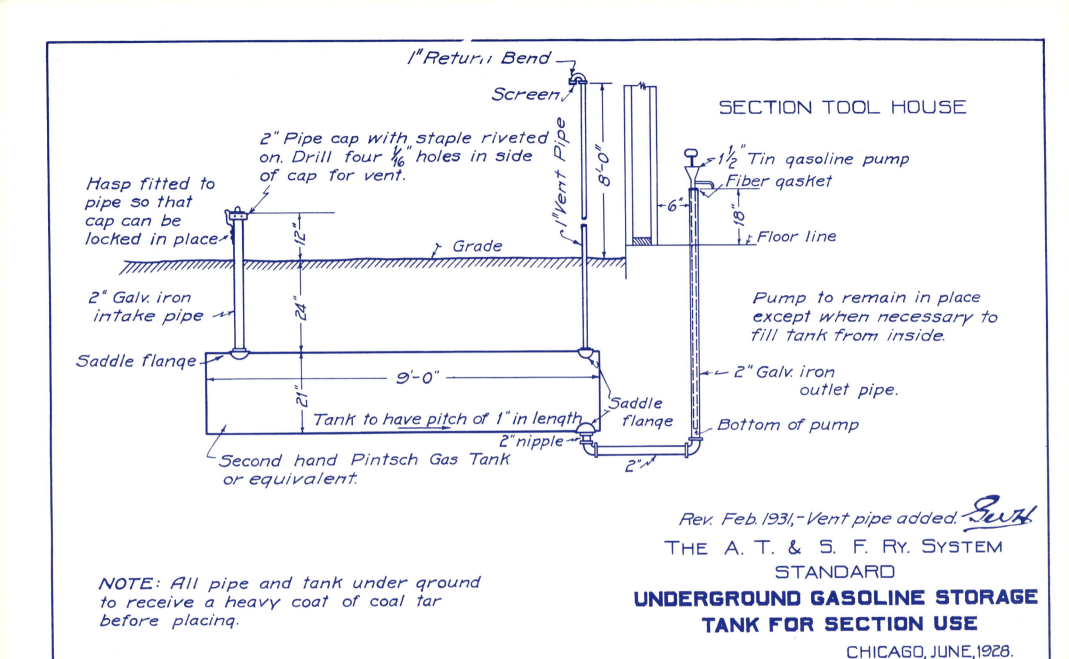

I. MAIN LINES

    (a) Main lines are those so classified in the Annual Mileage Statements.

    (b) "Main Line Construction" will be used on Main Lines not subject to change on account of grade reduction or improvement of alinement. For selection of bridges the Fourth and Parker Districts of the Albuquerque Division and the Cadiz District on the Los Angeles Division will be considered Main Line.

II. BRANCH LINES

    (a) The Annual Mileage Statements classify lines other than Main Lines, as Branch Lines, making no distinction as to which of the latter are Important and Unimportant.

    (b) The following Districts are classified as Important Branch Lines:

    Eastern Lines: Pekin-St.Joseph-Atchison-Girard-4th Dist. Eastern-Strong City-McPherson-Great Bend-Enid-Cushing-Cimarron Valley-Manter-Arkansas Valley-Las Animas-Boise City.

    Western Lines: Deming-Santa Rita-Carlsbad-Pecos (Carlsbad to Loving)-Medicine Lodge-Altus-Shattuck-Borger-Dumas-Hamlin-Sayard-Ft. Stockton-Longview-Silsbee (Silsbee to Beaumont)-Conroe-Dublin-San Angelo-Cresson-Dallas (Cleburne to Dallas)-Paris (Zacha Jct. to Farmersville).

    Coast Lines: Harbor

    (c) Branch Lines other than important, are classified as Unimportant.

GENERAL NOTES

    1. Applicable standard plans, and current specifications and instructions, shall be followed as to details of construction, limiting heights of fill, etc.

THE A. T. & S. F. RAILWAY SYSTEM

STANDARD

INSTRUCTIONS FOR SELECTION OF BRIDGES AND CULVERTS

Chicago, July 1966

APPROVED: APPROVED: APPROVED:

TYPE OF CONSTRUCTION

Structure	Main Line	Branch Lines — Important	Branch Lines — Unimportant
(a) Steel Bridges			
Spans: Truss-Girder-Beam			
Ballast Deck	x	x	On Curves or Spirals
Open Deck	-	-	On Tangent
Trestles: T-Rail			
Ballast Deck	x	x	On Curves or Spirals
Open Deck	-	-	On Tangent
(b) Timber Trestle Bridges			
Timber stringers on pile or framed bents or concrete piers and abutments if foundation conditions require			
Ballast Deck	x	On Curves or Spirals	On Curves or Spirals
Open Deck (5-Ply) See "Note"	x	-	-
Open Deck (4-Ply)	-	On Tangent	On Tangent
(c) Prestressed Concrete Ballast Deck Bridges	x	x	x
(d) Culverts			
Corrugated metal pipe, pipe arch, or arch	x	x	x
Reinforced Concrete Box	x	x	x
Reinforced Concrete Pipe	x	x	x

(e) Comparison of Building, Total, and Annual Costs of Standard Trestle Bridges, Office of Chief Engineer System, File 14408, to be considered when comparing costs of various types of openings to arrive at the most suitable and economical structure.

Note: Ballast deck should be used as specified above unless drift, center height limitation or unusual conditions require open deck.

THE A. T. & S. F. RAILWAY SYSTEM

STANDARD

INSTRUCTIONS FOR SELECTION OF BRIDGES AND CULVERTS

Chicago, July 1966

APPROVED: R D Shelton   APPROVED: R H Beeder   APPROVED: W E Robey

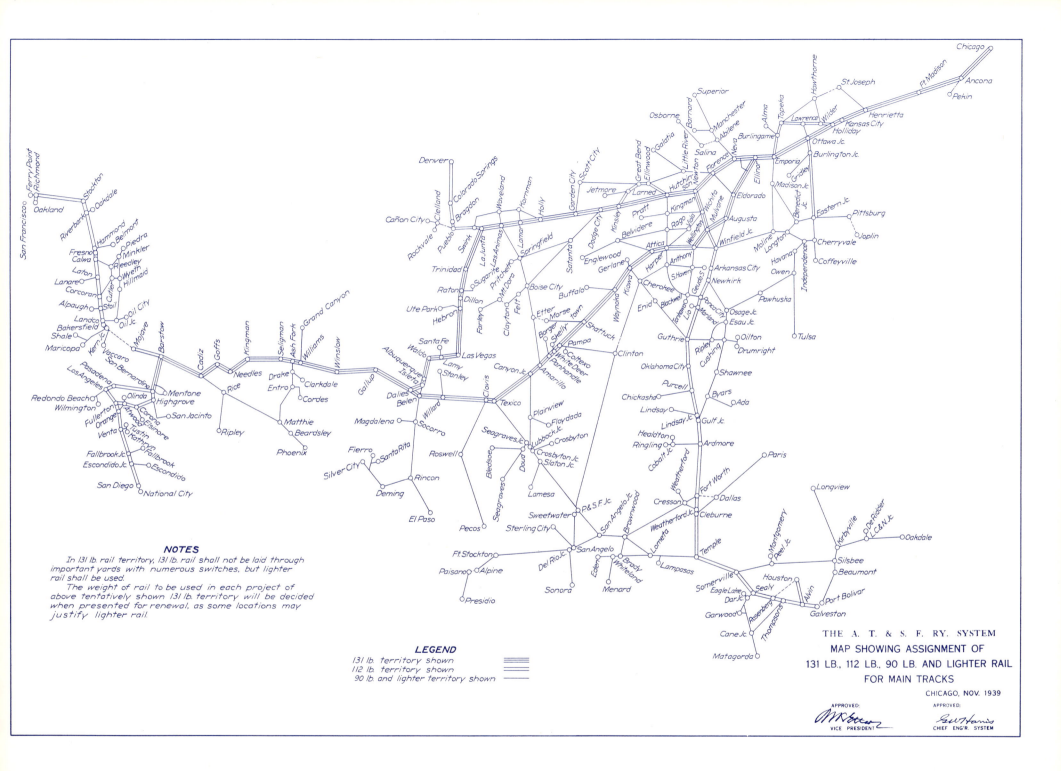

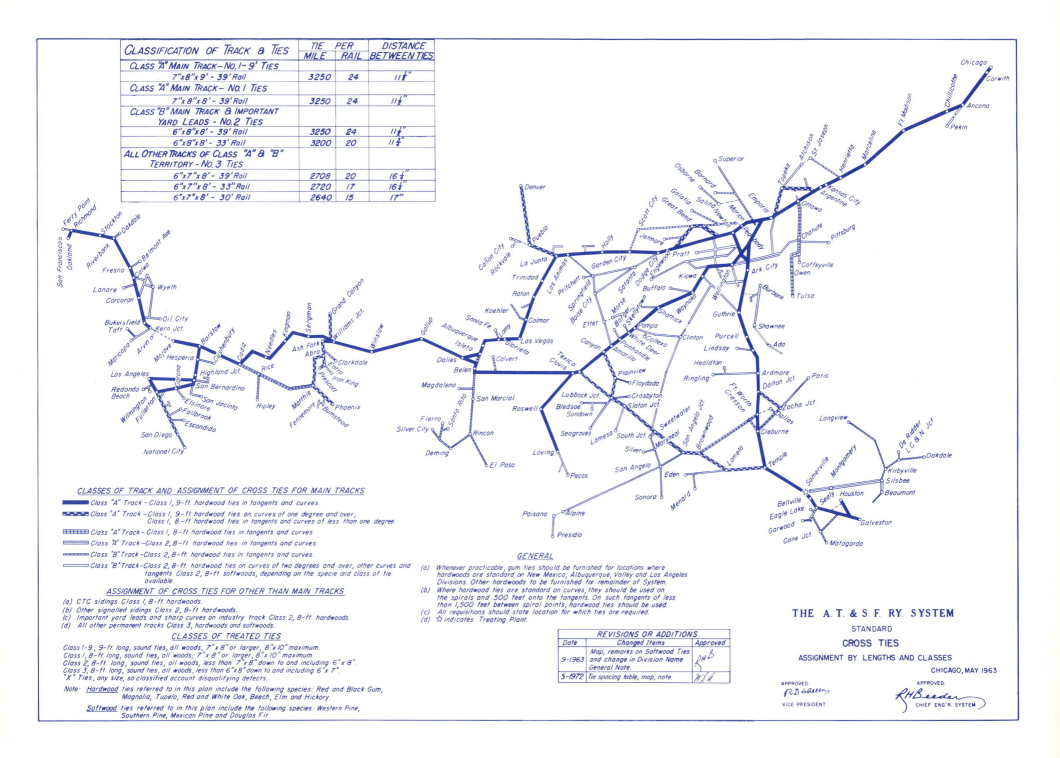

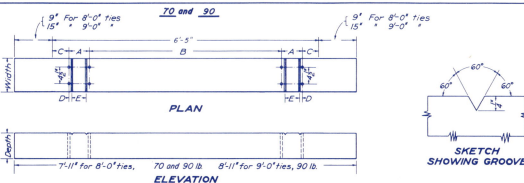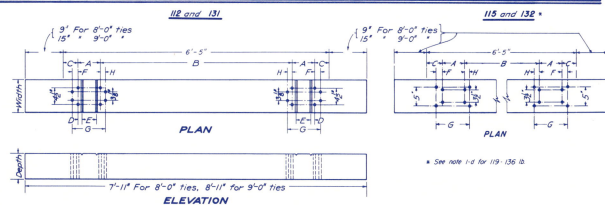

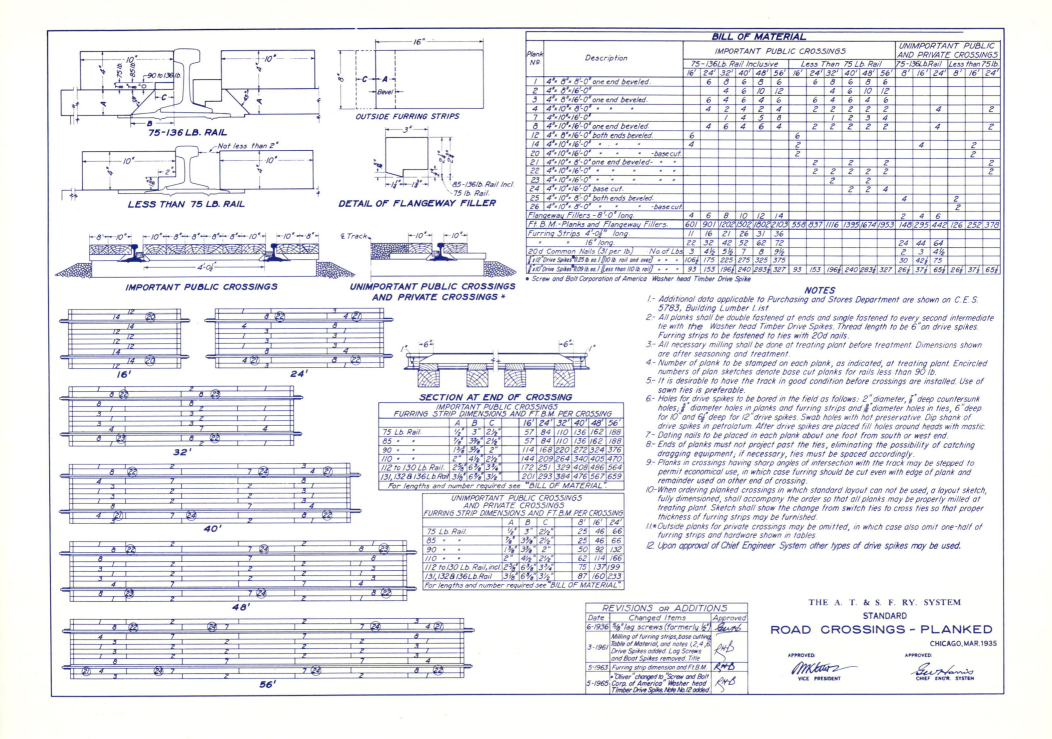

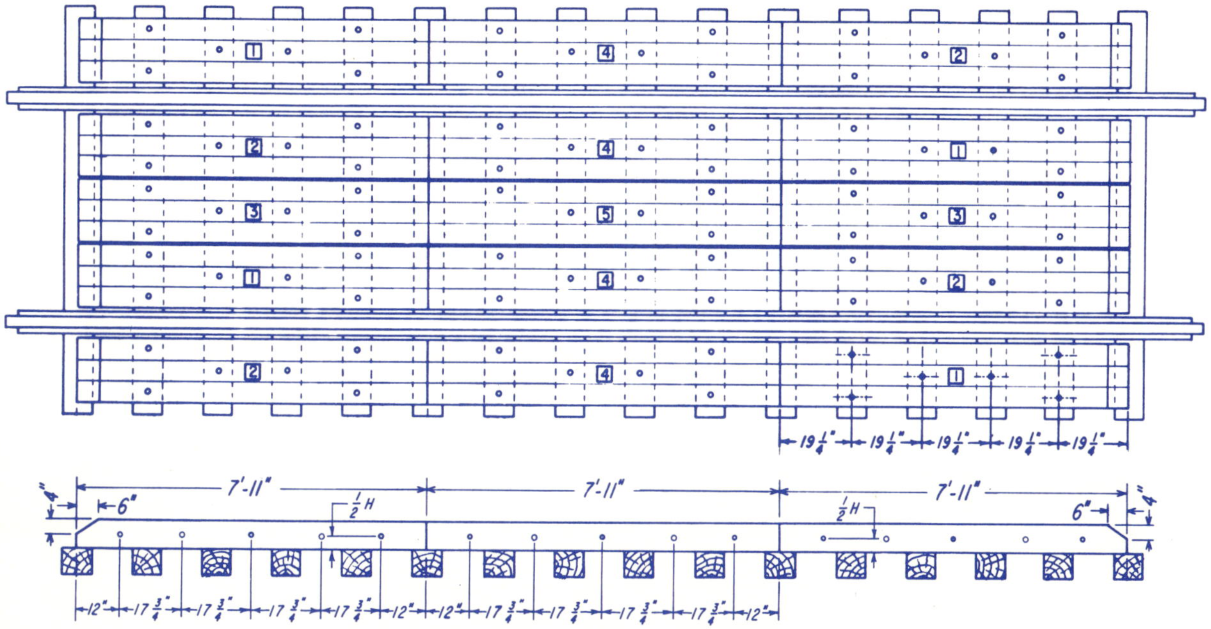

TYPICAL 24' ROAD CROSSING

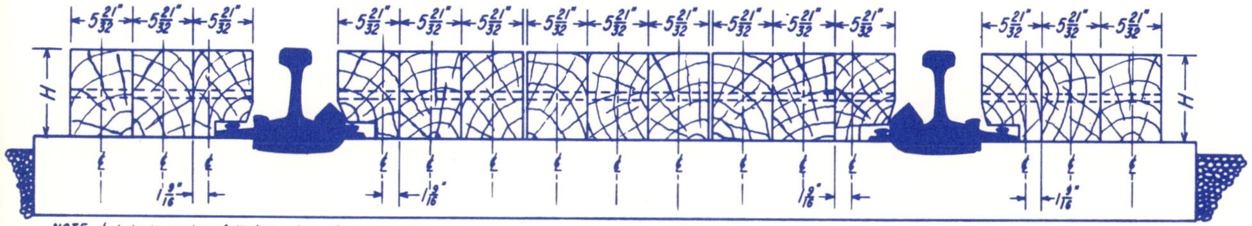

NOTE: ℄ hole in center of timber unless shown otherwise

SECTION THROUGH TYPICAL ROAD CROSSING

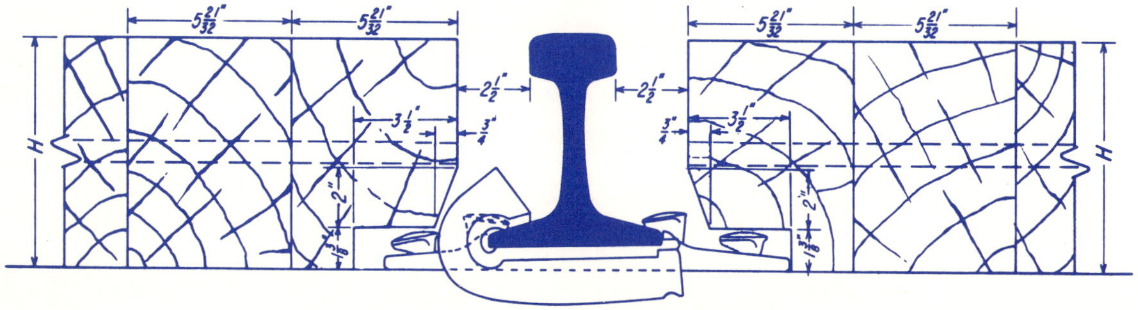

DETAIL OF ROAD CROSSING AT RAIL

BILL OF MATERIAL
IMPORTANT PUBLIC ROAD CROSSING
90-136 lb. Rail Inclusive

CROSSING LENGTH	END PANELS			CENTER PANELS		TOTAL NUMBER OF PANELS
	Outside RH Base Cut	Outside LH Base Cut	Inside Center	Outside Base Cut	Inside Center	
16'	4	4	2	—	—	10
24'	4	4	2	4	1	15
32'	4	4	2	8	2	20
40'	4	4	2	12	3	25
48'	4	4	2	16	4	30
56'	4	4	2	20	5	35
—	1	2	3	4	5	—

"H"	CROSSING LENGTH	16'		24'		32'		40'		48'		56'	
	Number of Ties Under Crossing (19¼" ctrs.)	11		16		21		26		31		36	
	Rail Section	TOTAL FT. B.M. PER CROSSING											
5⅝"	90 lb.	631		946		1262		1577		1893		2208	
6½"	110 lb.	729		1093		1458		1822		2187		2551	
7¼"	112, 115, 119, 130 lb.	813		1220		1626		2033		2439		2846	
7 11/16"	131, 132, 136 lb.	862		1293		1724		2155		2587		3018	
	HARDWARE	No.	Lb.	No.	Lb.	No.	Lb.	No.	Lb.	No.	Lb.	No.	Lb.
	¾" x 16" Square Head Machine Bolts (2.33 lbs. each)	50	116.5	75	175	100	233	125	291	150	350	175	408
	⅝" x 11" Notch Head Drive Spikes (1.2 lbs. each) 90 lb. Rail	60	72	90	108	120	144	150	180	180	216	210	252
	⅝" x 13" Notch Head Drive Spikes (1.36 lbs. each) 110 lb. Rail and Heavier	60	82	90	122	120	163	150	204	180	245	210	286
	¾" Cut Washers (10 per lb.)	100	10	150	15	200	20	250	25	300	30	350	35

NOTES

1. Sectional Panel Road Crossings are to be used at important main line road crossing where there is 90-lb. or heavier rail. Upon the approval of the General Manager they may also be used at other important road crossing.
2. All crossings are to be constructed from treated hardwood timbers.
3. All necessary milling and boring of holes for fastenings shall be done at the treating plant before the treatment of the timbers.
4. All dimensions shown are after seasoning and treatment.
5. Timbers are to be assembled into panels with machine bolts or dowels in the location shown. Each machine bolt will have two cut washers.
6. The identifying panel number, as indicated, is to be attached to each panel at the treating plant.
7. Sectional Panel Crossings shall be installed as follows: The track shall be placed in good condition before the crossing is installed. The crossing shall be placed on new (new meaning sound and with adequate remaining life to properly support the crossing) No. 1 - 9 ft., sawn, hardwood crossties. The crossties shall be spaced on 19¼" centers and the ends of the crossing must not project past the edge of the ties thus eliminating the possibility of catching dragging equipment. Each panel will be fastened to the crossties with 6 Notched Head Drive Spikes on 19¼" centers. The thread length will be 6" on all drive spikes. Upon approval of the Chief Engineer System other types of drive spikes may be used.
8. Field boring of holes for drive spikes, if necessary, will be as follows: ⅝" diameter holes in panels and 9/16" diameter holes in ties, 6" deep for 11" and 6½" deep for 13" drive spikes. Swab holes with preservative and dip the shank of drive spikes in petrolatum.

REVISIONS OR ADDITIONS		
Date	Changed Items	Appr'd
4-1970	Delete and reposition drive spike holes on panels, panel base cut and notes.	RHB
8-1970	Bill of Material, number and weight of Notch Head Drive Spikes, and Machine Bolts. Bolt Spacing.	RHB

THE A. T. & S. F. RY. SYSTEM

STANDARD

ROAD CROSSINGS - SECTIONAL PANEL

CHICAGO, JAN. 1969

APPROVED: L. Cena
VICE PRESIDENT

APPROVED: R. H. Beeder
CHIEF ENG'R. SYSTEM

NOTES

1. – Inside steel guard rails to be of relay rail.
2. – For new and renewal installations of guard rails, the following combinations of running rail and guard rail shall be used:

Running Rail.	Guard Rail.
Less than 75 lb.	Same as running rail.
75 lb.	75 lb.
85 lb.	75, 85 lb.
90 lb.	75, 85, 90 lb.
110 lb.	90, 110 lb.
112, 115, 119 lb.	90, 110, 112, 115, 119 lb.
131, 132, 136 lb.	110, 112, 115, 119, 130, 131, 132, 136 lb.

3. – When relaying the running rail with an increased section, the existing guard rails should not be changed if they fall within note 2 limits, except at option of General Manager, existing guard rails may be retained in service for the remainder of its life, as follows:

Increased running rail.	Existing guard rail.
90 lb.	75, 85 lb.
110 lb.	75, 85, 90 lb.
112, 115, 119 lb.	85, 90, 110, 112, 115 lb.
131, 132, 136 lb.	90, 110, 112, 115, 119, 130, 131, 132 lb.

4. – Inside steel guard rails must be fully spiked and each joint fully bolted.
5. – When available, second hand joints must be used in installing guard rails.
6. – All guard rail points to be furnished by the Newton Frog and Switch Shop, being reclaimed No. 10 frog points, beveled 45°.
7. – On double track bridges in automatic train control territory where there is a possibility of changing the direction of operation at will, guard rails must be installed on both tracks as shown in Case "A".
8. – When inside steel guard rails are required on any portion of a combination bridge of two or more types, they shall include the entire bridge structure.
9. – Where there is a curved approach to a bridge with girder, post or any structural member that might be seriously damaged by derailed equipment, the 45'-0" guard rail distance may be increased on the curved approach up to a maximum of 300', at option of General Manager.
10. – On high speed main track, inside steel guard rail at approach to bridge may be lengthened, at option of General Manager, from one to two rail lengths by increasing the parallel distance of 1'-8", retaining tapered portion as shown.

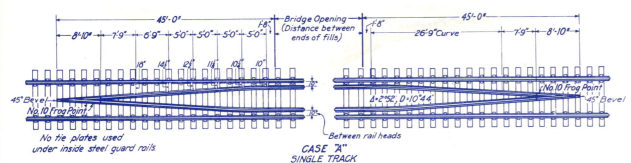

CASE "A"
SINGLE TRACK

INSIDE STEEL GUARD RAILS SHALL BE PLACED ON:

1. – Thru truss bridges and thru girder bridges regardless of length, height, location or alignment.
2. – Bridges on all lines regardless of length and location.
   (a) Having a center height greater than 35 feet.
   (b) On curves of 4° and over.
3. – Bridges that span important highways or important railroads at option of General Manager.

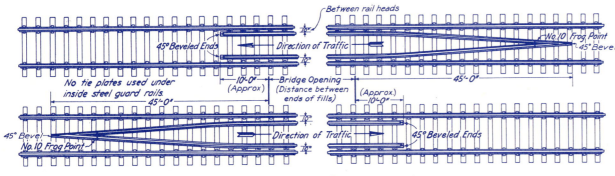

CASE "B"
DOUBLE TRACK

INSIDE STEEL GUARD RAILS TO BE PLACED ON:
Bridges of corresponding type, length and alignment described in Case "A", and all those with center girders, posts or any structural member forming an obstruction between the tracks.

REVISIONS OR ADDITIONS

Date	Changed Items	Approved
7-1931	Par. 6 of Case "A" and Gen. Note 2.	
6-1936	112 and 131 lb. rail added; Notes 1,2 and 3 re-written.	
10-1938	45° Bevel frog point, Note 8, Case "A" and "B".	
11-1940	Note 9 added.	
2-1944	10" Clearance, note 10 added, notes 2 and 3 revised.	
8-1957	Notes 2 and 3 revised to include 115, 119, 132 and 136 lb. rail.	
4-1966	Case "A" notes.	

THE A. T. & S. F. RY. SYSTEM
STANDARD
INSIDE STEEL GUARD RAIL FOR BRIDGES.
CHICAGO, DEC., 1927.

APPROVED: _____ VICE PRESIDENT.
APPROVED: _____ ACT. CHIEF ENG'R. SYSTEM.
APPROVED: _____ BRIDGE ENG'R. SYSTEM.

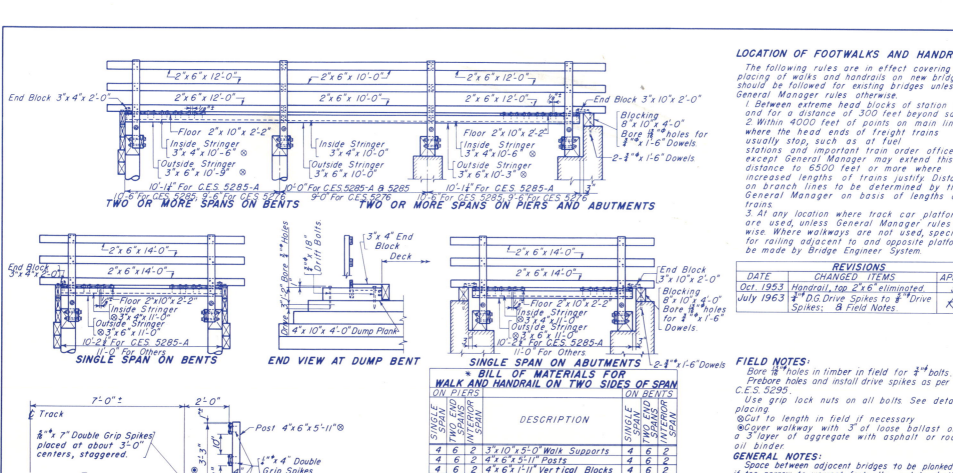
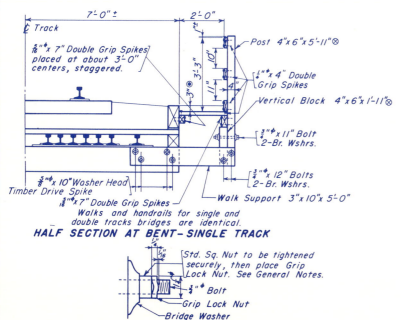

LOCATION OF FOOTWALKS AND HANDRAILS

The following rules are in effect covering the placing of walks and handrails on new bridges and should be followed for existing bridges unless General Manager rules otherwise.

1. Between extreme head blocks of station grounds and for a distance of 300 feet beyond same.
2. Within 4000 feet of points on main lines where the head ends of freight trains usually stop, such as at fuel stations and important train order offices, except General Manager may extend this distance to 6500 feet or more where increased lengths of trains justify. Distances on branch lines to be determined by the General Manager on basis of lengths of trains.
3. At any location where track car platforms are used, unless General Manager rules otherwise. Where walkways are not used, special plan for railing adjacent to and opposite platform to be made by Bridge Engineer System.

REVISIONS

DATE	CHANGED ITEMS	APPROVED
Oct. 1953	Handrail, top 2"x 6" eliminated.	
July 1963	$\frac{3}{4}$" D.G. Drive Spikes to $\frac{5}{8}$" Drive Spikes; & Field Notes.	

FIELD NOTES:

Bore $\frac{13}{16}$" holes in timber in field for $\frac{3}{4}$" bolts.
Prebore holes and install drive spikes as per C.E.S. 5295.
Use grip lock nuts on all bolts. See detail for placing.
⊗ Cut to length in field if necessary
⊙ Cover walkway with 3" of loose ballast or a 3" layer of aggregate with asphalt or road oil binder.

GENERAL NOTES:

Space between adjacent bridges to be planked over if too narrow to warrant footwalks and handrails.
For kinds and grades of timber, see C.E.S. 5786.
All timber shall have a preservative treatment.
Special Walk and Handrail plan for bridges on curves will be prepared by Bridge Engineer System.
Quantities in Bill of Materials are exact.
For General Notes on treated timber see C.E.S. 5285-A.
✱ Bill of materials is for bridges with 10'-0" panels. For bridges with 9'-0" panels, all stringers and handrails shall be ordered 1'-0" shorter, and number of pieces of flooring shall be decreased by 2 pieces per span.

THE A. T. & S. F. RY. SYSTEM
STANDARD
WALK AND HANDRAIL
FOR EXISTING BALLASTED DECK
T-RAIL BRIDGES

CHICAGO, JULY, 1952

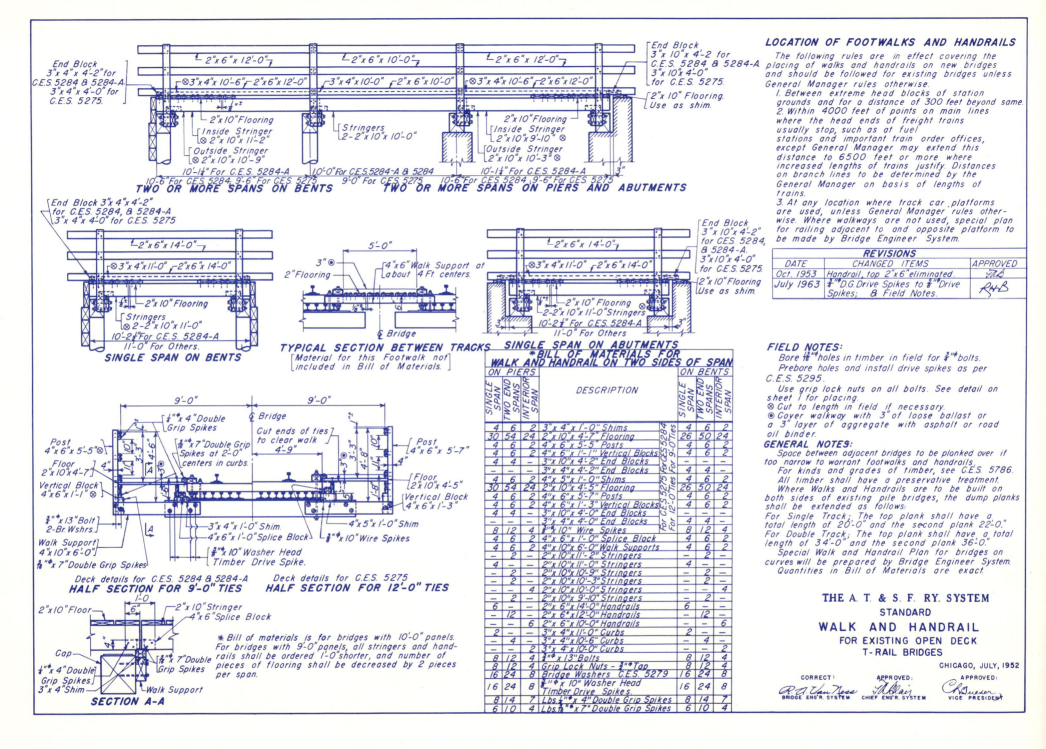

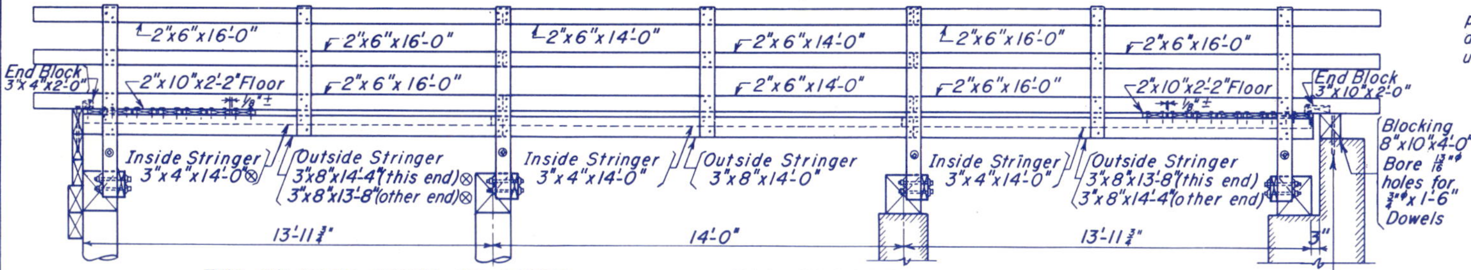

TWO OR MORE SPANS ON BENTS

TWO OR MORE SPANS ON PIERS AND ABUTMENTS

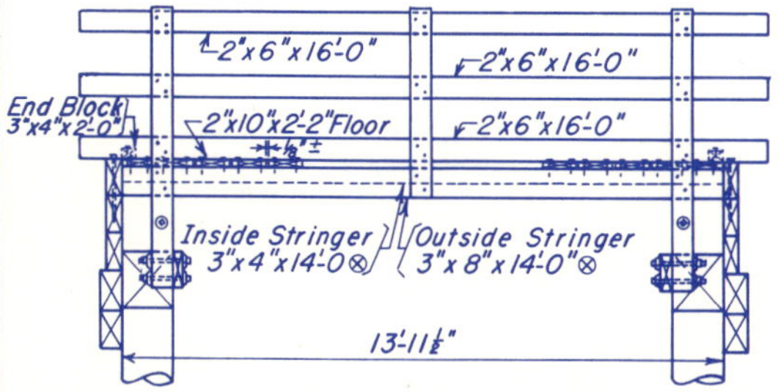

SINGLE SPAN ON BENTS

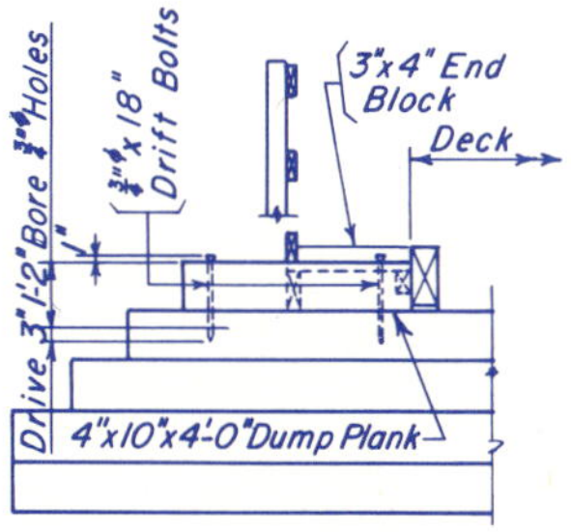

END VIEW AT DUMP BENT

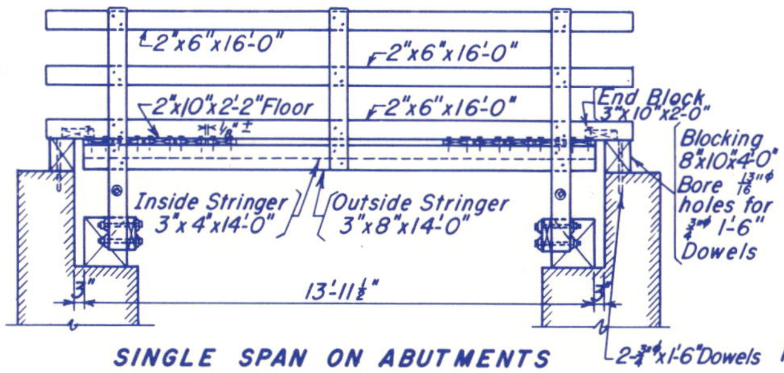

SINGLE SPAN ON ABUTMENTS

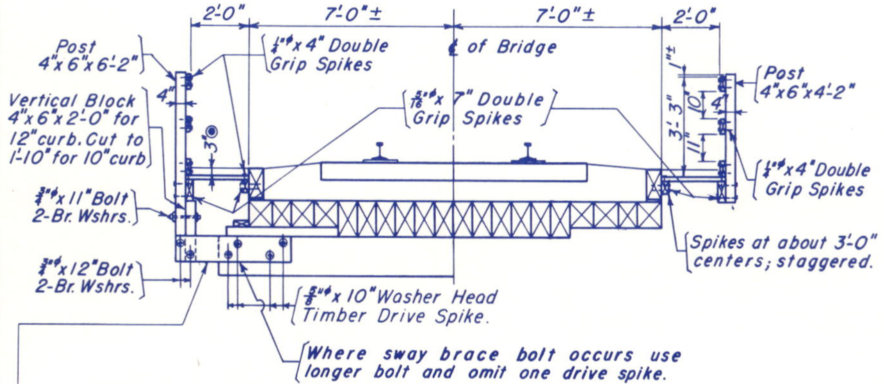

HALF SECTION AT BENT

HALF SECTION AT INT. POST

Walks and handrails for single and double track bridges are identical.

Walk Support 3"x10"x4'-0". Place on side opposite the end of sway brace on interior bents, and if pattern of sways at bents differ, make it uniform.

LOCATION OF FOOTWALKS AND HANDRAILS

The following rules are in effect covering the placing of walks and handrails on new bridges and should be followed for existing bridges unless General Manager rules otherwise.

1. Between extreme head blocks of station grounds and for a distance of 300 feet beyond same.
2. Within 4000 feet of points on main lines where the head ends of freight trains usually stop, such as at fuel stations and important train order offices, except General Manager may extend this distance to 6500 feet or more where increased lengths of trains justify. Distances on branch lines to be determined by the General Manager on basis of lengths of trains.
3. At any location where track car platforms are used, unless General Manager rules otherwise. Where walkways are not used, special plan for railing adjacent to and opposite platform to be made by Bridge Engineer System.

REVISIONS		
DATE	CHANGED ITEMS	APPROVED
Oct. 1953	Handrail, top 2"x6" eliminated.	[illegible]
July 1963	3/4"ϕ D.G. Drive Spikes to 5/8"ϕ Drive Spikes; & Field Notes.	RHB

FIELD NOTES:

Bore 13/16"ϕ holes in timber in field for 3/4"ϕ bolts.

Prebore holes and install drive spikes as per C.E.S. 5295.

Use grip lock nuts on all bolts. See detail on Sheet 1 for placing.

⊗ Cut to length in field if necessary.

◉ Cover walkway with 3" of loose ballast or a 3" layer of aggregate with asphalt or road oil binder.

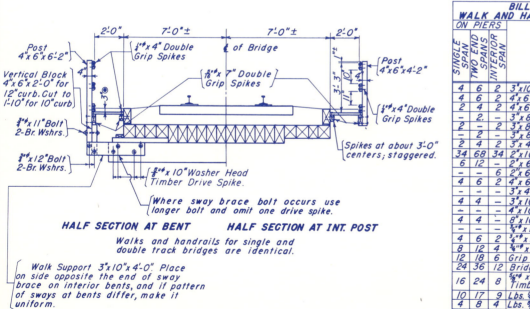

BILL OF MATERIALS FOR WALK AND HANDRAIL ON TWO SIDES OF SPAN

ON PIERS				ON BENTS		
SINGLE SPAN	TWO END SPANS	INTERIOR SPAN	DESCRIPTION	SINGLE SPAN	TWO END SPANS	INTERIOR SPAN
4	6	2	3"x10"x4'-0" Walk Supports	4	6	2
4	6	2	4"x6"x6'-2" Posts	4	6	2
2	4	2	4"x6"x4'-2" Posts	2	4	2
–	2.	–	3"x8"x14'-4" Stringers	–	2	–
2	–	2	3"x8"x14'-0" Stringers	2	–	2
–	2	–	3"x8"x13'-8" Stringers	–	2	–
2	4	2	3"x4"x14'-0" Stringers	2	4	2
34	68	34	2"x10"x2'-2" Flooring	34	68	34
6	12	–	2"x6"x16'-0" Handrails	6	12	–
–	–	6	2"x6"x14'-0" Handrails	–	–	6
4	6	2	4"x6"x2'-0" Vertical Blocks	4	6	2
–	–	–	3"x4"x2'-0" End Blocks	4	4	–
4	4	–	3"x10"x2'-0" End Blocks	–	–	–
–	–	–	4"x10"x4'-0" Dump Planks	4	4	–
4	4	–	8"x10"x4'-0" Blocking	–	–	–
–	–	–	3/4"ϕ x18" Drift Bolts C.E.S. 5262	8	8	–
4	6	2	3/4"ϕ x11" Bolts	4	6	2
8	12	4	3/4"ϕ x12" Bolts	8	12	4
12	18	6	Grip Lock Nuts 3/4"ϕ Tap	12	18	6
24	36	12	Bridge Washers C.E.S. 5279	24	36	12
16	24	8	5/8"ϕ x10" Washer Head Timber Drive Spikes	16	24	8
10	17	9	Lbs. 1/4"ϕ x4" Double Grip Spikes	10	17	9
4	8	4	Lbs. 5/16"ϕ x7" Double Grip Spikes	4	8	4
8	8	–	3/4"ϕ x1'-6" Dowels	–	–	–

GENERAL NOTES:

For kinds and grades of timber, see C.E.S. 5786.

All timber shall have a preservative treatment.

Special Walk and Handrail plan for bridges on curves will be prepared by Bridge Engineer System.

Quantities in Bill of Materials are exact.

For General Notes on treated timber see C.E.S. 5282-A.

Space between adjacent bridges to be planked over if too narrow to warrant footwalks and handrails.

THE A. T. & S. F. RY. SYSTEM

STANDARD

WALK AND HANDRAIL

FOR EXISTING BALLASTED DECK TIMBER TRESTLE BRIDGES

CHICAGO, JULY, 1950

CORRECT: BRIDGE ENG'R. SYSTEM — APPROVED: CHIEF ENG'R. SYSTEM — APPROVED: VICE PRESIDENT

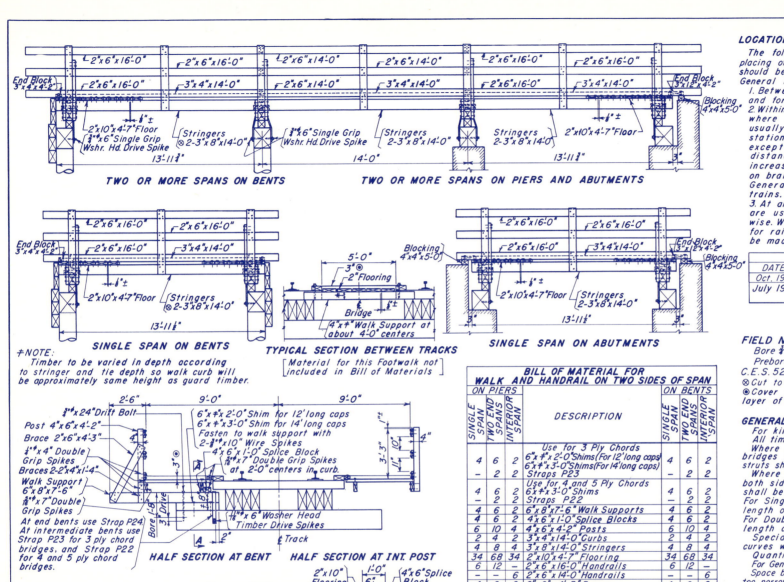

LOCATION OF FOOTWALKS AND HANDRAILS

The following rules are in effect covering the placing of walks and handrails on new bridges and should be followed for existing bridges unless General Manager rules otherwise.

1. Between extreme head blocks of station grounds and for a distance of 300 feet beyond same.
2. Within 4000 feet of points on main lines where the head ends of freight trains usually stop, such as at fuel stations and important train order offices, except General Manager may extend this distance to 6500 feet or more where increased lengths of trains justify. Distances on branch lines to be determined by the General Manager on basis of lengths of trains.
3. At any location where track car platforms are used, unless General Manager rules otherwise. Where walkways are not used, special plan for railing adjacent to and opposite platform to be made by Bridge Engineer System.

REVISIONS

DATE	CHANGED ITEMS	APPROVED
Oct. 1953	Handrail, top 2"x6" eliminated.	
July 1963	¾"⌀ S.G. Drive Spikes to 11/16"⌀ Drive Spikes; & Field Notes.	R+B

FIELD NOTES:
Bore ⅝" holes in timber in field for ¾" drift bolts.
Prebore holes and install drive spikes as per C.E.S. 5295.
⊗ Cut to length in field if necessary.
⊙ Cover walkway with 3" of loose ballast or a 3" layer of aggregate with asphalt or road oil binder.

GENERAL NOTES:
For kinds and grades of timber see C.E.S. 5786.
All timber shall have a preservative treatment.
Where walks and handrails are to be built on existing bridges built from plans C.E.S. 1457, the longitudinal struts shall be lowered flush with top of the caps.
Where Walks and Handrails are to be built on both sides of existing pile bridges, the dump planks shall be extended as follows:
For Single Track; The top plank shall have a total length of 20'-0" and the second plank 22'-0".
For Double Track; The top plank shall have a total length of 34'-0" and the second plank 36'-0".
Special Walk and Handrail Plan for bridges on curves will be prepared by Bridge Engineer System.
Quantities in Bill of Materials are exact.
For General Notes on treated timber see C.E.S. 5281-A.
Space between adjacent bridges to be planked over if too narrow to warrant footwalks and handrails.

THE A.T. & S.F. RY. SYSTEM
STANDARD
WALK AND HANDRAIL
FOR EXISTING OPEN DECK
TIMBER TRESTLE BRIDGES

CHICAGO, JULY, 1950

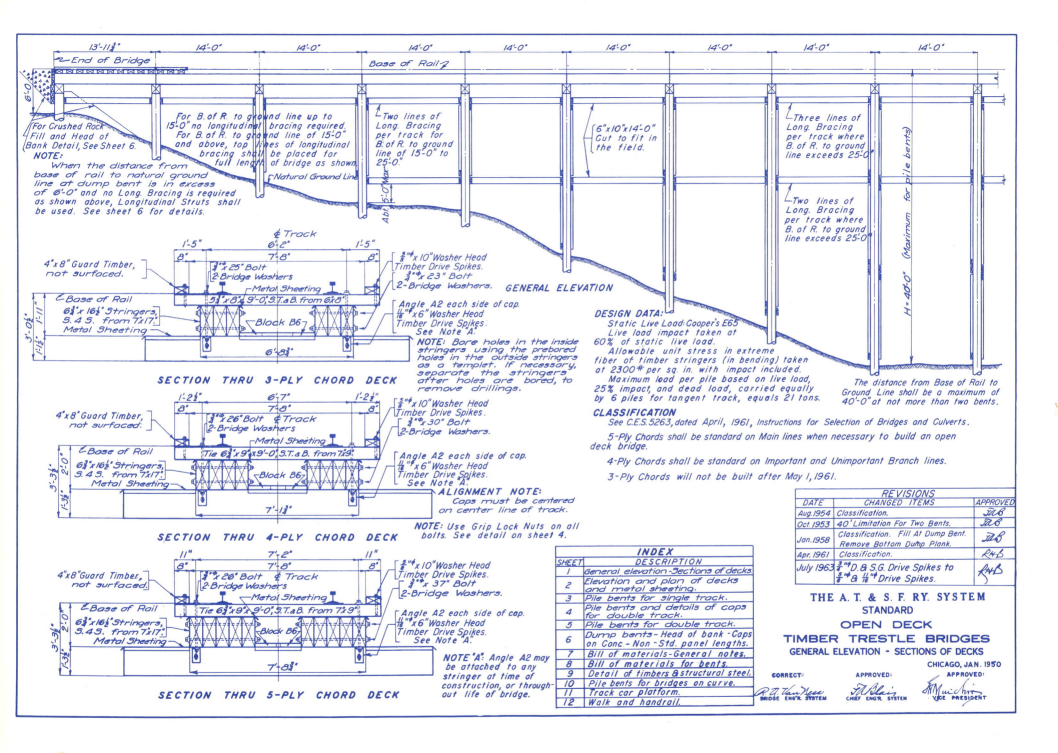

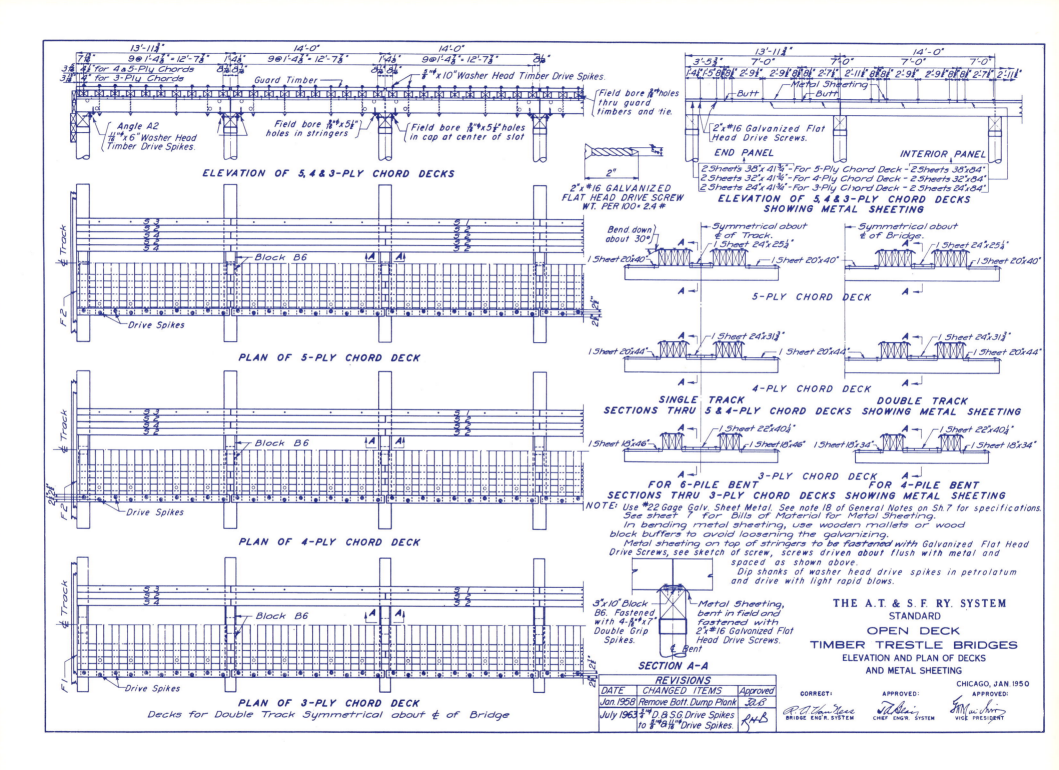

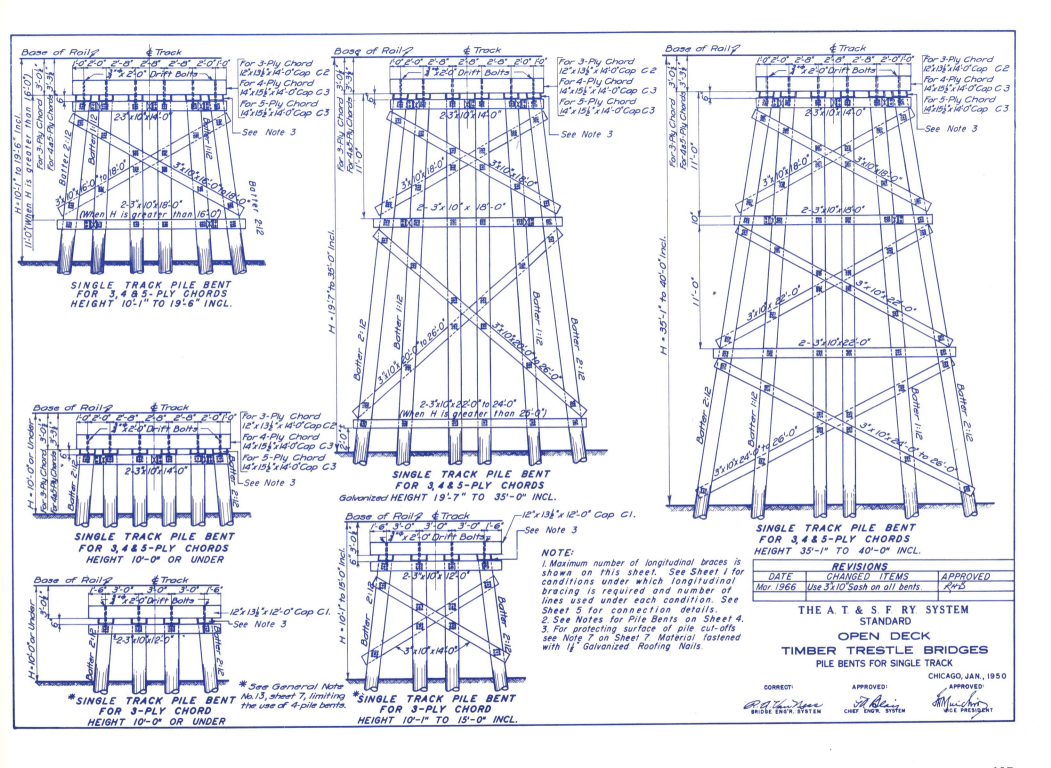

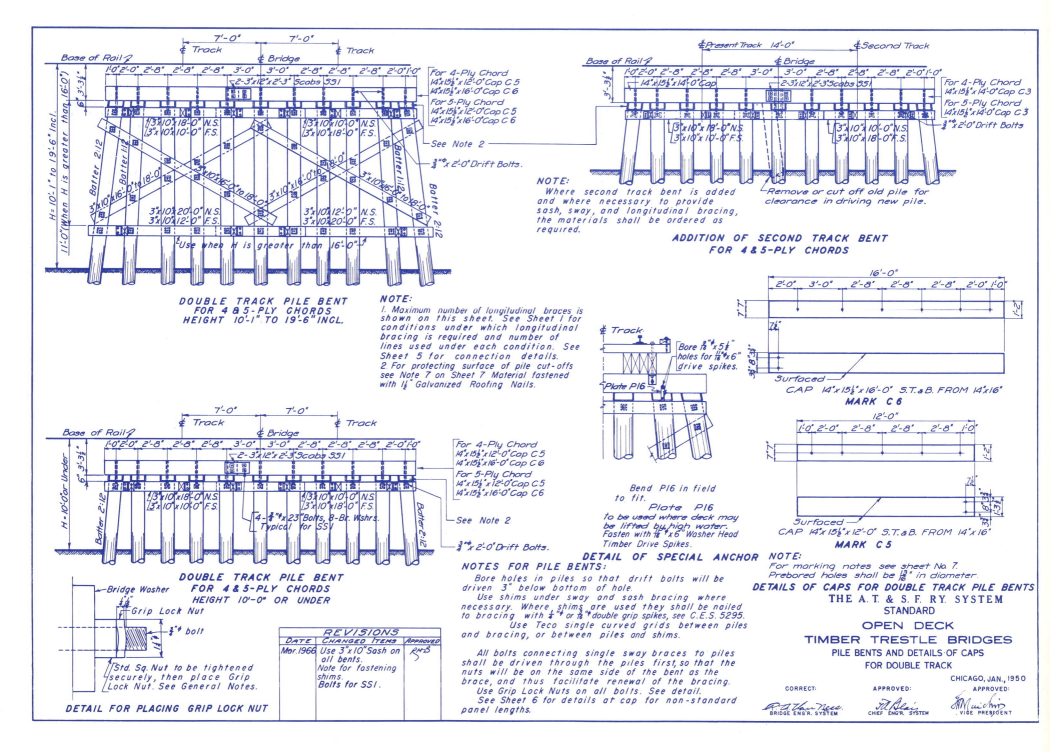

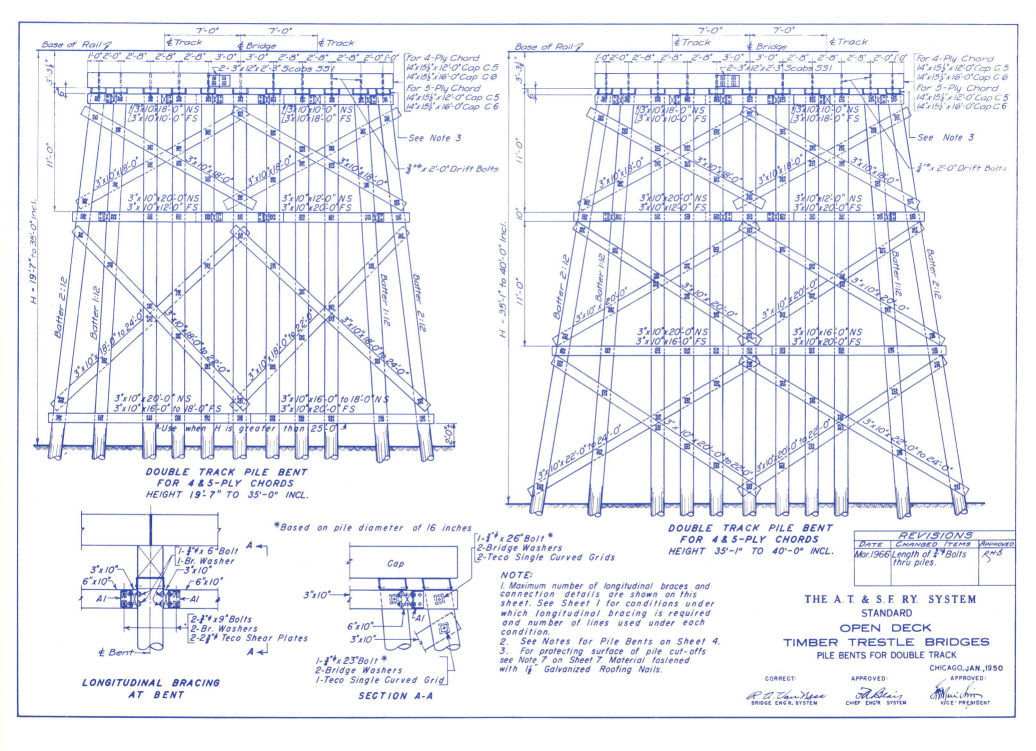

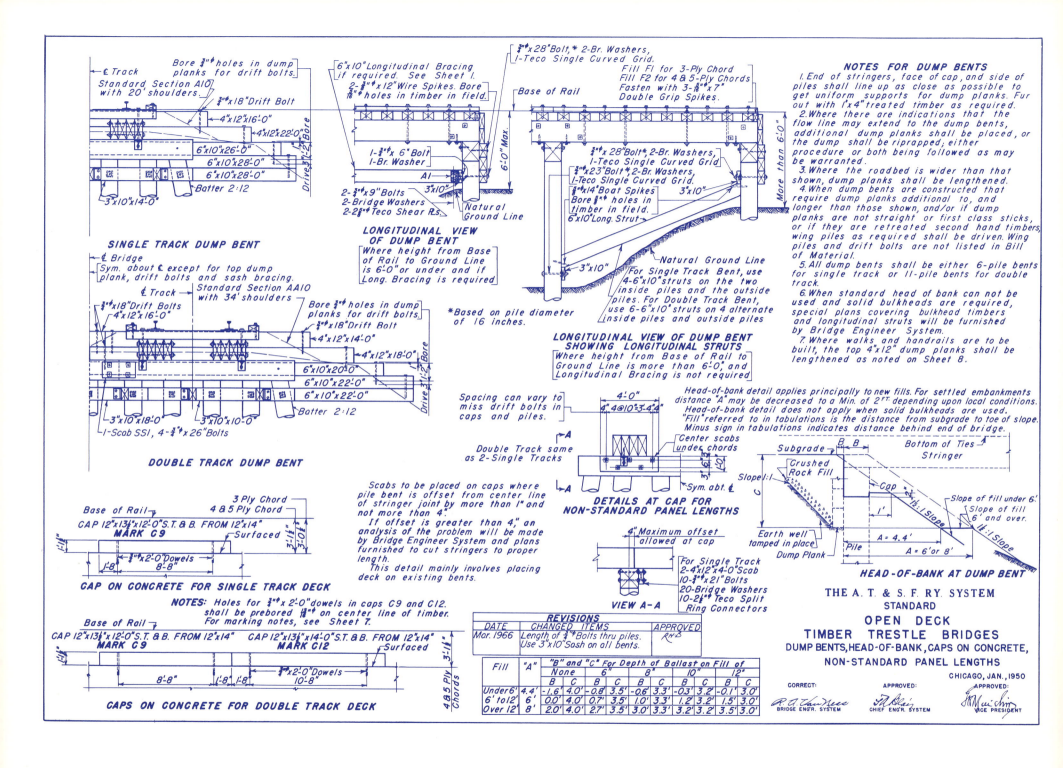

BILL OF MATERIALS FOR SINGLE TRACK 3-4 & 5 PLY CHORD DECKS EXCEPT METAL SHEETING AND STRINGERS

	SINGLE SPAN			TWO END SPANS			ONE INTERIOR SPAN		
	3-PLY	4-PLY	5-PLY	3-PLY	4-PLY	5-PLY	3-PLY	4-PLY	5-PLY
TREATED TIMBER									
Guard Timbers G1	2	2	2	4	4	4	2	2	2
*Ties T1	10	—	—	20	—	—	10	—	—
*Ties T2	—	10	10	—	20	20	—	10	10
Fills F1	2	—	—	2	—	—	—	—	—
Fills F2	—	2	2	—	2	2	—	—	—
Blocks B6	4	4	4	6	6	6	2	2	2
STRUCTURAL STEEL									
Angles A2	4	4	4	8	8	8	4	4	4
HARDWARE									
7/8"⌀x7" Double Grip Spikes	22	22	22	30	30	30	8	8	8
3/4"⌀x6" Washer Head Timber Drive Spikes	8	8	8	16	16	16	8	8	8
3/4"⌀x10" Washer Head Timber Drive Spikes	20	20	20	40	40	40	20	20	20
7/8"⌀ x 25" Bolts	8	—	—	16	—	—	8	—	—
7/8"⌀ x 26" Bolts	—	8	8	—	16	16	—	8	8
7/8"⌀ x 23" Bolts	8	—	—	16	—	—	8	—	—
7/8"⌀ x 30" Bolts	—	8	—	—	16	—	—	8	—
7/8"⌀ x 37" Bolts	—	—	8	—	—	16	—	—	8
Bridge Washers C.E.S. 5279	32	32	32	64	64	64	32	32	32
Grip Lock Nuts - 7/8"⌀ Tap.	16	16	16	32	32	32	16	16	16

STRINGERS REQUIRED FOR SINGLE TRACK (N = TOTAL NO. OF PANELS)

	ONE PANEL BRIDGE			TWO PANEL BRIDGE			MORE THAN A TWO PANEL BRIDGE					
							ODD NO. OF PANELS			EVEN NO. OF PANELS		
	3-Ply	4-Ply	5-Ply	3-Ply	4-Ply	5-Ply	3-Ply	4-Ply	5-Ply	3-Ply	4-Ply	5-Ply
Stringers S1	—	—	—	2	2	2	2	2	2	2	2	2
Stringers S2	—	—	—	4	6	8	2(N-1)	3(N-1)	4(N-1)	2(N-1)	(3N-2)	4(N-1)
Stringers S3	2	2	2	—	—	—	2	2	2	4	4	4
Stringers S4	4	6	8	—	—	—	4	6	8	4	6	8

BILL OF MATERIALS FOR METAL SHEETING

	5-PLY CHORD DECK					4-PLY CHORD DECK					3-PLY CHORD DECK									
											FOR 6-PILE BENT					FOR 4-PILE BENT				
	SHEETS 38"x 41 3/4"	SHEETS 38"x 84"	SHEETS 20"x 40"	SHEETS 24"x 25 1/4"	2"x #16 GALV. FLAT HEAD DRIVE SCREWS	SHEETS 32"x 41 3/4"	SHEETS 32"x 84"	SHEETS 20"x 40"	SHEETS 24"x 44"	2"x #16 GALV. FLAT HEAD DRIVE SCREWS	SHEETS 24"x 41 3/4"	SHEETS 24"x 84"	SHEETS 18"x 46"	SHEETS 22"x 40 1/4"	2"x #16 GALV. H.D. DRIVE SCREWS	SHEETS 24"x 41 3/4"	SHEETS 24"x 84"	SHEETS 18"x 34"	SHEETS 22"x 40 1/4"	2"x #16 GALV. H.D. DRIVE SCREWS
SINGLE SPAN	4	2	4	2	66	4	2	4	2	52	4	2	4	2	52	4	2	4	2	52
TWO END SPANS	4	6	6	3	114	4	6	6	3	88	4	6	6	3	88	4	6	6	3	88
ONE INT'R SPAN	—	4	2	1	48	—	4	2	1	36	—	4	2	1	36	—	4	2	1	36

*When ties are ordered, weight of rail shall be specified and ties shall be prebored and grooved similar to C.E.S. 5670. Bolt holes and holes for drive spikes in guard timbers and ties shall be bored in the field.

Double track quantities same as two single tracks.

GENERAL NOTES:

1. All timber and piles shall have a preservative treatment.
2. Before timber is treated, all pieces shall be cut to exact lengths, surfaced, and prebored as required.
3. Damaging of the surface of treated timber or piles by the unnecessary use of timber hooks, peavies, etc., should be avoided. When possible, treated timber or piles should be handled by rope slings. The dropping of treated timber or piles from any appreciable height is not permitted.
4. When it becomes necessary to work from scaffolding in constructing the bridge, such scaffolding should be hung by ropes and not nailed to the treated timber or piles.
5. When necessary to disturb the surface of treated timber or piles, or when the surface has been damaged through handling, such surfaces must be mopped with a liberal quantity of preservative, followed by 1/4 coat of coal tar plastic cement.
6. Swab field holes with preservative. Clean bolt of dirt and rust scale, coat shank with plastic cement and dip end of bolt in same so as much as possible will be pushed ahead of bolt when inserted in hole. Unused holes to be fitted at each end with 1 1/8"⌀ x 4" treated wooden plugs coated with plastic cement before inserting.
7. Tops of piles to be coated with preservative followed shortly by about 1/4" thickness of plastic cement. Lay on a 30"x 30" piece of coal tar-pitch saturated cotton fabric, pressing it smooth to contact pile. Lap fabric on side of pile and nail 4" down from top, trimming 2" below nails. Apply 1/4" of plastic cement on top surface of fabric. After cap is drifted, apply 1/4" of plastic cement to exposed area of fabric.
8. Cracks above ground in piles, and cracks in timbers, 1/8" and wider, to be cleaned of dirt and sprayed with preservative.
9. Preservative, plastic cement and treated wooden plugs not included in Bill of Material and will be supplied on requisition to the Store Department. Coal tar plastic cement to be as per current A.R.E.A. Waterproofing Specifications.
10. Just before completion of the work, all bolts shall be gone over and tightened securely and a Grip Lock Nut shall be placed over each nut; see detail on sheet 4.
11. Inaccessible surfaces of structural steel and washers shall be given a heavy coat of petrolatum before placing, exposed portions of all steel and hardware shall be given a heavy coat of petrolatum just before completion of the work.
12. Inside steel guard rails shall be provided in accord with C.E.S. 5278 when necessary.
13. On unimportant branch lines, four-pile bents may be used up to and including a height of 15'-0" base of rail to ground line, if authorized by the Chief Engineer System.
14. If piles cannot be driven to a satisfactory penetration, framed bents may be used, or caps may be supported on concrete piers.
15. In the case of bridges having framed bents on piles or on concrete piers, the timber for the framed bents shall be framed and bored before treatment, and the plans shall be made by the Bridge Engineer System.
16. Short-toe joint bars only shall be used on the bridge, and the most distance possible shall be maintained between ends of bars and spikes immediately beyond ends of bars.
17. For kinds and grades of timber and piling, see C.E.S. 5786.
18. Metal sheeting shall be zinc-coated (Galvanized) #22 gage, coating Class C, as per current Specification A.S.T.M. A 525.
19. Teco single curved grids, shear plates, split rings, and cutter heads and pilots to groove for shear plates and split rings, are secured from the Timber Engineering Company, Washington, D.C.
20. For detail and installation of drive spikes see C.E.S. 5295.
22. Bridges in hot and dry desert territory shall have caps protected by placing new #22 gage or second hand #20 to #26 gage galvanized sheet metal on the ends.
23. For details and location of Shims see C.E.S. 5294.
24. Quantities in Bill of Materials are exact.

REVISIONS

DATE	CHANGED ITEMS	APPROVED
Mar. 1966	Corrected Stringer Table. Notes 7, 8, 12 & 18.	RHB

NOTES ON MARKING OF TIMBER

1. Ties, stringers, caps, guard timbers, and piles shall be branded at the treating plant, before treatment, to show the class of treatment, the kind of timber, the assembly mark, and the year of treatment.
   (a.) Ties, stringers, caps, and guard timbers shall have shown on one end the assembly mark number, and the year of treatment.
   (b.) The class of treatment, the kind of timber, and the year of treatment shall be shown on the top and bottom of the stringers, three feet from one end, and on one edge of the guard timbers, two feet from one end. The class of treatment and the kind of timber shall be shown on one side of the caps, three feet from one end.
   (c.) Piles shall have shown on the butt end the year of treatment; and on the side, four, ten and sixteen feet from the butt end, the class of treatment, the kind of timber, and the year of treatment.
2. After construction of a bridge, dating nails indicating the year of construction shall be placed by field forces as called for by C.E.S. 5733.

THE A.T. & S.F. RY. SYSTEM
STANDARD
OPEN DECK TIMBER TRESTLE BRIDGES
BILL OF MATERIALS & GENERAL NOTES
CHICAGO, JAN., 1950

CORRECT: BRIDGE ENG'R SYSTEM
APPROVED: CHIEF ENG'R SYSTEM
APPROVED: VICE PRESIDENT

BILL OF MATERIALS FOR SINGLE TRACK PILE BENTS 3, 4 & 5-PLY CHORD DECKS

Height Base of Rail to Ground Line	10'-0" and Under	10'-1" to 13'-0"	13'-1" to 16'-0"	16'-1" to 19'-6"	19'-7" to 25'-0"	25'-1" to 27'-0"	27'-1" to 30'-0"	30'-1" to 33'-0"	33'-1" to 35'-0"	35'-1" to 37'-0"	37'-1" to 40'-0"
TREATED TIMBER											
Cap C2 For 3-Ply Chord	1	1	1	1	1	1	1	1	1	1	1
Cap C3 For 4-Ply Chord	1	1	1	1	1	1	1	1	1	1	1
Cap C3 For 5-Ply Chord	1	1	1	1	1	1	1	1	1	1	1
Piles	6	6	6	6	6	6	6	6	6	6	6
Bracing 3"x10"x14'-0"	2	2	2	2	2	2	2	2	2	2	2
Bracing 3"x10"x16'-0"	–	2	–	–	–	–	–	–	–	–	–
Bracing 3"x10"x18'-0"	–	–	2	4	4	4	4	4	4	4	4
Bracing 3"x10"x20'-0"	–	–	–	–	2	–	–	–	–	–	–
Bracing 3"x10"x22'-0"	–	–	–	–	–	2	4	–	–	4	4
Bracing 3"x10"x24'-0"	–	–	–	–	–	–	–	4	2	2	–
Bracing 3"x10"x26'-0"	–	–	–	–	–	–	–	–	2	–	2
Longitudinal Bracing 6"x10"x14'-0"	See Sheets 1, 3, 4 & 5										
HARDWARE											
1"⌀ x 24" Drift Bolts C.E.S. 5262	6	6	6	6	6	6	6	6	6	6	6
3/4"⌀ x 23" Bolts *	–	12	12	12	24	24	24	24	24	36	36
3/4"⌀ x 26" Bolts *	6	6	6	12	12	18	18	18	18	18	18
Teco Single Curved Grids	12	24	24	36	48	60	60	60	60	72	72
Bridge Washers C.E.S. 5279	12	36	36	48	72	84	84	84	84	108	108
Grip Lock Nuts 3/4" Tap	6	18	18	24	36	42	42	42	42	54	54
Lbs. 1 1/2" Galvanized Roofing Nails	0.5	0.5	0.5	0.5	0.5	0.5	0.5	0.5	0.5	0.5	0.5
1/4"⌀ x 6" Wshr. Hd. Timber Drive Spike											
Hardware for Longitudinal Bracing	See Sheets 1, 3, 4 & 5										
MISCELLANEOUS											
30"x30" Sheets of Coal Tar-Pitch Saturated Cotton Fabric	6	6	6	6	6	6	6	6	6	6	6
STRUCTURAL STEEL											
Plates P16											

* Based on pile diameter of 16 inches.

For Dump Bents:
① Use 26" Bolts in place of 23" Bolts, see sh. 6;
△ Use 28" Bolts in place of 26" Bolts, see sh. 6;
☐ Order half of quantities shown.
† Based on using #12 gage nails with 3/8"⌀ heads, at 249 per Lb.

BILL OF MATERIALS FOR DOUBLE TRACK PILE BENTS 4 & 5-PLY CHORD DECKS

Height Base of Rail to Ground Line	10'-0" and Under	10'-1" to 12'-0"	12'-1" to 16'-0"	16'-1" to 19'-6"	19'-7" to 21'-0"	21'-1" to 25'-0"	25'-1" to 29'-0"	29'-1" to 32'-0"	32'-1" to 35'-0"	35'-1" to 37'-0"	37'-1" to 40'-0"
TREATED TIMBER											
Cap C5 For 4-Ply Chord	1	1	1	1	1	1	1	1	1	1	1
Cap C6 For 4-Ply Chord	1	1	1	1	1	1	1	1	1	1	1
Cap C5 For 5-Ply Chord	1	1	1	1	1	1	1	1	1	1	1
Cap C6 For 5-Ply Chord	1	1	1	1	1	1	1	1	1	1	1
Scabs SS1	2	2	2	2	2	2	2	2	2	2	2
Piles	11	11	11	11	11	11	11	11	11	11	11
Bracing 3"x10"x10'-0"	2	2	2	2	2	2	2	2	2	2	2
Bracing 3"x10"x12'-0"	–	–	–	2	2	2	2	2	2	2	2
Bracing 3"x10"x16'-0"	–	4	4	–	–	–	–	2	–	2	2
Bracing 3"x10"x18'-0"	2	2	6	6	10	6	6	6	8	6	8
Bracing 3"x10"x20'-0"	–	–	–	2	2	6	8	6	4	10	8
Bracing 3"x10"x22'-0"	–	–	–	–	–	–	–	2	2	2	2
Bracing 3"x10"x24'-0"	–	–	–	–	–	–	–	–	2	–	–
Longitudinal Bracing 6"x10"x14'-0"	See Sheets 1, 3, 4 & 5										
HARDWARE											
1"⌀ x 24" Drift Bolts C.E.S. 5262	11	11	11	11	11	11	11	11	11	11	11
3/4"⌀ x 23" Bolts *	4	24	24	24	44	44	44	44	44	64	64
3/4"⌀ x 26" Bolts *	11	13	13	24	26	26	37	37	37	39	39
Teco Single Curved Grids	22	46	46	68	92	92	114	114	114	138	138
Bridge Washers C.E.S. 5279	30	74	74	96	140	140	162	162	162	206	206
Grip Lock Nuts 3/4" Tap	15	37	37	48	70	70	81	81	81	103	103
Lbs. 1 1/2" Galvanized Roofing Nails	1.0	1.0	1.0	1.0	1.0	1.0	1.0	1.0	1.0	1.0	1.0
1/4"⌀ x 6" Wshr. Hd. Timber Drive Spike											
Hardware for Longitudinal Bracing	See Sheets 1, 3, 4 & 5										
MISCELLANEOUS											
30"x30" Sheets of Coal Tar-Pitch Saturated Cotton Fabric	11	11	11	11	11	11	11	11	11	11	11
STRUCTURAL STEEL											
Plates P16											

BILL OF MATERIALS FOR SINGLE TRACK 4-PILE BENT 3-PLY CHORD DECK

Height Base of Rail to Ground Line	10'-0" and Under	10'-1" to 15'-0"
TREATED TIMBER		
Cap C1	1	1
Piles	4	4
Bracing 3"x10"x12'-0"	2	2
Bracing 3"x10"x14'-0"	–	2
HARDWARE		
1"⌀ x 24" Drift Bolts C.E.S. 5262	4	4
3/4"⌀ x 23" Bolts *	–	8
3/4"⌀ x 26" Bolts *	4	4
Teco Single Curved Grids	8	16
Bridge Washers C.E.S. 5279	8	24
Grip Lock Nuts 3/4" Tap	4	12
Lbs. 1 1/2" Galvanized Roofing Nails	0.5	0.5
MISCELLANEOUS		
30"x30" Sheets of Coal Tar-Pitch Saturated Cotton Fabric	4	4

BILL OF ADDITIONAL MATERIALS FOR TWO DUMP BENTS

	Single Track	Double Track
TREATED TIMBER		
Dump Plank 4"x12"x14'-0"	–	2
Dump Plank 4"x12"x16'-0"	2	2
Dump Plank 4"x12"x18'-0"	–	4
Dump Plank 4"x12"x22'-0"	2	–
Dump Plank 6"x10"x20'-0"	–	4
Dump Plank 6"x10"x22'-0"	–	8
Dump Plank 6"x10"x26'-0"	2	–
Dump Plank 6"x10"x28'-0"	4	–
HARDWARE		
1"⌀ x 18" Drift Bolts C.E.S. 5262	16	24
1/2"⌀ x 12" Wire Spikes	4	4

Bill of Materials for Dump Bents is for bents where height from Base of Rail to Ground Line is 6'-0" or under. Where height is greater than 6'-0" material will be required as shown by longitudinal view of dump bent on sheet 6.

⊠ Where walks and handrails are to be built on both sides, the 4"x12" dump plank shall be as follows: For Single Track; Top Plank 4"x12"x20'-0" For Double Track; Top Planks 1-4"x12"x16'-0" & 1-4"x12"x18'-0"

NOTES:
1. Where caps are placed on concrete instead of piles, the caps will be prebored, see sheet 6. These caps are not listed in the Bill of Materials and shall be ordered as required.
2. Bill of Materials given on this sheet does not include any timber or hardware for the longitudinal struts shown on Sheet 6 nor any timber or hardware for details at cap for non-standard panel lengths shown on Sheet 6.

⊛ 8 Drive spikes and 4 Plates P16 shall be ordered per track for each bent if field conditions require account of high water. See detail Sheet 4.

4. A sufficient number of 1"x10"x1'-0" and 2"x10"x1'-0" treated timber shims, and 3/4"⌀ or 7/8"⌀ double grip spikes shall be ordered for sash and sway brace shimming as noted on pile bents on sheet 4.
5. Galvanized sheet metal for ends of caps as called for in the General Notes on Sheet 7 is not included in Bill of Materials.

¤ Coal tar-pitch saturated cotton fabric weighing not less than 11 oz. per. sq. yd. to be as per current A.R.E.A. Waterproofing Specifications.

REVISIONS

DATE	CHANGED ITEMS	APPROVED
Mar. 1966	Length of 3/4"⌀ Bolts thru piles. Use 3"x10" Sash on all bents. Note 3 & 4. Bolts for SS1.	RHB

THE A. T. & S. F. RY. SYSTEM
STANDARD
OPEN DECK TIMBER TRESTLE BRIDGES
BILLS OF MATERIALS FOR BENTS

CHICAGO, JAN., 1950

CORRECT: R.A. Van Ness, BRIDGE ENG'R. SYSTEM
APPROVED: CHIEF ENG'R. SYSTEM
APPROVED: VICE PRESIDENT

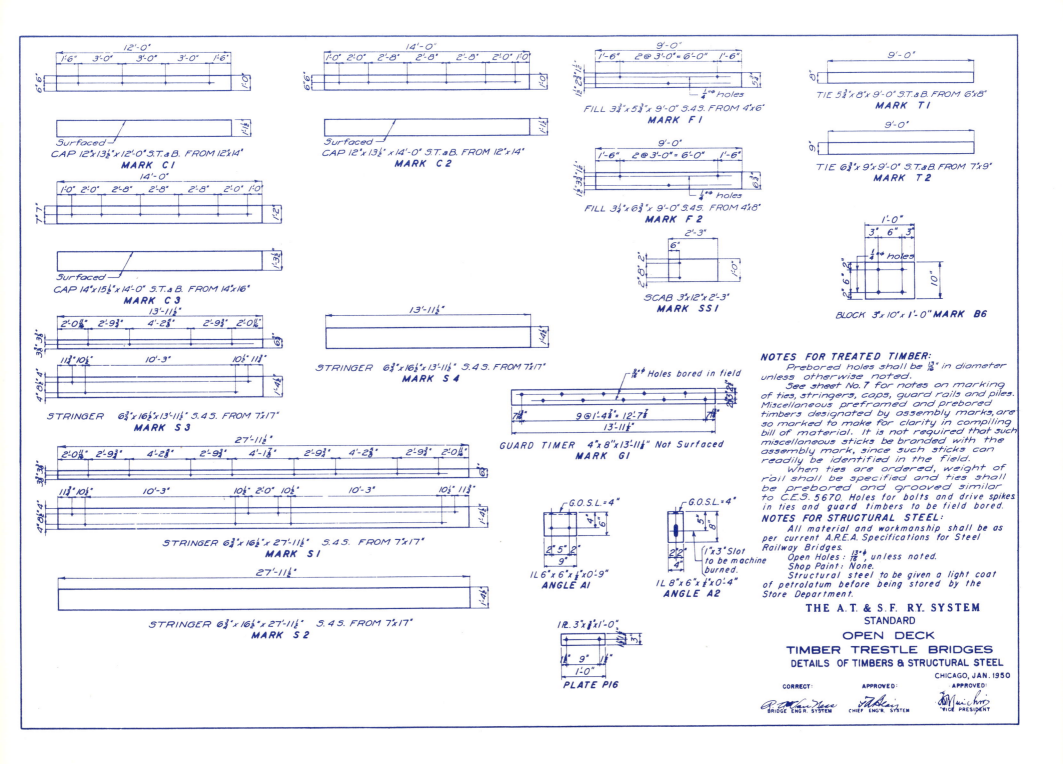

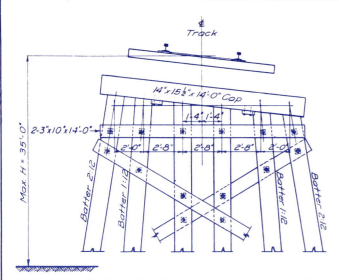

SINGLE TRACK 6-PILE BENT ON CURVE
SEE TABLE ON THIS SHEET GIVING MAXIMUM PERMISSIBLE VALUES OF "H" FOR DIFFERENT DEGREES OF CURVATURE

SINGLE TRACK 6-PILE BENT ON CURVE
HEIGHT 10'-0" OR UNDER

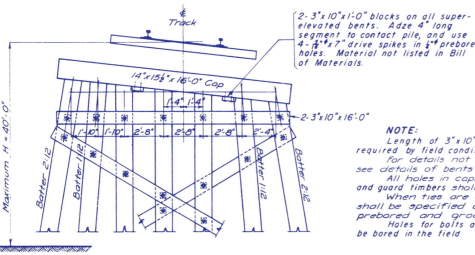

SINGLE TRACK 7-PILE BENT ON CURVE
SEE TABLE ON THIS SHEET GIVING MAXIMUM PERMISSIBLE VALUES OF "H" FOR DIFFERENT DEGREES OF CURVATURE

NOTE:
Length of 3"x10" sway bracing to be as required by field conditions.
For details not shown on this sheet, see details of bents on tangent track.
All holes in caps, piles, bracing, stringers, and guard timbers shall be bored in the field.
When ties are ordered, weight of rail shall be specified and ties shall be prebored and grooved similar to C.E.S. 5670
Holes for bolts and drive spikes in ties shall be bored in the field.

BENTS FOR BRIDGES CARRYING CURVED TRACKS
SINGLE TRACK BRIDGES

1. Single track open deck bridges carrying curved track shall be built to follow the curve. The bents shall be placed on radial lines, and so spaced that the outside stringers will be the same length as for bridges on tangent; the remainder of the stringers being cut to fit in the field. The stringers in the chords shall be interlaced, and spread as much as may be necessary to permit the chords to follow the curve concentrically. The chords shall be spaced 5'-0" center to center. Where the chord bolts pass thru the stringers spreaders shall be used, if necessary. These spreaders shall be made of treated timber blocks, beveled to suit the conditions. If required on account of spreading the stringers, length of ties may be increased.

2. Caps shall be 14"x15½" and shall be placed on the same slope as the ties. Piles shall be cut off on the correct bevel to give the required superelevation to the track. Particular care shall be taken to cut piles to correct elevation and bevel to avoid placing caps or chords on shims.

3. Bent shall be constructed with either six or seven piles, as shown on this sheet, depending on the degree of curve and height of bent. The maximum permissible height of bent for different degrees of curve shall be as given in the following table:

DEGREE OF CURVE	MAXIMUM PERMISSIBLE VALUE OF "H"	
	6-PILE BENTS	7-PILE BENTS
0°-30'	35'-0"	40'-0"
1°-00'	25'-0"	40'-0"
2°-00'	20'-0"	35'-0"
3° to 8°	16'-0"	20'-0"

For degrees of curvature between the values specified in the foregoing, the maximum permissible values of "H" may be obtained by linear interpolation.

4. For bridges not included in the above noted limitations, special designs of bents will be prepared by the Bridge Engineer System.

DOUBLE TRACK BRIDGES

Since double track open deck bridges on curves are of rare occurrence, no standard plans for double track bents on curves have been prepared. Where such bridges are required, they may be constructed, if feasible, as two separate single track bridges, with bents staggered; otherwise, designs of special double track bents will be prepared by the Bridge Engineer System.

THE A.T. & S.F. RY. SYSTEM
STANDARD
OPEN DECK
TIMBER TRESTLE BRIDGES
PILE BENTS FOR
BRIDGES ON CURVED TRACK

CHICAGO, JAN., 1950

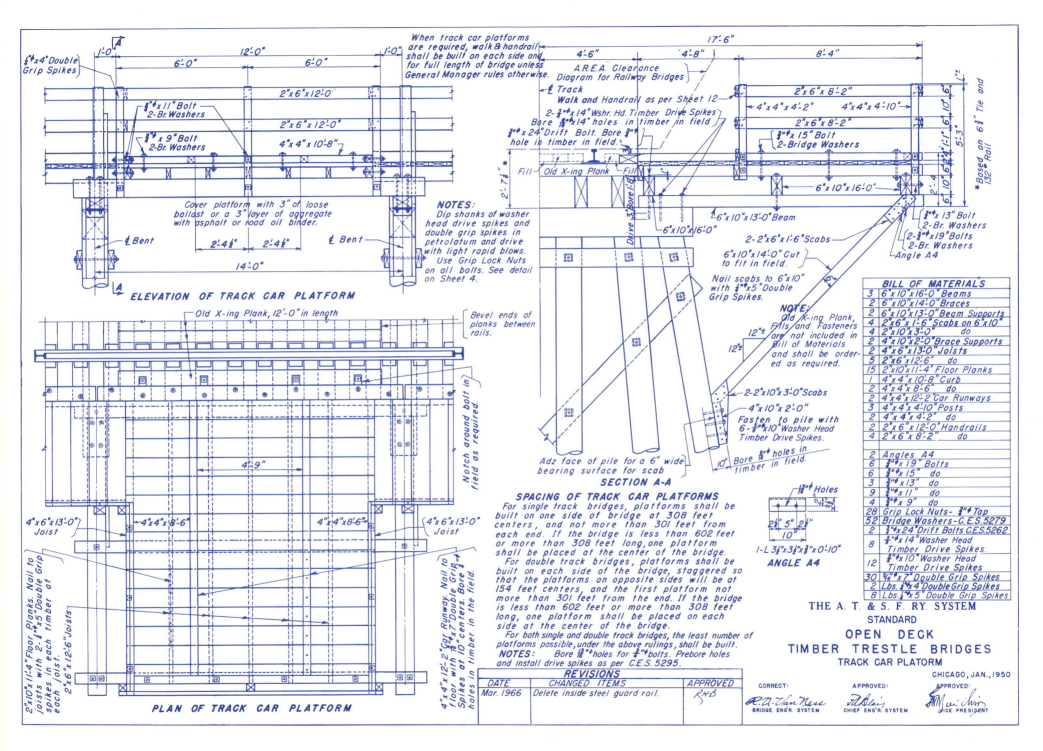

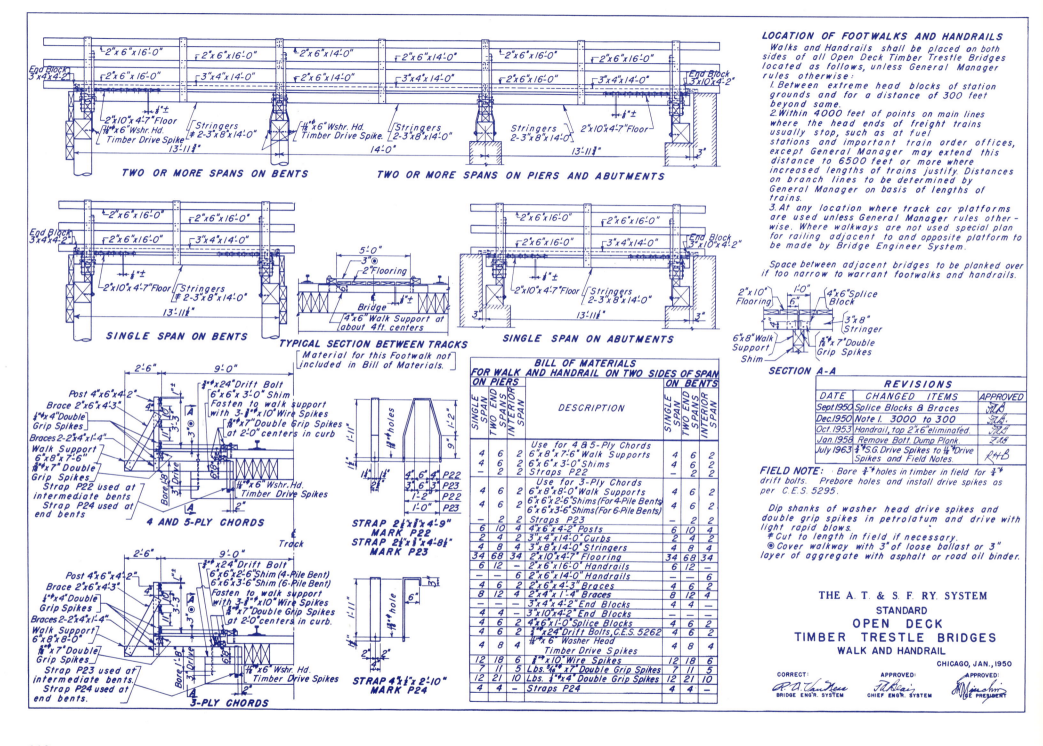

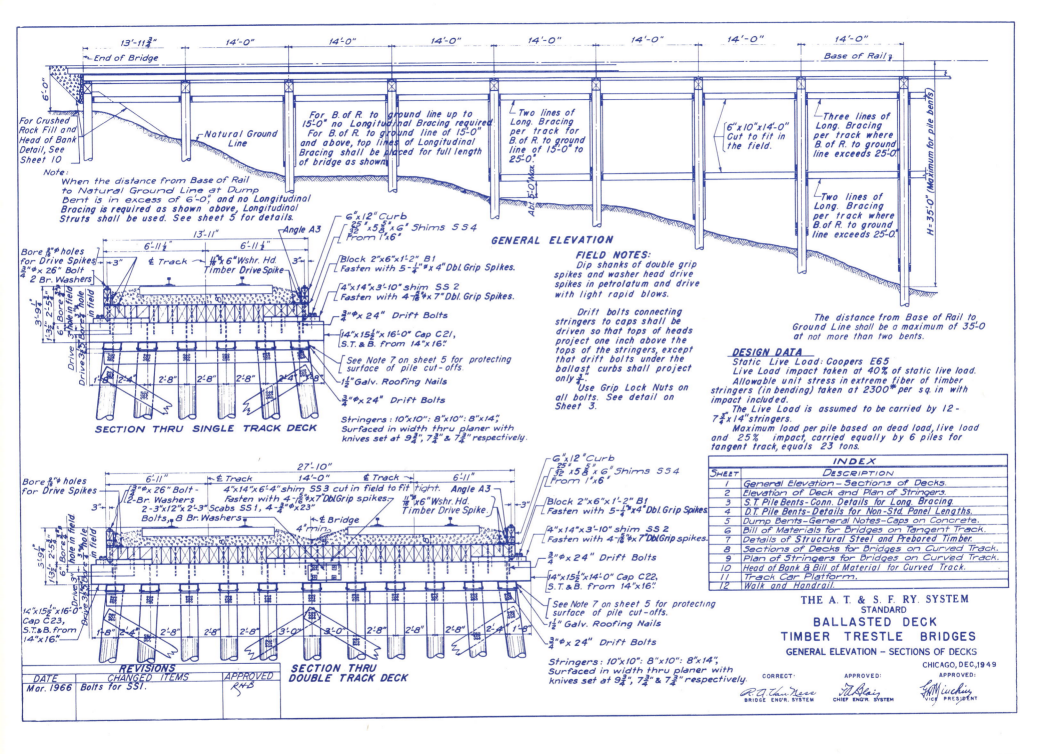

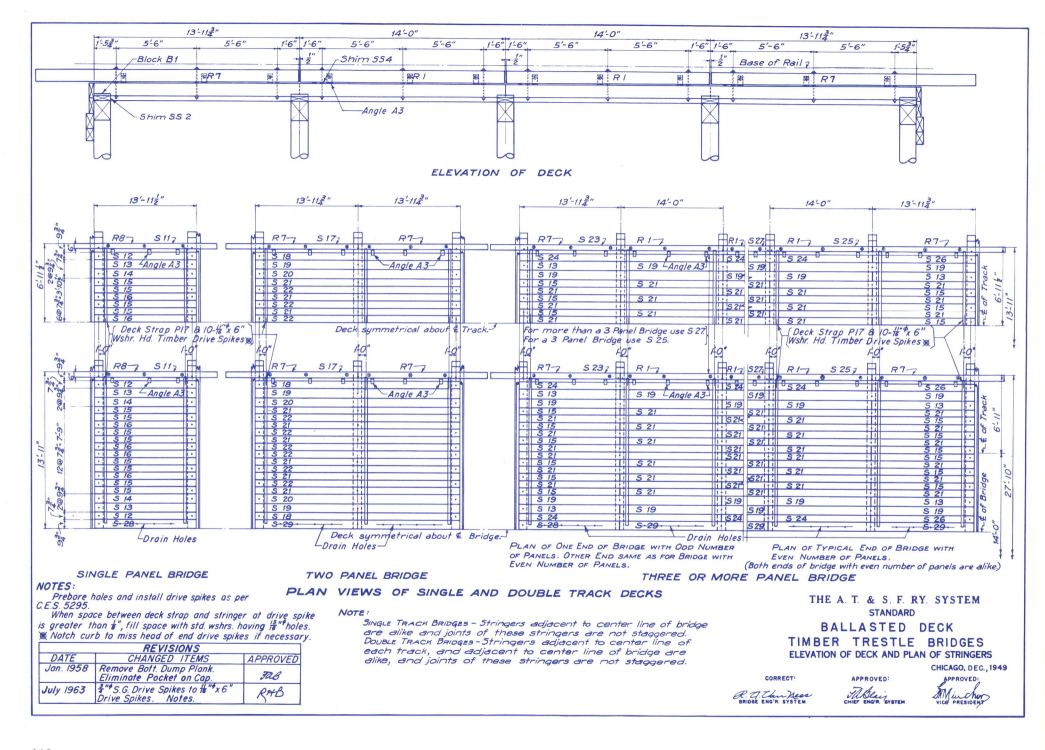

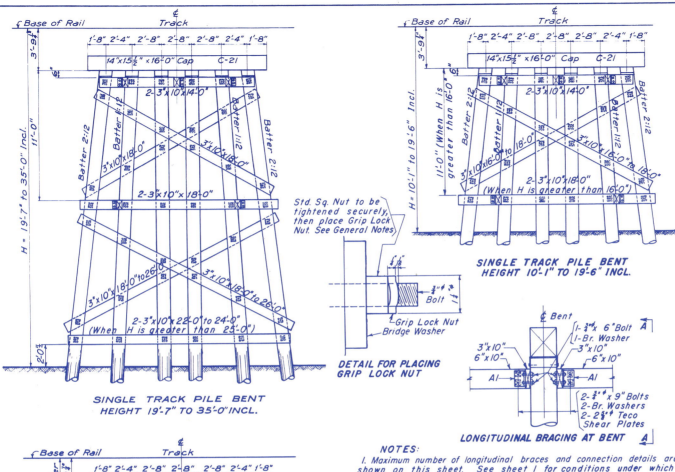

NOTES
BENTS FOR BRIDGES CARRYING CURVED TRACKS
SINGLE TRACK BRIDGES
For single track bridges carrying curved track, the bents shall be constructed the same as for bridges under tangent track, except as follows:

The maximum values of "H" shall be as follows:

Degree of Curve	Type C1	Type C2	
0°–30'	30'-0"	25'-0"	For construction of Types C1 and C2, see sheet number 8.
1°–00'	20'-0"	18'-0"	
2°–00'	16'-0"	14'-0"	
3° to 8° inclusive	12'-0"	10'-0"	

(a) For degrees of curvature between the values specified in the foregoing, the maximum permissible values of "H" may be obtained by linear interpolation.
(b) For bridges not covered by the above noted limitations, plans will be prepared by Bridge Engineer System.

DOUBLE TRACK BRIDGES
For double track bridges carrying curved track, the bents shall be constructed the same as for bridges under tangent track, except the 14'-0 cap shall always be placed under the outside track. Maximum value of "H" shall be 30'-0" for all degrees of curvature.

* Based on pile diameter of 16 inches.

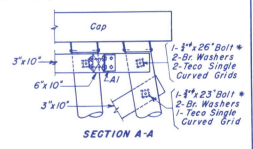

SECTION A-A

NOTES:
1. Maximum number of longitudinal braces and connection details are shown on this sheet. See sheet 1 for conditions under which longitudinal bracing is required and number of lines used under each condition.
2. Use shims under sway and sash bracing where necessary. Where shims are used they shall be nailed to bracing with ⅜" or 7/16" double grip spikes, see C.E.S. 5295. Use Teco single curved grids between piles and bracing, or between piles and shims.
3. All bolts connecting single sway braces to piles shall be driven through the piles first, so the nut will be on the same side of the bent as the brace, and thus facilitate renewal of the bracing.
4. Use Grip Lock Nuts on all bolts. See detail above.
5. See sheet 4 for details at cap for non-standard panel lengths.

THE A.T. & S.F. RY. SYSTEM
STANDARD
BALLASTED DECK TIMBER TRESTLE BRIDGES
S.T. PILE BENTS-CONN. DETAILS FOR LONG. BRACING.
CHICAGO, DEC., 1949

REVISIONS		
DATE	CHANGED ITEMS	APPROVED
Mar. 1966	Length of ¾"ø Bolts thru piles. Use 3"x10" Sash on all bents. Note 2. Notes for Curved Tracks.	R+B

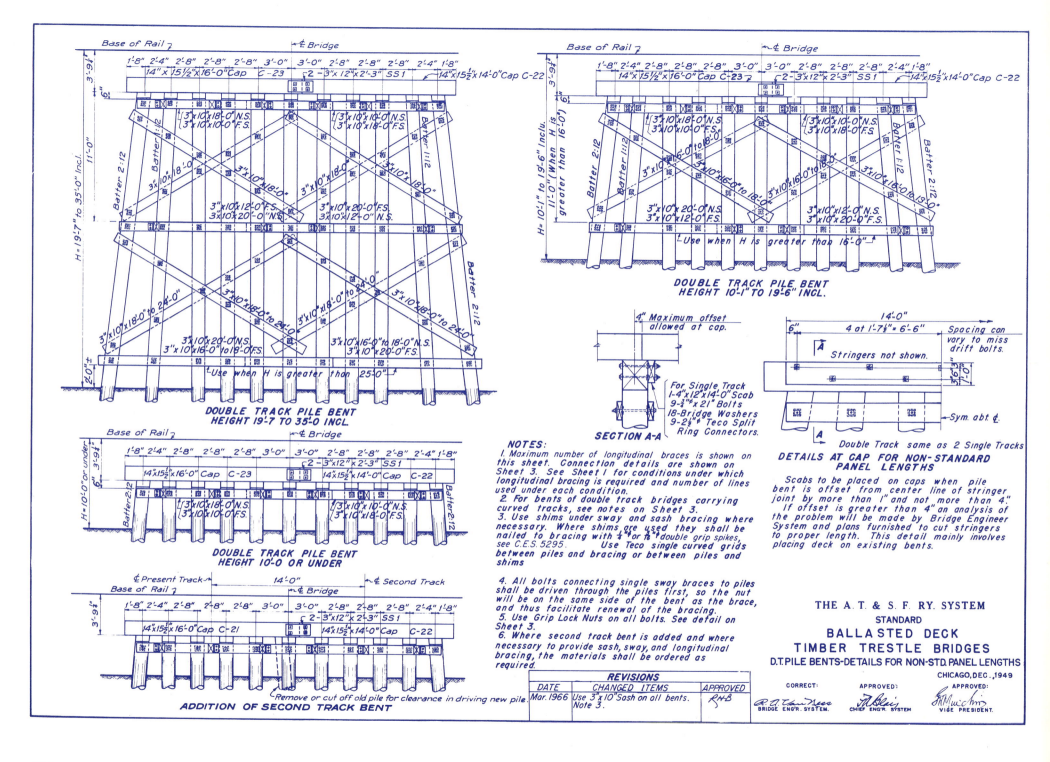

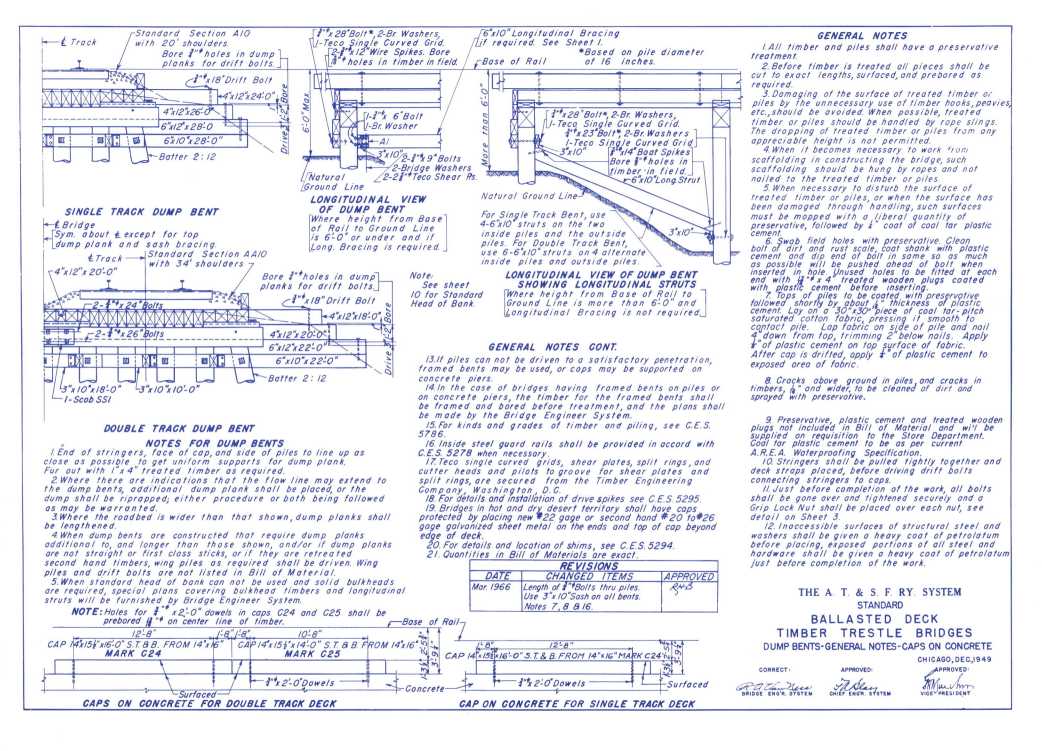

BILL OF MATERIALS FOR DECK STRINGERS NOT INCLUDED

	SINGLE SPAN		2-END SPANS		1-INT. SPAN	
	ST	DT	ST	DT	ST	DT
TREATED TIMBER						
Blocks B1	4	4	6	6	2	2
Curbs R1	-	-	-	-	2	2
Curbs R7	-	-	4	4	-	-
Curbs R8	2	2	-	-	-	-
Shims SS2 ‡	4	4	6	6	2	2
Shims SS3	-	2	-	3	-	1
Shims SS4	6	6	12	12	6	6
HARDWARE						
¾"x24" Drift Bolts, C.E.S. 5262	30	58	34	64	12	22
¾"x26" Bolts	6	6	12	12	6	6
11/16"x6" Wshr. Hd. Timber Drive Spikes	32	52	54	84	22	32
Bridge Washers, C.E.S. 5279	12	12	24	24	12	12
Grip Lock Nuts - ¾" Tap	6	6	12	12	6	6
½"x4" Double Grip Spikes	20	20	30	30	10	10
5/8"x7" Double Grip Spikes	16	24	24	36	8	12
STRUCTURAL STEEL						
Angles A3	6	6	12	12	6	6
Deck Straps P17	2	4	3	6	1	2

STRINGERS REQUIRED (N = Total No. of Panels)

	ONE PANEL BRIDGE		TWO PANEL BRIDGE		MORE THAN A TWO PANEL BRIDGE			
					ODD NO. OF PANELS		EVEN NO. OF PANELS	
STRINGERS	ST	DT	ST	DT	ST	DT	ST	DT
S11	2	2	-	-	-	-	-	-
S12	2	4	-	-	-	-	-	-
S13	2	4	-	-	4	8	4	8
S14	2	4	-	-	-	-	-	-
S15	8	16	-	-	12	24	12	24
S16	4	8	-	-	-	-	-	-
S17	-	-	2	2	-	-	-	-
S18	-	-	2	4	-	-	-	-
S19	-	-	2	4	2(N-1)	4(N-1)	2(N-1)	4(N-1)
S20	-	-	2	4	-	-	-	-
S21	-	-	6	12	6(N-1)	12(N-1)	6(N-1)	12(N-1)
S22	-	-	6	12	-	-	-	-
S23	-	-	2	2	-	-	-	-
S24	-	-	-	-	(N-1)	2(N-1)	(N-2)	2(N-2)
S25	-	-	-	-	2	2	4	4
S26	-	-	-	-	2	4	4	4
S27	-	-	-	-	(N-3)	(N-3)	(N-4)	(N-4)
S28	-	2	-	-	-	2	-	-
S29	-	-	-	2	-	(N-1)	-	N

BILL OF ADDITIONAL MATERIALS FOR TWO DUMP BENTS

SINGLE TRACK		DOUBLE TRACK	
TREATED TIMBER		**TREATED TIMBER**	
Dump Plank 4"x12"x24'-0"	2	Dump Plank 4"x12"x18'-0"	2
Dump Plank 4"x12"x26'-0"	2	Dump Plank 4"x12"x20'-0"	6
Dump Plank 6"x10"x28'-0"	2	Dump Plank 6"x10"x22'-0"	4
Dump Plank 6"x12"x28'-0"	2	Dump Plank 6"x12"x22'-0"	4
HARDWARE		**HARDWARE**	
¾"x18" Drift Bolts, C.E.S. 5262	12	¾"x18" Drift Bolts, C.E.S. 5262	12
½"x12" Wire Spikes	4	½"x12" Wire Spikes	4

Bill of Materials for Dump Bents is for bents where height from Base of Rail to Ground Line is 6'-0" or under. Where height is greater than 6'-0" material will be required as shown by longitudinal view of dump bent on Sheet 5.

BILL OF MATERIALS FOR SINGLE TRACK PILE BENT

Height Base of Rail to Ground Line	10'-0" and Under	10'-1" to 11'-6"	11'-7" to 16'-0"	16'-1" to 19'-6"	19'-7" to 21'-0"	21'-1" to 25'-0"	25'-1" to 30'-0"	30'-1" to 33'-0"	33'-1" to 35'-0"
TREATED TIMBER									
Cap C21	1	1	1	1	1	1	1	1	1
Piles	6	6	6	6	6	6	6	6	6
□ Bracing 3"x10"x14'-0"	2	2	2	2	2	2	2	2	2
Bracing 3"x10"x16'-0"	-	2	-	-	-	-	-	-	-
Bracing 3"x10"x18'-0"	-	-	2	4	6	4	4	4	4
Bracing 3"x10"x20'-0"	-	-	-	-	-	2	-	-	-
Bracing 3"x10"x22'-0"	-	-	-	-	-	-	4	-	-
Bracing 3"x10"x24'-0"	-	-	-	-	-	-	-	4	2
Bracing 3"x10"x26'-0"	-	-	-	-	-	-	-	-	2
Longitudinal Bracing 6"x10"x14'-0"	See Sheets 1, 3 & 4								
HARDWARE									
¾"x24" Drift Bolts, C.E.S. 5262	6	6	6	6	6	6	6	6	6
¾"x23" Bolts *	-	12	12	12	24	24	24	24	24
△ ¾"x26" Bolts *	6	6	12	12	12	18	18	18	18
□ Teco Single Curved Grids	12	24	24	36	48	48	60	60	60
Bridge Washers, C.E.S. 5279	12	36	36	48	72	72	84	84	84
Grip Lock Nuts - ¾" Tap	6	18	18	24	36	36	42	42	42
† Lbs. 1½" Galv. Roofing Nails	.50	.50	.50	.50	.50	.50	.50	.50	.50
Hardware for Longitudinal Bracing	See Sheets 1, 3 & 4								
MISCELLANEOUS									
⊙ 30"x30" Sheets of Coal Tar-Pitch Saturated Cotton Fabric	6	6	6	6	6	6	6	6	6

BILL OF MATERIALS FOR DOUBLE TRACK PILE BENT

Height Base of Rail to Ground Line	10'-0" and Under	10'-1" to 12'-0"	12'-1" to 16'-0"	16'-1" to 19'-6"	19'-7" to 25'-0"	25'-1" to 28'-6"	28'-7" to 31'-0"	31'-1" to 35'-0"
TREATED TIMBER								
Cap C22	1	1	1	1	1	1	1	1
Cap C23	1	1	1	1	1	1	1	1
□ Scabs SS1	2	2	2	2	2	2	2	2
Piles	11	11	11	11	11	11	11	11
□ Bracing 3"x10"x10'-0"	2	2	2	2	2	2	2	2
Bracing 3"x10"x12'-0"	-	-	-	2	2	2	2	2
Bracing 3"x10"x16'-0"	-	4	-	-	-	2	2	-
Bracing 3"x10"x18'-0"	2	2	6	6	10	6	6	8
Bracing 3"x10"x20'-0"	-	-	-	-	2	2	8	4
Bracing 3"x10"x22'-0"	-	-	-	-	-	-	4	-
Bracing 3"x10"x24'-0"	-	-	-	-	-	-	-	4
Longitudinal Bracing 6"x10"x14'-0"	See Sheets 1, 3 & 4							
HARDWARE								
¾"x24" Drift Bolts, C.E.S. 5262	11	11	11	11	11	11	11	11
① ¾"x23" Bolts *	4	24	24	24	40	40	40	40
△ ¾"x26" Bolts *	11	13	13	24	28	39	39	39
□ Teco Single Curved Grids	22	46	46	68	92	114	114	114
Bridge Washers, C.E.S. 5279	30	74	74	96	136	158	158	158
Grip Lock Nuts - ¾" Tap	15	37	37	48	68	79	79	79
† Lbs. 1½" Galv. Roofing Nails	1.0	1.0	1.0	1.0	1.0	1.0	1.0	1.0
Hardware for Longitudinal Bracing	See Sheets 1, 3 & 4							
MISCELLANEOUS								
⊙ 30"x30" Sheets of Coal Tar-Pitch Saturated Cotton Fabric	11	11	11	11	11	11	11	11

*Based on pile diameter of 16" inches.
For Dump Bents:
① Use 2-¾"x24" & 2-¾"x26" Bolts, see sh. 5;
△ Use 28" Bolts in place of 26" Bolts, see sh. 5;
□ Order half of quantities shown.
† Based on using 12 gage nails with ⅜" head, at 249 per pound.
‡ Where bridge is to have footwalk and handrail, shim SS2 shall be replaced by walk support WS1.

NOTES:
1. Where caps are placed on concrete instead of piles, the caps will be prebored, see Sheet 5. These caps are not listed in the Bill of Materials and shall be ordered as required.
2. Bill of Materials given on this sheet does not include any timber or hardware for the longitudinal struts shown on Sheet 5, nor any timber or hardware for details at cap for non-standard panel lengths shown on Sheet 4.
4. A sufficient number of 1"x10"x1'-0" and 2"x10"x1'-0" treated timber shims, and ¾"# or 7/16"# double grip spikes shall be ordered for sash and sway brace shimming as noted on pile bents, Sheets 3 and 4.
5. Galvanized sheet metal for ends and top of caps as called for in the General Notes on Sheet 5, is not included in Bill of Material.

REVISIONS

DATE	CHANGED ITEMS	APPROVED
Mar. 1966	Length of ¾"# Bolts thru piles. Use 3"x10" Sash on all bents. Note 3 & 4. Bolts for SS1	RHB

NOTES ON MARKING OF TIMBER
1. Stringers, caps, ballast curbs, and piles shall be branded at the treating plant, before treatment to show the class of treatment, the kind of timber, the assembly mark, and the year of treatment.
   (a) Stringers, caps, and ballast curbs shall have shown on one end the assembly mark number and the year of treatment.
   (b) The class of treatment, the kind of timber, and the year of treatment shall be shown on the top and bottom of the stringers, two feet from one end, and on each side of the ballast curbs, two feet from one end. The class of treatment and the kind of timber shall be shown on one side of caps, three feet from one end.
   (c) Piles shall have shown on the butt end the year of treatment; and on the side, four, ten, and sixteen feet from the butt end, the class of treatment, the kind of timber, and the year of treatment.
2. After construction of a bridge, dating nails indicating the year of construction shall be placed by field forces as called for by C.E.S. 5733.

⊙ Coal tar-pitch saturated cotton fabric weighing not less than 11 oz. per sq. yd. to be as per current A.R.E.A. Waterproofing Specifications.

THE A. T. & S. F. RY. SYSTEM
STANDARD
BALLASTED DECK TIMBER TRESTLE BRIDGES
BILL OF MATERIALS FOR BRIDGES ON TANGENT TRACK
CHICAGO, DEC., 1949

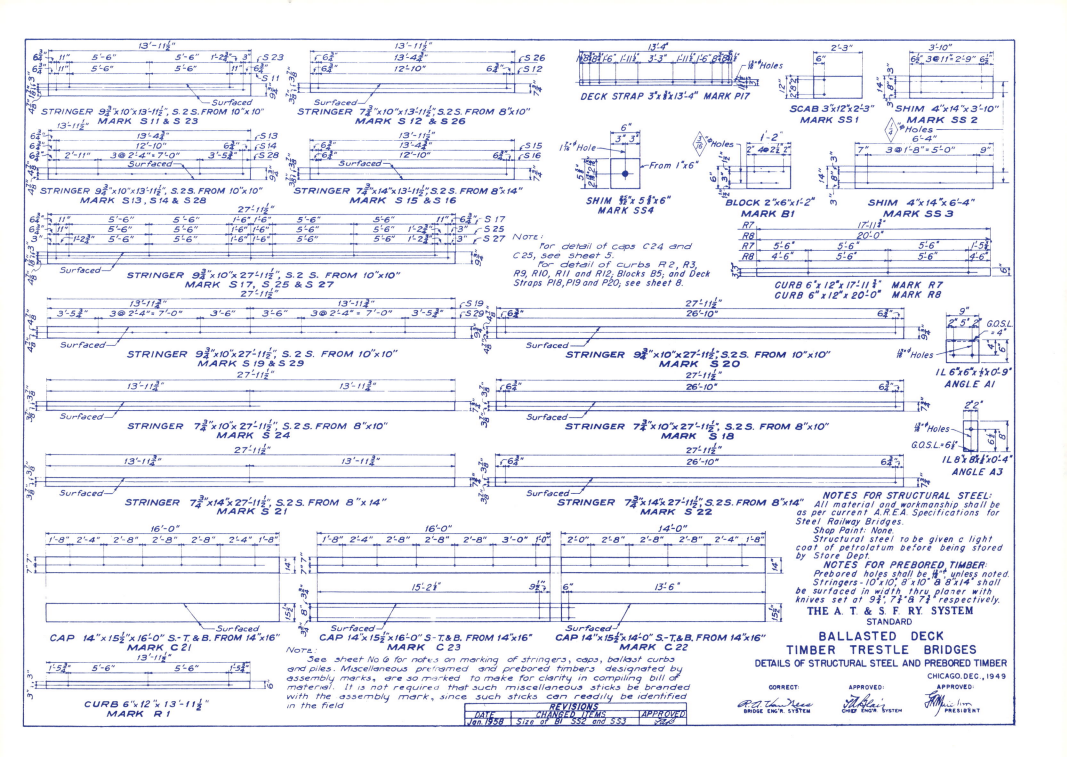

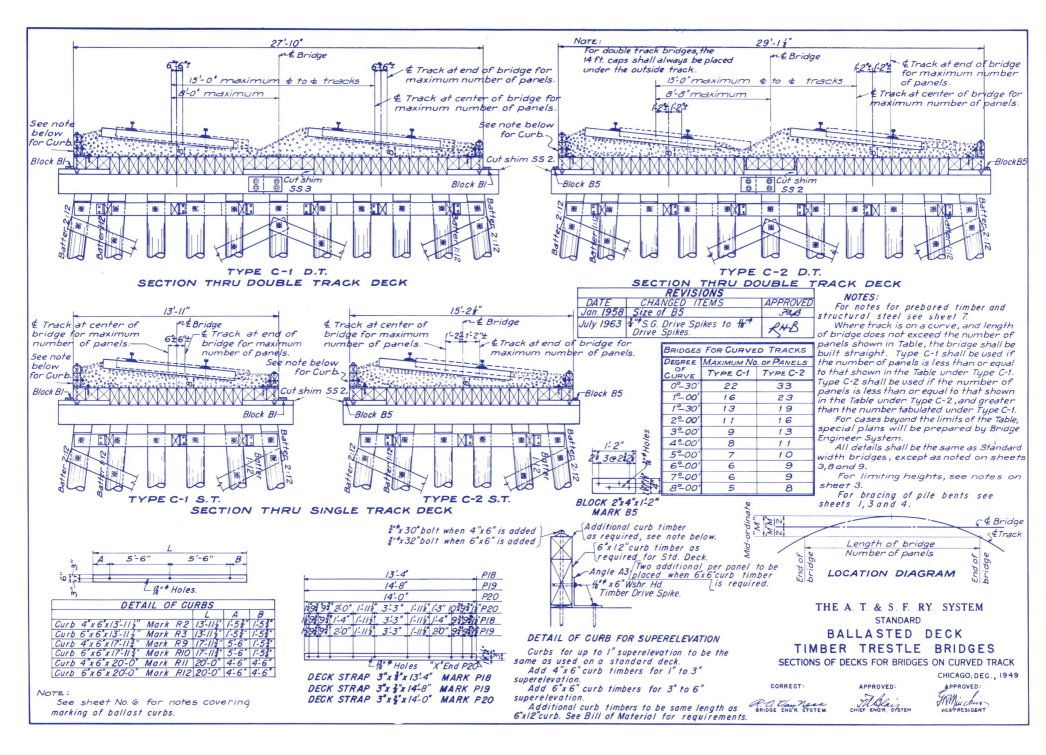

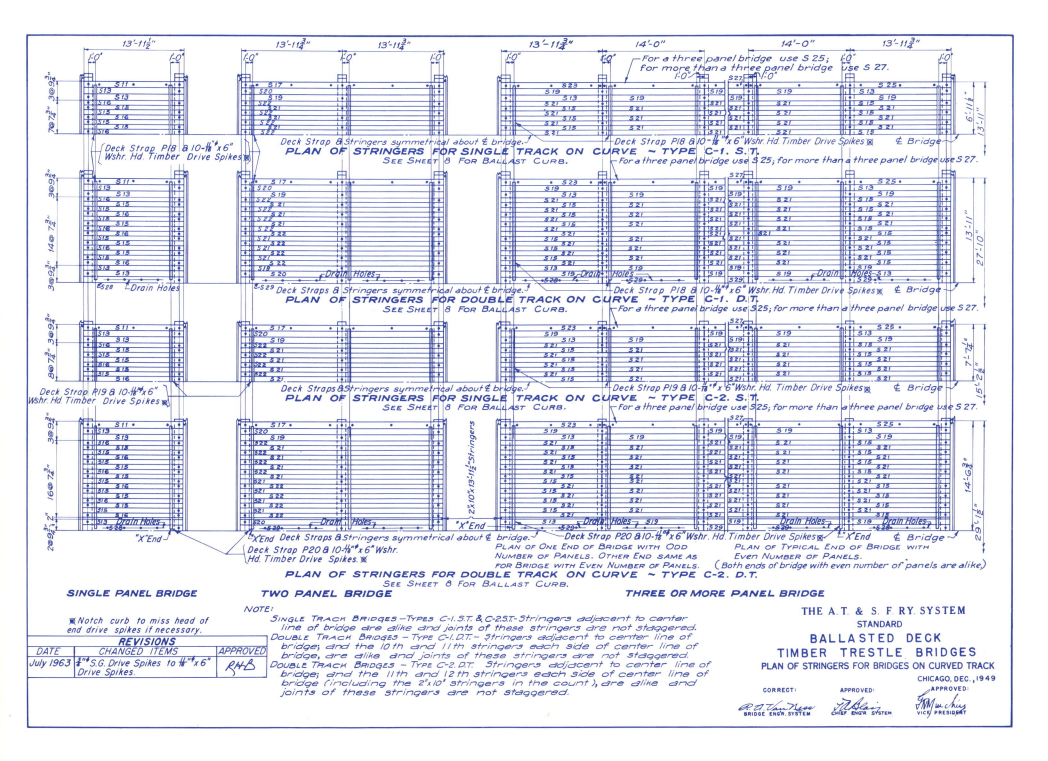

BILL OF MATERIALS FOR DECK STRINGERS NOT INCLUDED

		TYPE C1 DECK						TYPE C2 DECK					
		SINGLE SPAN		TWO END SPANS		ONE INT. SPAN		SINGLE SPAN		TWO END SPANS		ONE INT. SPAN	
		ST	DT	ST	DT	ST	DT	ST	DT	ST	DT	ST	DT
TREATED TIMBER													
Blocks B1		4	4	6	6	2	2	–	–	–	–	–	–
Blocks B5		–	–	–	–	–	–	4	4	6	6	2	2
Shims SS2		4	4	6	6	2	2	4	6	6	9	2	3
Shims SS3		–	2	–	3	–	1	–	–	–	–	–	–
Shims SS4		6	6	12	12	6	6	6	6	12	12	6	6
For up to 1" Superelevation	Curbs R1	–	–	–	–	–	–	2	2	–	–	2	2
	Curbs R7	–	–	4	4	–	–	–	–	4	4	–	–
	Curbs R8	2	2	–	–	–	–	2	2	–	–	–	–
For 1" to 3" Superelevation	Curbs R1	–	–	–	–	–	–	2	2	–	–	2	2
	Curbs R2	–	–	–	–	–	–	1	1	–	–	1	1
	Curbs R7	–	–	4	4	–	–	–	–	4	4	–	–
	Curbs R8	2	2	–	–	–	–	2	2	–	–	–	–
	Curbs R9	–	–	2	2	–	–	–	–	2	2	–	–
	Curbs R11	1	1	–	–	–	–	1	1	–	–	–	–
For 3" to 6" Superelevation	Curbs R1	–	–	–	–	–	–	2	2	–	–	2	2
	Curbs R3	–	–	–	–	–	–	1	1	–	–	1	1
	Curbs R7	–	–	4	4	–	–	–	–	4	4	–	–
	Curbs R8	2	2	–	–	–	–	2	2	–	–	–	–
	Curbs R10	–	–	2	2	–	–	–	–	2	2	–	–
	Curbs R12	1	1	–	–	–	–	1	1	–	–	–	–
HARDWARE													
For up to 1" Superelevation	3/4"⌀ x 26" Bolts	6	6	12	12	6	6	6	6	12	12	6	6
For 1" to 3" Superelevation	3/4"⌀ x 26" Bolts	3	3	6	6	3	3	3	3	6	6	3	3
	3/4"⌀ x 30" Bolts	3	3	6	6	3	3	3	3	6	6	3	3
For 3" to 6" Superelevation	3/4"⌀ x 26" Bolts	3	3	6	6	3	3	3	3	6	6	3	3
	3/4"⌀ x 32" Bolts	3	3	6	6	3	3	3	3	6	6	3	3
3/4"⌀ x 24" Drift Bolts C.E.S. 5262		28	54	34	64	12	22	30	56	36	66	14	24
7/16" x 7" Double Grip Spikes		16	22	24	33	8	11	12	20	18	30	6	10
Bridge Washers C.E.S. 5279		12	12	24	24	12	12	12	12	24	24	12	12
Grip Lock Nuts - 3/4" Tap		6	6	12	12	6	6	6	6	12	12	6	6
1/4" x 4" Double Grip Spikes		20	20	30	30	10	10	16	16	24	24	8	8
For up to 3" Superelevation	11/16"⌀ x 6" Washer Head Timber Drive Spikes	32	52	54	84	22	32	32	52	54	84	22	32
For 3" to 6" Superelevation	11/16"⌀ x 6" Washer Head Timber Drive Spikes	36	56	62	92	26	36	36	56	62	92	26	36
STRUCTURAL STEEL													
Deck Straps P18		2	4	3	6	1	2	–	–	–	–	–	–
Deck Straps P19		–	–	–	–	–	–	2	–	3	–	1	–
Deck Straps P20		–	–	–	–	–	–	–	4	–	6	–	2
For up to 3" Superelevation	Angles A3	6	6	12	12	6	6	6	6	12	12	6	6
For 3" to 6" Superelevation	Angles A3	8	8	16	16	8	8	8	8	16	16	8	8

STRINGERS REQUIRED (N = Total No. of Panels)

	TYPE C1 DECK								TYPE C2 DECK							
	ONE PANEL BRIDGE		TWO PANEL BRIDGE		MORE THAN A TWO PANEL BRIDGE				ONE PANEL BRIDGE		TWO PANEL BRIDGE		MORE THAN A TWO PANEL BRIDGE			
					ODD NO. OF PANELS		EVEN NO. OF PANELS						ODD NO. OF PANELS		EVEN NO. OF PANELS	
STRINGERS	ST	DT	ST	DT	ST	DT	ST	DT	ST	DT	ST	DT	ST	DT	ST	DT
S11	2	2	–	–	–	–	–	–	2	2	–	–	–	–	–	–
S13	4	8	–	–	4	8	4	8	4	6	–	–	4	6	4	8
S15	8	16	–	–	14	28	16	32	10	20	–	–	16	32	16	32
S16	6	12	–	–	–	–	–	–	6	12	–	–	–	–	–	–
S17	–	–	2	2	–	–	–	–	–	–	2	2	–	–	–	–
S19	–	–	2	4	2(N-1)	4(N-1)	2(N-1)	4(N-1)	–	–	2	2	2(N-1)	3(N-1)	2(N-1)	(3N-2)
S20	–	–	2	4	–	–	–	–	–	–	2	4	–	–	–	–
S21	–	–	6	12	7(N-1)	14(N-1)	(7N-8)	2(7N-8)	–	–	8	16	8(N-1)	16(N-1)	8(N-1)	16(N-1)
S22	–	–	8	16	–	–	–	–	–	–	8	16	–	–	–	–
S23	–	–	–	–	2	2	–	–	–	–	–	–	2	2	–	–
S25	–	–	–	–	2	2	4	4	–	–	–	–	2	2	4	4
S27	–	–	–	–	(N-3)	(N-3)	(N-4)	(N-4)	–	–	–	–	(N-3)	(N-3)	(N-4)	(N-4)
S28	–	2	–	–	–	–	–	–	–	2	–	–	–	–	–	4
S29	–	–	–	2	(N-1)	N	–	–	–	–	–	2	–	(N-1)	–	(N-2)
2" x 10" x 13'-11½"	–	–	–	–	–	–	–	–	–	–	2	4	–	2N	–	2N

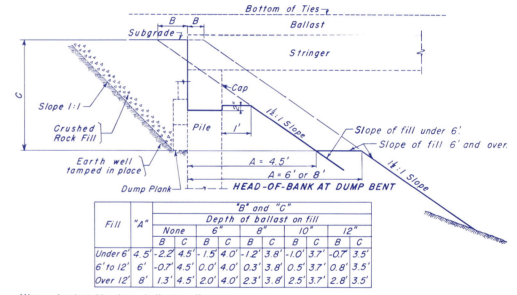

HEAD-OF-BANK AT DUMP BENT

Fill	"A"	"B" and "C" Depth of ballast on fill									
		None		6"		8"		10"		12"	
		B	C	B	C	B	C	B	C	B	C
Under 6'	4.5'	-2.2'	4.5'	-1.5'	4.0'	-1.2'	3.8'	-1.0'	3.7'	-0.7'	3.5'
6' to 12'	6'	-0.7'	4.5'	0.0'	4.0'	0.3'	3.8'	0.5'	3.7'	0.8'	3.5'
Over 12'	8'	1.3'	4.5'	2.0'	4.0'	2.3'	3.8'	2.5'	3.7'	2.8'	3.5'

Minus sign in table above indicates distance behind end of bridge.
"Fill" referred to in tabulations is the distance from subgrade to toe of slope.
Head-of-Bank detail does not apply when solid bulkheads are used.
Head-of-Bank detail applies principally to new fills. For settled embankments distance "A" may be decreased to a minimum of two feet depending upon local conditions.

REVISIONS

DATE	CHANGED ITEMS	APPROVED
Jan. 1958	Depth of fill & Remove bott. dump plank.	
July 1963	3/4"⌀ S.G. Drive Spikes to 11/16"⌀ x 6" Drive Spikes.	

THE A. T. & S. F. RY. SYSTEM
STANDARD
BALLASTED DECK TIMBER TRESTLE BRIDGES
HEAD OF BANK & BILL OF MATERIAL FOR CURVED TRACK
CHICAGO, DEC., 1949

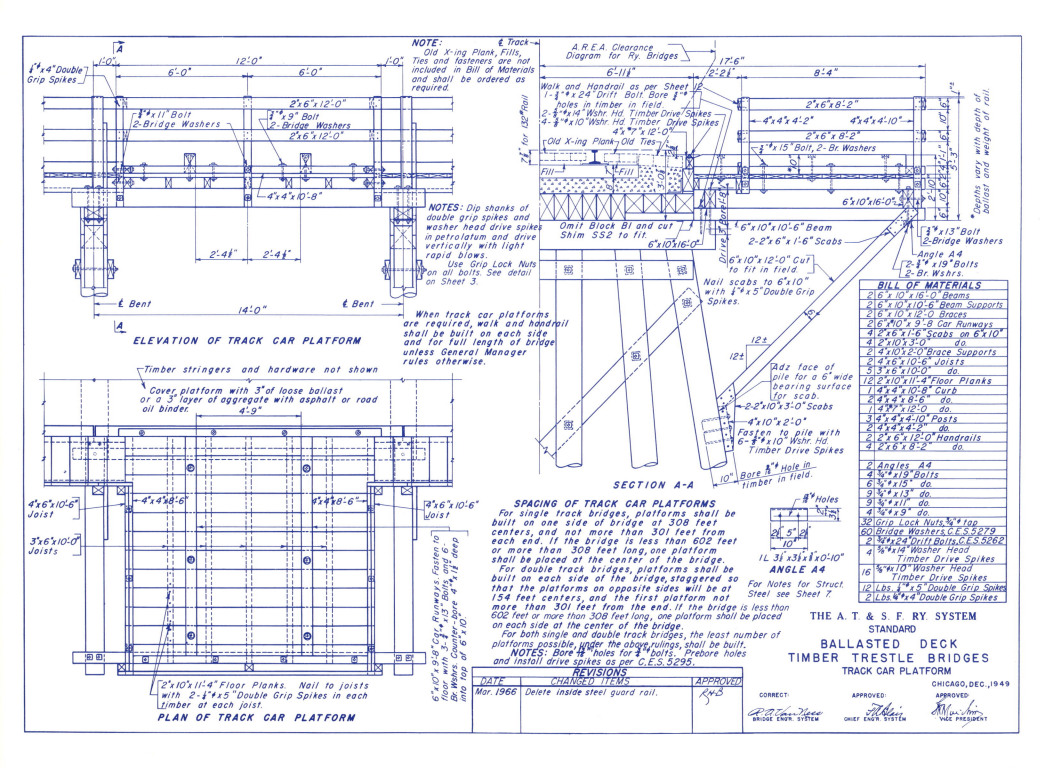

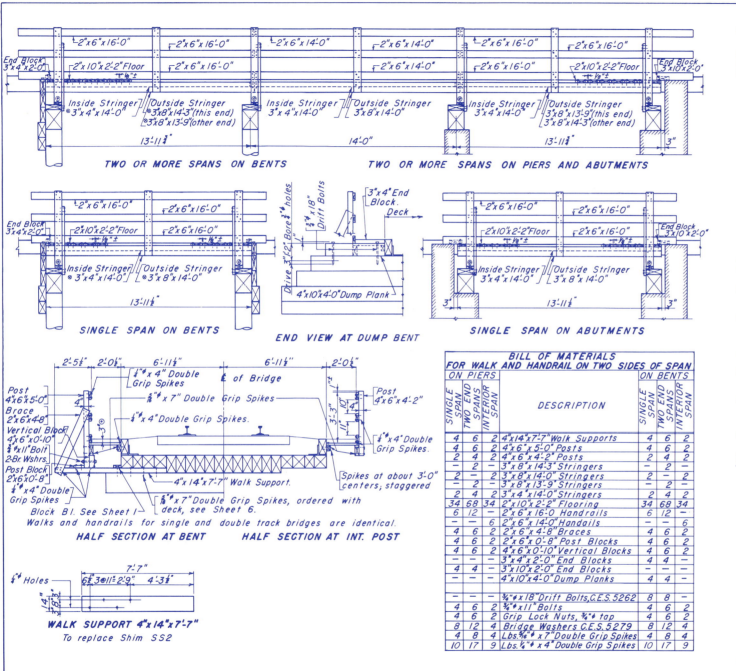

LOCATION OF FOOTWALKS AND HANDRAILS

Walks and Handrails shall be placed on both sides of all Ballasted Deck Timber Trestle Bridges located as follows, unless General Manager rules otherwise:

1. Between extreme head blocks of station grounds and for a distance of 300 feet beyond same.
2. Within 4000 feet of points on main lines where the head ends of freight trains usually stop, such as at fuel stations and important train order offices, except General Manager may extend this distance to 6500 feet or more where increased lengths of trains justify. Distances on branch lines to be determined by General Manager on basis of lengths of trains.
3. At any location where track car platforms are used, unless General Manager rules otherwise. Where walkways are not used special plan for railing adjacent to and opposite platform to be made by Bridge Engineer System.

Space between adjacent bridges, to be planked over if too narrow to warrant footwalks and handrails.

FIELD NOTES:

Bore $\frac{13}{16}$" holes in timber in field for $\frac{3}{4}$" bolts.
Prebore holes and install drive spikes as per C.E.S. 5295.

Dip shanks of double grip spikes in petrolatum and drive with light rapid blows.
Use grip lock nuts on all bolts. See detail on Sheet 3 for placing.
⊗ Cut to length in field if necessary.
⊙ Cover walkway with 3" of loose ballast or a 3" layer of aggregate with asphalt or road oil binder.

NOTE:

Special walk and handrail plan for bridges on curves will be prepared by Bridge Engineer System.

REVISIONS		
DATE	CHANGED ITEMS	APPROVED
Sept.1950	3"x6" Inside Stringers to 3"x4"	J.L.
Oct.1953	Handrail, top 2"x6" eliminated.	J.L.
Jan.1958	Eliminate Pockets on Caps. Size of Walk Supports.	J.L.B.
July 1963	Field Notes	R+B

THE A.T. & S.F. RY. SYSTEM
STANDARD
**BALLASTED DECK
TIMBER TRESTLE BRIDGES**
WALK AND HANDRAIL

CHICAGO, DEC., 1949

If you would like to receive future announcements about new books to be published by KACHINA PRESS, fill out and mail this card _____

And, for that friend who wants to receive announcements, too, here is an extra card _____

☐ YES, please add my name to your list to receive future announcements about new publications from Kachina Press.

Name: _____

Address: _____

City: _____ State _____ Zip _____

Be sure to place stamp here; post office will not deliver without stamp.

KACHINA PRESS
P. O. BOX 50011
DALLAS, TEXAS 75250

Be sure to place stamp here; post office will not deliver without stamp.

KACHINA PRESS

P. O. BOX 50011

DALLAS, TEXAS 75250

☐ YES, please add my name to your list to receive future announcements about new publications from Kachina Press.

Name: _____

Address: _____

City: _____ State _____ Zip _____

If you would like to receive future announcements about new books to be published by KACHINA PRESS, fill out and mail this card _____

☐ YES, please add my name to your list to receive future announcements about new publications from Kachina Press.

Name: _____

Address: _____

City: _____ State _____ Zip _____

And, for that friend who wants to receive announcements, too, here is an extra card _____

Be sure to place stamp here; post office will not deliver without stamp.

KACHINA PRESS
P. O. BOX 50011
DALLAS, TEXAS 75250

Be sure to place stamp here; post office will not deliver without stamp.

KACHINA PRESS

P. O. BOX 50011

DALLAS, TEXAS 75250

☐ YES, please add my name to your list to receive future announcements about new publications from Kachina Press.

Name: _____

Address: _____

City: _____ State _____ Zip _____